W9-BAG-197

MAXING OUT

ALSO BY COLETTE DOWLING

The Cinderella Complex
Perfect Women
You Mean I Don't Have To Feel This Way?
Red Hot Mamas

MAXING OUT

Why Women Sabotage
Their Financial Security

COLETTE DOWLING

Little, Brown and Company

Boston   New York   Toronto   London

Copyright © 1998 by Colette Dowling

All rights reserved. No part of this book may be reproduced in any form or by any electronic or mechanical means, including information storage and retrieval systems, without permission in writing from the publisher, except by a reviewer who may quote brief passages in a review.

First Edition

Library of Congress Cataloging-in-Publication Data
Dowling, Colette.
    Maxing out : why women sabotage their financial security / by Colette Dowling.
        p.   cm.
    ISBN 0-316-19120-5
    1. Women — Finance, Personal.   2. Debt — Psychological aspects.
3. Compulsive behavior.   4. Dependency (Psychology).   I. Title.
HG179.D696   1998
332.024'042 — dc21   97-49409

10   9   8   7   6   5   4   3   2   1

MV-NY

Printed in the United States of America

CONTENTS

AUTHOR'S NOTE

I decided to begin this book with my own money story, painful as it is, because it shows so vividly how accomplishment and financial success aren't necessarily proof that one is comfortable with having to support oneself.

If you had suggested to me ten years ago, even five, that I would methodically (if unconsciously) set about destroying my financial security, losing all the money I'd made on a bestselling book, losing, even, my furniture, I would have laughed. I would have told you I was *over* my biggest hurdles, that I *knew* who I was and had the financial comfort and psychological equanimity to prove it. I'd raised my kids, after all. I'd learned a profession, taught myself a difficult craft, done marriage, done the single life. I'd even faced the difficult task of putting my parents to rest.

But there was something else, it turned out. I remained deeply conflicted about financial independence. Making money as a single mother was fine. Someone had to support the children, after all. Someone had to put them through school. But once they were on their own, and I was responsible for no one but me, my psychological reality silently shifted. What did it mean that I didn't need anyone for support? And was I really prepared to go on supporting myself for decades to come?

Such questions lay at the heart of my book *The Cinderella Complex*. But when it was published, in the early eighties, I didn't understand that my resistance to taking care of myself financially was only burrowing deeper as I "mastered" life and built an increasingly brittle facade of independence. Concerns about success, money, and my desirability as a woman continued to fester. Eventually, the anxiety drove me to destroy everything I'd built up. It turned out I was more comfortable *without* money of my own piling up in an investment account. Why would this be? And was I so different from other women? I didn't think so.

Our history with money has not been the same as men's, obviously. What has been less obvious is how our entire sense of ourselves as female has been tied to *not* having money, *not* managing it, *not* being financially independent. As I interviewed women around the country for *Maxing Out*, I came to see how confused we remain on the subject of what constitutes femininity, of how much independence one can achieve and still feel like a "real" woman. I would find that women are afraid to make the ultimate commitment to themselves for fear of ending up alone, unloved and uncared for.

I decided to write this book to find out why that fear, in spite of what we know intellectually, remains so emotionally gripping. True femininity, true security, depends on our getting past the fear of supporting ourselves and being able, instead, to commit to it, enjoy it, feel powerful — and desirable — *because* we can take care of ourselves. Without getting to the bottom of this conflict, I was sure, women would continue in a state of financial precariousness and insecurity, struggling indefinitely with the discomfiting sense of being out of control.

MAXING OUT

Chapter 1

A WOMAN'S CRISIS

"Poor Little Rich Girl," screamed the headline of the *New York Post*. There was a photograph of a thin woman in jewelry and jeans striding purposefully down a New York street. "Gloria Vanderbilt, heiress to one of America's most famous fortunes, has moved into a small 2-bedroom apartment after having to sell two luxury homes in order to pay her taxes," the caption read.

It's the sort of front page I've always ignored, but not this time. This time I was riveted. I had just finished selling two homes to pay off part of a debt to the IRS and was still reeling from the shock. Other people had such problems, but not me. Now I was having to acknowledge a whole hidden part of myself. I was a fifty-five-year-old woman who, when it came to money, had been behaving like a teenager with her first credit card.

Three years earlier I had owned two country properties, a co-op in Manhattan, and a retirement fund worth a quarter of a million dollars. Now I had neither the retirement fund nor the houses nor any credit worth a damn.

I am no heiress, but I certainly felt identified with Gloria Vanderbilt. Even after selling everything I'd worked so hard for and handing over the profits to the government, I still owed the IRS twenty-six thousand dollars.

For years I was able to ignore the fact that I was avoiding dealing with money. I had so little of it — as a struggling writer and as the wife of a struggling writer — that no one could see how I was mismanaging things, least of all me. I thought I was courageous because I wouldn't let the lack of money beat me down. Like so many women, I had learned to scrimp and save. I could make the *best* linguine with clam sauce for the quarters and dimes it took to buy a half pound of spaghetti, a can of clams, and a bunch of parsley. I could clothe myself in dresses made from *Vogue* patterns and remnants bought on Fourteenth Street. A certain principle was operating here: doing well at doing without is the same thing as doing.

My husband and I were poor, proud, and intellectual. Our values precluded *caring* about the fact that we were down and out. And besides, we knew how to do things with style. A party for a baby's christening would involve cognac and oysters by the half bushel. Julia Child was our goddess, and when we weren't eating spaghetti for supper, we were serving *blanquette de veau* to friends on our sawhorse dining table. There was a kind of righteousness about our money situation. I once went to a bank's loan officer and convinced him, after a lie had been detected on our loan application, that freelance artists had no recourse but to lie, since the system was stacked against us. He relented and gave us the loan. I was pregnant, then, and I marched back home along West Twenty-first Street with belly bulging and head held high, feeling I had triumphed over no less an instrument of capitalism than Fifth Avenue's Irving Trust Bank.

After nine difficult years the marriage broke up. Of course, I had to continue scrimping. I also continued fudging and evading. Three children were now my sole responsibility — *and* I was developing a career as a freelance magazine writer. How could I acknowledge the fear, doubt, and panic gathering beneath my heroic exterior? I was fighting the good fight. If there were days when buying milk for the kids meant searching for quarters under the couch cushions, it wasn't because I was mismanaging my income; it was because writers in this country didn't get adequate support from society and the government.

After being on my own a couple of years, I began spending money. There was no one looking over my shoulder, no parents, no roommates, no husband. Only *I* was accountable for me, and I wasn't enough. Without some authority to keep me in tow, I was soon out of control. If I went shopping for a dress to wear to a business affair, I'd leave with not only a dress but a fabulous stretch-lace shirt the saleswoman had convinced me I looked great in, plus pants, belt, jewelry, and a big felt hat.

My shopping binges felt deliciously freeing. It was like a delayed adolescence, only it wasn't baby-sitting money I was spending with such abandon — it was babies' money. Of course, I didn't look at it that way. I was able to convince myself I needed to dress well for lunches with editors. I denied the manic high I got from trying on outfits brought to me by the cooing boutique owner — and then succumbing to her pitch because it made me feel so good. I could *see* myself attracting attention, and oh, how I wanted attention! At night, with Carly Simon cranked on the stereo, I would prance in front of the mirror with my new black hat, brim turned this way and that. I wanted to look younger, freer, and more adventurous than I was, or could be, given my life circumstances. I wanted to be a girl again.

The actual stress of having to support myself and my family, though I did it for five years, didn't fully manifest itself until I entered a new relationship — whereupon ambition crashed and I instantly returned to the womblike comfort of being a housewife again. I still wrote, but without any urge to turn my writing into money. I made no calls to editors proposing ideas for articles. My new love was paying most of my bills. I felt dreamy, secure, and blissfully free of anxiety. For challenge, I made cakes with the artful addition of Jell-O pudding mixes.

This regression almost cost me the relationship. The man I was with had come of age at feminist Sarah Lawrence College, and wasn't thrilled by having to support all five of us while I experimented with espalier and stapling designer sheets to the walls of our rented house. I entered psychoanalysis and began to understand my problems with dependency. Women I knew, and women I eventually interviewed, were struggling with the same issue. Under the guise of our new independence, many of us still wanted to be taken care of. It was something we didn't talk about, couldn't talk about, couldn't admit.

Feminism, at that point, hadn't acknowledged the conflicts women were experiencing with the new push to gain freedom. Uncovering those conflicts became the focus of *The Cinderella Complex*. Women were acting as if they were sassy and free, while beneath the surface they harbored a wish to be rescued that was bred from their traditional upbringings. Unwittingly, because the responsibility attached to freedom made them anxious, many were sabotaging their attempts at living independently.

I certainly was.

Paradoxically, the success and money that came to me after *The Cinderella Complex* was published obscured my continuing problems with financial responsibility. Also, I was in a relationship with a man who was circumspect and careful in his handling of money. So long as I was with him, I stayed on the straight and narrow, but once the relationship broke up, it wasn't long before I was off and prancing again. Suddenly my closet was blooming with dresses, expensive shoes, good suits. I decorated. I renovated. I bought antiques. I stopped putting money into my retirement account. At tax time I was always short. I'd call up my agent, and she'd say, "I'll go out and rattle my gourds." By this she meant looking around among my various book contracts to see if anyone owed me money. To me, finances were ephemeral. No matter how hard I might work for it, money retained a magical quality.

By the time it all came crashing down, I was so removed from reality I saw no connection between what was happening now and the vagueness with which I'd approached money my entire life. I felt caught, trapped, victimized. I hadn't been in debt before, but I hadn't saved nearly as much as I might have. And most of what I'd saved hadn't been invested; it sat languishing in a money market fund making little interest.

I thought of myself as hardworking (I was), driven by concerns about money (I was), and utterly without fault (I wasn't). Suddenly, the IRS was after me for back taxes. How could this have happened? I felt virtuous, good, and innocent. I also felt wounded (Why me?). And weary (I knew it would come to this!). And wronged.

Anything, that is, but responsible. Anything but the creator of my own situation. Anything but culpable. Here was the truth: I didn't want to have to manage my money. I would work like a dog if need be, and I did. But something about a plan or budget or consideration of the future was more than I wanted to contend with.

This financial crisis would be one of the most difficult struggles I have ever had to face. I re-entered therapy and eventually joined a financial recovery program. Slowly I would feel better-grounded, more in control, more confident about the future. As I began getting a handle on the patterns of self-deception that had been grinding me under, I started to think about how other women were dealing with money. We were all joined in this.

I began poor, and then, when I never expected it would happen in my lifetime, I made money. In the early eighties, after years of struggling as a full-time writer and full-time mother, I had my surprise bestseller, *The Cinderella Complex.* It's the sort of thing a writer may dream of but never expects. For the first time in my life I had money. I hardly knew how to relate to it. "Get it out of that bank account and into something that earns interest," the man I lived with kept saying. (We had agreed that he would not handle the money for me.)

I was afraid to get it out of the bank account. Just handling the money, moving it from one place to another, or finding someone to handle it — a broker, an investment manager, even a lawyer or an accountant — any move at all, at first, seemed dangerous.

As a child I had never been exposed to large amounts of money. When suddenly I was receiving more royalty checks than I knew how to reckon with (there ended up being twenty foreign publishers of *The Cinderella Complex*) I remember once thinking, Can I afford a fur coat? It wasn't that I wanted a fur coat; the question reflected my confusion. I had no idea what I could afford or couldn't afford. When I thought of buying a co-op in Manhattan, my accountant said it wasn't a good idea. "You have to keep your funds liquid for your kids," was his advice.

"That's ridiculous," my analyst countered. "Accountants are notoriously conservative."

I went with the analyst. I bought in Brooklyn Heights, a garden duplex that I ended up selling only twelve months later for a hefty profit. With that sale, I thought I had it all figured out. But those twelve months just happened to be the apex of the eighties real estate market. And with closing costs both when I bought and sold, and capital gains taxes to pay, was it really a good move, or was the whole thing merely a distraction?

The decision to sell was based primarily on my wish to follow my lover out of the city, and to Woodstock, New York. I had been through this eight years earlier, leaving New York and going with him to the country. When I did it then, I became utterly financially dependent on him. Now I was following him again, but this time with the illusory feeling of independence produced by having money in my bank account. When we bought a house in Woodstock, I not only paid my half of the down payment, I lent him his share.

It seemed that for a decade or more, in spite of not knowing what I was doing, I had managed pretty well. My career, at that point, was nothing if not ego-enhancing. When I arrived in Brazil to promote the publication of my book, bunting strung up over the streets announced, "Welcome Cinderella!" in Portuguese. I soon had enough money from domestic and foreign royalties to be able to stop worrying about money for the first time in my life.

The trouble was, I also stopped *thinking* about it. I hired a bookkeeper, an accountant. Printouts appeared magically. Taxes got calculated smoothly each spring. Slowly the details began more and more to elude me. I rationalized that I was more interested in ideas, in creativity, in having the peace of mind to be able to *think*. Someone else could take care of the details.

Ah, the joys of what twelve-step programs refer to as "terminal vagueness." And the joys of grandiosity! For some years, it was like living in warm amniotic fluid. I couldn't see outside the sac I was floating in, but who wanted to?

CINDERELLA HITS BOTTOM

The trouble first became apparent in 1992. For the longest time I thought that everything else that was to follow stemmed from not having a penny to put toward that year's seventy-thousand-dollar tax bill. The high tax wasn't because my income was so great (though it was not insubstantial). Because I'd borrowed from my Keogh account to finish the renovation on a small house I owned and rented out, and which I planned to occupy in an effort to "scale down," my huge tax debt included interest on and penalties for removing the money from my retirement account early.

I pursued the renovation against my accountant's advice. I did it because demolition was under way before I discovered that I couldn't simply "improve" the attic space, making myself a pretty new bedroom and bath. Because the roof was too low to meet the building code, if I wanted to change that space at all, it would mean adding a new second floor.

My architect was supremely challenged by this idea and whipped into action. Soon the thrill and sense of aggrandizement made possible by raising up a huge new four-gabled roof on my little 1860 farmhouse seemed more than I could pass up. "Let's go for it," I said to the contractor.

Arriving at the decision caused me only one sleepless night.

ILLUSIONS OF POWER

The house renovation that brought down my own house of cards was part of what I call the Romance Myth. I had been creating a little fairy tale house. Not just "creating," as in window treatments and faux finishes, but actually *building* — or, rather, supervising the building. I loved the heft of the project, bulldozers digging out the old foundation and readying the site for a new one, masons extending the chimney to a new height, carpenters raising up the roof beams. That roof was pure glory. It was twenty-eight feet square and designed with four steeply pitched gables, one on each side of the square. The architect had worked out a system wherein each beam was notched to fall precisely into place. The old attic had been razed, and now there was just the mountain rising up in the background and a flat platform on which would be constructed the miraculous assemblage of fitted beams. Watching from where I lived, on the property across the road, I was like a little girl watching a game being played by the big boys. But crossing the street, and then the bridge over the little stream, and entering the house with its luscious odor of fresh sawdust and racket of hammers and power machines, I grew bigger. I was allowed to join them!

"Come on up," the head man would yell from above, and I would climb the ladder rungs and suddenly be up there with them, with the leaves all around us turning gold and wood smoke wafting over from a neighboring chimney, the sky blue as crystal above. And those fabulous many-beamed gables going up so fast it was enough to take your breath away. This was living, out in the elements, racing against the arrival of the first snow, a dance company of men in jeans and plaid shirts whose every movement was choreographed. At its apogee, the job had eleven guys all dashing about doing what they were supposed to be doing. And I felt like one of them, up there on the platform in the sky. I was making this thing happen, I was the boss of bosses, the woman with the money.

It was like being my father, only more so: more in charge, more important, more powerful. No more was I the envious little girl in the midst of boys with their trucks and their engine growls. These guys accepted me. I was smart, but also reasonable. I was funny. They didn't have to squelch themselves when I climbed the ladder to join them on their platform in the sky. I laughed at their dirty jokes. I tsk-tsked them like a benevolent mother. But I was the one who determined what grade of lumber would be used, whose unerring eye for aesthetics dominated. The architect wanted to curve the arch between dining room and kitchen. I said no curves. He wanted the kitchen to have no wall-hung cabinets. I said, don't be ridiculous, have you ever *worked* in a kitchen? When he countered with the impracticality of my idea of French doors leading to the master bath, I said they were beautiful and if people wanted privacy, they could curtain them.

All of this was a major high. Major. Cars slowed to watch the progress of my beautiful house. Friends came for tours. Toward the end, a manic high prevailed, infecting everyone down to the lowest gofer on the totem pole, the boy who swept up the debris each evening so the guys would have a clean site when they arrived in the morning. *This* was a project. Gleaming floors, soaring gables, massive bluestone walls, a chimney of hand-hoisted river stone. The *energy* that went into this, the sheer male enthusiasm. Whistle while you work. Heigh-ho, heigh-ho. Blow, blow, blow the man down. It was Daddy's energy that was happening all around, and I was with it, and of it, at last.

Putting the ultimate spin on the experience was the gamble, the thrill of the deadline. Here was the situation: the project had to be finished in time for me to get a certificate of occupancy before the bank closing, which was scheduled on the last day an 8 percent interest rate was being offered. In my mind, the entire project had been made viable by that 8 percent. It was thirty-six hours to countdown and the building department still hadn't made its final inspection. I went to the inspector's office to find that he had just left town on a trip. Tears sprang to my eyes. His secretary became alarmed. "Let me see if I can get him on the car phone. Maybe Marty can sign the C of O."

Marty was his assistant. They'd both been out to look at the renovation a million times. We were down to doorknobs now. I couldn't believe how close I was playing it. I sat by the secretary's desk, looking glumly out the window at the darkening November afternoon. And then, success! She reached him. He was on his way for a weekend of hunting and drinking. He said yes, Marty could do it. I was ecstatic, buoyant, triumphant beyond all measure. I had done it. I had succeeded against the odds.

Somehow, looking back on all this is like looking back on a wild dream, a dream of high-wire acrobatics and less-than-noble desires. A nightmare of unanswered questions. Would the low-end heating system work? Would the building inspector discover the sewage seeping from an old abandoned cistern?

And, finally, when I seemed to be getting away with it all by meeting the mortgage deadline, would I be able to make up the thousands of dollars I'd taken out of my retirement account to fund this romantic storybook house?

I was working on a book when the tax bill came due that year, though that was not in itself unusual. I used the work to deny the money crisis. "I can't afford to get too anxious," I told myself. "I just have to put down my head and finish this manuscript."

Put down my head I did. The Prozac I was taking helped keep anxiety at bay. I slept restlessly at night but during the day was cool. Cool and "in denial." I'm sure you've heard that expression. I thought of it when I read how Gloria Vanderbilt had described her situation to a newspaper reporter: " 'I'm not broke. This is just a temporary situation until I liquidate my house and other assets to pay off my debt.' " Meanwhile, she was living in a two-bedroom apartment with her brother. " 'I have my career. I have my health . . . my talent and my energy. All this is going to be resolved very soon.' "

Apparently she felt she had an eternity in which to make up the shortfall. She was seventy-one at the time.

I know about this sort of fuzzy thinking. At first one treats the situation as if an accident has occurred, something in which one has played no real part. Or perhaps only the smallest, most human part. It is as if a gap has occurred in one's thought processes. For the longest time life was rosy. And then . . . it was not.

While the IRS waited for its money, the amounts I continued tallying up on my American Express card were huge, between two and three thousand dollars a month. They'd been huge for so long I no longer thought of them as huge. "Everything is a matter of scale," I would tell myself. "I simply live on a different scale than I used to."

The scale didn't change until the IRS came knocking on my door. And not immediately, even then. I had no sense that it was necessary to cut back, only that a debt loomed off in the distance somewhere. This was an extension of a psychological block that had been going on for years. My income was no longer as grandly inflated as it had been in the eighties. At the same time, my expenses were higher, since I'd stopped sharing them with my partner when our relationship broke up, in 1989. Who among us wants to acknowledge that the good life is no longer so good?

I have since learned that women, who often feel deprived to begin with, find it difficult, when they move out of a relationship, to trade down to the single life. I certainly did. Not wanting to experience myself as diminished by the loss of a relationship, I traded up, spending more grandly than I ever would have permitted myself when I was with my more conservative partner. The year the tax bill hit, I rented a house on a barrier island off South Carolina for Christmas and bought plane tickets for myself and two of my grown children. It seemed the only thing to do — the "right" thing to do. It was my mother's first Christmas as a widow, and we needed to pull together. (Forget about *my* need to pull together.)

For several years I'd spent all my free time helping my parents through what would be their final illnesses. As they grew closer to the ends of their lives, I focused entirely on their needs and avoided my own problems, which were not so slowly spiraling out of control. As panic gathered beneath the surface, I had a little acronym I'd begun repeating like a charm: DTRT. It stood for Do the Right Thing. I said it like a mantra, and I continued spending. That year, we raised up a big Christmas tree and crammed the floor beneath it with presents.

But I no longer had the wherewithal to be playing Lady Bountiful. By then I was scrambling to pay my monthly bills. I had large mortgage payments. Although I had tenants in one house and the New York co-op, the income barely covered my expenses. Still, I tried to be a beneficent landlord. I maintained things well and told myself, as I threw up a new stone wall or bought fruit trees, that I was enhancing my assets.

Such expansiveness might have been justified in the heyday of the eighties, but in the nineties it was crazy. The truth is, I was out of control with money, but because I'd made it before, I assumed (as had, apparently, Vanderbilt) that I could right myself in a heartbeat. We fool ourselves, we debting women. We want to insist that any distress caused by our debacles is transient and minor. But health, energy, and yes, even talent, are affected by the losses we bring down upon ourselves. I would go through rigorous self-examination before coming to terms with what I was doing to myself.

Vanderbilt said her troubles began the day she handed over her personal and business affairs to her lawyer (now dead) and her psychiatrist, whose first name (unbelievably) was Christ. According to judgments against them, Christ and the lawyer formed a partnership to earn money from the Gloria Vanderbilt name and ended up stealing or losing millions from her bank account.

But where was Gloria during all this?

And where, on a smaller though no less painful scale, was I? For nine years I had lived in a five-bedroom house by a rushing stream in Woodstock. When my partner and I split up, he bought a house he could afford and continued building his business. I bought out his share of our valuable 1775 colonial, saddling myself with enormous expense because I thought it would be better, psychologically, if I didn't take on too much change all at once. A sixteen-year relationship was ending, and though I had chosen the separation, I felt I needed the comfort of staying in the house to maintain my equilibrium. "Just for a while," I said.

But I didn't just hang out, waiting for things to sift out and settle. I went on a rampage. Something was driving me. I had the driveway circle regraded, lined with river stone, and planted up with dozens of Festiva Maxima peonies. When five bedrooms seemed like a ridiculous arrangement of space for one person, I decided to combine two bedrooms to make myself a grand twenty-five-foot office. Ceilings came down, permitting a view that expanded upward. Of course, collar ties had to be installed to allow the structure to support that view. French doors opened a passage to my bedroom. Floor-to-ceiling bookcases were built. When it was finished, there was no question I had the nicest work space ever. I deserved it, I told myself. The price tag? A mere twelve thousand dollars.

After 1992 went by without my having enough money to pay my taxes, one thing led to another, and 1993 ended up that way, too, although I continued to acknowledge only 1992 as a problem. After all, 1993 was "current," I told myself. I wasn't paying my quarterly estimates, but I didn't count that as debt, either. I had *never* paid my quarterly estimates. At the end of every year, I would scratch to come up with the whole wad, plus the penalties for paying late, often having to ask my agent for advances against future royalties. Though I worked hard for what I earned, I made no real connection between working and earning, earning and spending, spending and debting. I didn't even *mind* paying the government extra money if doing so allowed me to go a year without having to think about it.

When the time came to cough up the debt, I actually prided myself on always having something to tap into as a way of getting the necessary sum together. My bookkeeper would try to suggest ways of putting aside money as the year went along, so that I could pay my tax bill in a timely fashion and stop accruing penalties. I would always nod, but I never took action. I had more important things to think about. When the bookkeeper came once a month to pay the bills, I signed the checks, winced when she showed me the balance in my bank account, and went on. Onward and upward, as I chose to think of it.

Part of the process, here, was denial — denial and compensation. Since the mounting debts were affecting my self-esteem, I needed to do things to stave off depression. What I did was spend money. The house I was renovating became more and more beautiful. I bought the most expensive paints, thrilled by the Martha Stewart effects I was achieving. As the renovation proceeded, I told myself I was "growing," and in some ways I suppose I was. At least I was going through things from which I would later be able to extract a lesson. Each week I handed over a fistful of cash, literally thousands of dollars, to the contractor, whom I'd hired on a time-and-materials basis. I had chosen this payment method rather than contracting on a firm bid, gambling that I could save the 10 percent buffer the builder told me he always built into any guaranteed estimate to make sure he didn't lose anything. In fact, the entire venture was a gamble. I think, now, that that was part of the thrill.

The scariest period came toward the end, when eleven men were working on the house simultaneously, and "time and materials" were costing me five or six thousand dollars a week. Now I *was* losing sleep. The deadline on my mortgage commitment was running out, and I needed that mortgage money to live on, since by then I was spending every last cent I had on the nails and molding and the last doorknobs the building inspector required before giving me the certificate of occupancy the bank needed to close on the mortgage.

By the end I was really down to the wire. I was also living out of my car, carrying a suitcase full of clothes and my computer in the trunk. The whole project had been intended to put me in a less costly living situation. I had rented out my larger house and was planning to live in the smaller, renovated one — if it ever got finished. I actually had the fantasy of writing a piece about this project and calling it "Scaling Down." Meanwhile, friends were taking turns taking me in.

As November rolled into December, it became harder to escape the fact that I was living like a migrant while the pine floors in my new living room were being refinished by hand and a third coat of Pratt and Lambert paint was going down in the dining room. The fact I *could* escape was how much all this was costing, and what the penalties would be for removing that ill-fated money early from my retirement account.

Vanderbilt says she has learned some things since losing all her money. She learned " 'never to give over my power of attorney to anyone' " and she became " 'cured' " of psychiatrists forever. " 'I was too trusting,' " she says.

Of course, it was more than that. The picture she paints is of a misguided, gullible woman, a romantic heroine led down the path of destruction by greedy and evil men. But come on! This was a woman savvy enough to build a garment-manufacturing empire.

At first we all want to look for scapegoats. If I could have drummed up a few I would have. The whole saga ended, finally, with my having a beautiful new house (albeit a smaller one) and overwhelming debt.

Suddenly, I felt frightened. Very frightened. The fear was not just about the debt — and the menacing image of the IRS, which, by 1994, was really coming down on me. It was a deeper terror: *I was sure that if I ever made any money again, the same thing would happen.*

I was out of control with money. I felt victimized by some rapacious, unknown part of myself that lurked beneath the level of consciousness.

FACING THE TAX MAN

I moved into the little renovated house before Christmas. It was pristine, it was perfect; but when my taxes came due the following April I went into a state of shock. I owed the government fifty thousand dollars! And after spending all my money on the renovation, I was having a slower year. Simply, there was no money to pay the tax bill. By now I was trying to catch up with the book manuscript I'd laid aside but was finding work difficult because

I'd become depressed. Yet I knew the only way out of my morass was to get the book finished. In spite of my low mood and many interruptions, I kept writing. Whatever money came in went to hiring people to transcribe interviews and put my endless changes into the computer.

Anxiety was high, my mood low. The two women who came, cheerfully, each morning to work alongside me provided structure and human contact that got me through the Dark Night of this period. Also, I entered therapy again. Eventually, I completed the manuscript and felt proud of what I'd accomplished. But I was still in the tax bind, with notices from the IRS becoming ever more urgent. By the end of the year, of course, I owed an additional four quarters' worth of taxes.

Looking back, I'm surprised the government didn't crash down on me earlier, but when it did, placing liens on both properties, I owed almost eighty thousand dollars. I thought, God only knows how I'm going to get out of this. In the back of my mind lurked the freelance writer's ultimate rescue fantasy — a windfall, a publishing coup, a bestseller. I chose not to dwell on the statistical unlikelihood of this occurring. I needed every crumb of false hope I could generate.

I had no faith that I could get out of debt the slow, hard way, through cutting back on spending and making regular payments to the tax man. I had no understanding that committing to such a process, mundane though it seemed, would put me in control. I thought salvation could come in the fluke of a big hit or not at all.

Salvation is the operative word here. I needed someone to come along and take charge of my affairs, the way my daddy had when he put me on a weekly allowance in college. Well, I wanted Big Daddy and I got him: Big Daddy, Uncle Sam, the U.S. government. I got him in the form of Mark Hinds, a strict though surprisingly kind IRS agent, who sat me down in his office, looked over everything, and told me I had to sell both houses and give whatever I made on the sales directly to the government. Once I did that, he said, the IRS would allow me to go on an installment plan, the amount of monthly payments to be determined by Hinds. In addition, of course, I would be expected to pay my quarterly taxes on time. If I failed to do this, the installment program would be stopped and more drastic measures levied. Specifically, the government would begin going after my income directly, intercepting it as soon as it came into my agent's office from publishers.

Hinds's announcement had an immediate and bracing effect. I felt relieved not to be skidding on thin ice any longer, like a kid out of control. The nightmare had come to an end. Strict as it was, a plan had been put forth whereby I could actually mend my fences.

I set about putting first one house on the market and then the next. I was as creative in writing my ad copy as if I were going to put the profits into my own bank account. In fact, the profits *were* going to me, since they were going toward my debt, and debt was destroying me.

The very thought that I could get back into control, even though crawling back, restored some of my dignity. I decided not to alert people, least of all the real estate brokers, to the direness of my situation. The market was flat as hell, so I knew I wasn't going to make any hefty profits, but I wasn't going to be cheated, either. There would be no fire sale here. Having put long, hard effort and cold hard cash into improving both properties, I valued them. And I knew enough not to be persuaded by the broker's computerized printouts on how many houses of the same square footage had sold for what in the previous twelve months. My properties were special, with water and gardens, lovely views. And they had been meticulously maintained.

As I expected, a serious buyer for the big house came forth almost immediately. I hung tough in the negotiations until the end. Even in the eleventh hour, when the buyer was still trying to get concessions and the broker was begging me to go along with the buyer so as "not to lose the deal," I stuck. The buyer was a lawyer, using everything in his arsenal to shave a few thousand off the price. I, by then, had arranged a sale of my furniture to pay my monthly bills, but he had no way of knowing how hard up I was.

The morning of the big furniture sale, the broker arrived unexpectedly, at 9 A.M., to present a list of antiques the buyer wanted me to give him in lieu of lopping more money from a price he'd already agreed to. I said no.

I think that I was in the process of learning a big lesson. You can't afford to cave in when others show muscle. Nor, playing the passive good daughter who compliantly stays in her place, can you simply rely on virtue and good intentions to see you through. Even though something terrible had happened to me — perhaps *because* something terrible had happened to me — my cowering days were over. The veils were lifting from my eyes. I was awakening from a dream — a dream of rescue. At last I was beginning to understand how things really operate.

Real estate can be a kind of game people play to see who can gain the most benefit. But there are some who go through the motions of negotiating, fearing that *not* to would look naive. It was in this category that I positioned my lawyer-buyer. He wasn't actually a cutthroat type, he was just trying to appear hard-nosed. His wife was salivating for the house.

And I? I had business to take care of. The more I walked away with at the closing — actually, the more the IRS walked away with, since they would be right there at the closing to intercept the check — the shorter the time I would have to be on the pressing installment plan.

My life was going to be far different than it had been, but at last I was seeing things clearly. Very clearly.

After the sale of the two properties, which together put $50,000 toward my tax debt, I gathered up six months of bills and canceled checks so Mark Hinds could see what my monthly expenses were. He also required proof of my income. With these documents and a fast, greasy pencil, he would determine what I had to come up with each month toward my tax bill. *He* would decide whether my $250 phone bill was too high to be considered a legitimate monthly expense. (He did, saying, "I'm going to allow you one seventy-five.") It was, to some small extent, a negotiating table. He wanted me to pay no more than $600 in rent. I stuck to my claim that I couldn't find a place to live and work in Woodstock for less than $1,000. Finally he agreed to the figure I wanted, making up for it by chiseling away at the allotments he'd given me for other categories, such as food and entertainment. No more eating out for me, I thought, although it would turn out that by watching my money closely, I would be able to do a great deal more than I might have thought.

Finally, Hinds came up with the magic figure. On the sixteenth of every month, I would owe $760 to the IRS, over and above the payment of my regular quarterly estimates.

Strangely, I was not undone by the news. Going through the process with Hinds had given me a sense of financial groundedness. For the first time in my life, I knew how much I would be spending and on what. I had a program for making good on my transgressions. The mandate was clear. For me, the experience had been like going to confession to expiate guilt. Hinds was giving me a penance and absolving me of my sins.

For some months I would have an anxiety attack every time the $760 was due. Did I have enough? If not, where would I get it? Sometimes other creditors had to be put off. Unpleasant telephone exchanges ensued. As I juggled and struggled, someone always ended up feeling mistreated. Interest payments were attached to bank loans I was paying late. But as Mark Hinds had advised me, the IRS had to come first. *No* one, he cheerfully pointed out, would charge me more interest and penalties than the U.S. government.

I went back to his office for one more meeting so he could make sure I was on track. I told him I'd joined a financial recovery program, knowing that while I might prove myself capable of meeting Mark's mandate, I didn't trust myself to remain free of financial trouble in the future. I was excited about beginning the process of cleaning up my financial mess, and I felt hopeful that I could come to understand and change my ways. I greeted Hinds, at our follow-up session, with something close to affection. "This hasn't exactly been fun," I told him, "but it's been good for me. I'm going to write about it all someday."

"You're really something," he beamed at me. I beamed back. Then came an insight! *Once again I was getting gratification from being the star pupil, the little girl with her hand in the air waving for teacher's attention.*

If I were really going to change, I needed to take a long hard look at my motives. Was it possible to take charge of my life while I was still playing the "good girl"?

Obviously, it wasn't.

FINANCIAL INDEPENDENCE: THE LAST FRONTIER

Among my friends and acquaintances no one else has racked up quite the numbers I have, but the feeling of being out of control with money, and the specter of eventual destitution, is remarkably strong among women I know. It seems to make little difference how much money they're earning. They aren't *dealing* with it. At twenty-eight, a friend's daughter makes $70,000 a year in the television business, puts 20 percent into her retirement account — *and* lets her mother pay for her health insurance. Her mother feels this is all right. Her mother isn't *sure* this is all right. Her mother said, finally, that she hopes her daughter will come to her before long and say, "I don't need this anymore. I can do it myself."

At least this young woman has a retirement account. There are those who just spend, spend, spend — and get in trouble with their landlords. "I will follow you to the ends of the earth," my daughter's landlord told her in his gravelly voice on her message tape. In the meantime, she was wearing the most incredible new pair of boots. *And* imitating the way her landlord sounded on her answering machine, emphasizing the monster quality. "The son of a bitch," I said, when I first heard about it. She was three months behind on her rent. "Have you kept the tape?"

That was before I entered Debtors Anonymous and began to straighten out my skewed attitudes. I envisioned litigation. I saw victimization. I did *not* see, *What the hell are you doing with your money?*

And as I had gone down the path of increasing debt, so, not surprisingly, had she.

In a survey whose results were published in 1996, women were asked about their fears and attitudes toward money. "Almost without exception, those who responded to my questionnaire displayed a deep *intellectual* or *political* understanding of the gendered inequities around money, and of how discriminatory attitudes affect them," says the researcher, Margaret Randall. But "dealing with the *emotional* residue is clearly more difficult."[1]

Randall sees deception — self- and otherwise — as part of that residue. "Excuses and cover-ups develop, as well as the silences, secrets, or outright fabrications. Almost everyone who responded to my questionnaire listed a few financial lies — committed, or by omission."

" 'I sometimes say things cost more or less than they actually did, depending on who I am talking to,' " said one of Randall's survey respondents. " 'I am silent about how much I owe on my credit card, which I keep using despite resolving not to. I pretend I have more money than I do, and thus spend too much.' "

Jane, an artist and graphics designer in her mid-forties, told Randall, " 'The greatest secret I have about money is that I lie to myself about it. I don't look at the facts. I don't review my books, or make a financial plan, going month to month. If I'm nice enough and do good work, the clients will come.' "

Jane's attitude, says Randall, mirrors that held by many women, "who have been conditioned to believe that ignoring a possible trouble spot will keep it from erupting."

The power that comes from managing one's money is something women have a hard time with. " 'I think that I play the "poor" role with my children to avoid saying I don't want to spend for something,' " one mother admitted. " 'Instead I say we can't afford that. It's easier but not honest.' "

How many times do we say we can't afford something "when what we really mean is, 'I have the money but prefer to use it for something else?' " muses Randall. "Or, 'I'm afraid my choice may seem selfish to you, and I depend for my self-esteem on what you think.' "

A combination of magical and catastrophic thinking is surprisingly prevalent among women. " 'I don't like to admit how much my husband makes,' " one woman told Randall. " 'I downplay how much we pay for things.' " The subject of money, and its implicit power, was so disturbing she maintained superstitions about it. " 'If I got a gift of $100, it was almost for sure that one of the kids would need a doctor visit, or the car would need tires. It worked the other way too. If I had to buy my son a new soccer uniform, I'd almost magically get an extra on-the-side typing job offered to me. This superstition causes me some trouble now that we are beginning to have more money than we spend every month — it feels like it invites disaster. Surely one of us will have an accident, or the house will burn down. Something.' "

A COMPULSIVE SPENDER

I have flinched, seeing my resistance to financial independence crop up again and again. This, I think, is the last taboo for women to overcome: to let it be known, once and for all, that we are capable of taking care of ourselves financially. It is the final frontier in the battle for equality, and it is also the last hole in the sieve preventing inner security.

There are various psychological underpinnings to women's compulsion to spend. One is image related. Spending money can have the effects of seeming to gloss over gaps in self-esteem. Because spending produces a momentary uplift, the strategy becomes self-perpetuating. Like eating candy for the sugar high or drinking coffee for the caffeine, spending seems to work for a while as a method of elevating our spirits — through a perceived improvement in status.

But then, inevitably, comes the crash, as financial problems come slamming down — and with them, our creakily supported feelings of self-worth. A vicious cycle ensues. We spend to feel better about ourselves, and as we go deeper into debt, we become desperate, grabbing on to expensive palliatives — the vacation escape, the great (read "important") suit, the soft leather interior of a foreign car.

The debtor doesn't acknowledge what's going on until she's seriously out of control, bill-ridden, anxious, and getting by week to week via ever-finer manipulations of her credit sources — a modus operandi that used to be called "living hand-to-mouth."

I discovered that one can earn a lot of money and still be living hand-to-mouth.

My way of dealing with debt had always been to drive myself harder to make more money. There was a year not long ago when I grossed close to four hundred thousand dollars. Now, I send off monthly checks to the IRS, slowly chipping away at the balance of my debt. I buy my clothes at Marshalls and color my own hair. No more Madison Avenue salons for me. I live in a rented house that I heat with wood in the winter.

But life is not, by any means, bad. In fact, it is better, more real, more gratifying, than it's been for a long time. I joined Debtors Anonymous, an organization that is structured to help tame the untamable — layer by layer, day by day.

I've been given tools that helped me to learn to function in a different way. I have learned to spend money on the things that provide true pleasure — the Pilates training that strengthens my body and contributes to a profound new sense of well-being, the therapy that has helped me, at midlife, to become a different kind of person, the plants I grow from seed in the spring. I don't care that my car looks its age; it runs, and not having to make car payments affords me the money for more important things. It sounds obvious. It sounds simple. It isn't.

To finally grow up, financially, I had to revisit my childhood and adolescence and uncover the fears I'd developed about taking care of myself. In the course of my research I learned how systematically girls and young women are trained to disengage from their most fundamental desires and feelings of competence. They are taught to be Cinderellas — today, no less than they were when I first began my research on women's problems with dependency, in the 1970s.

If anything, females' training into dependency is more confusing in the nineties, because teachers and other adults pay lip service to equality while permitting an aggressiveness and independence in boys that they discourage in girls.

In addition, girls entering sexual maturity often face ridicule and disparagement — from adults, as well as from boys their age. Many experience actual trauma, as has finally been documented for the first time. It is not surprising, then, given their demeaning introduction to the adult world, that on some hidden level young women try to remain girls — girls in grown-ups' clothing.

In my research for *Maxing Out*, I found that women suffer from a destructive lack of confidence about taking care of ourselves. *Our inhibitions against achieving financial independence, which result from a complex web of social and psychological conditions, are wreaking havoc with inner security and our ability — even our wish! — to become mistresses of our own fate.*

The bind in which women find themselves derives not only

from bias-distorted economics, but also comes from the ways in which women conspire in undermining their financial security. Until women uncover the roots of their financial passivity, they'll continue to view prosperity as linked to fate rather than as something they create in an active, conscious, self-liberating way. Cinderella had nothing but her dreams. The bag lady has nothing but her shopping cart. Cinderella and the bag lady: these are the opposing myths that haunt women today — women who, though we have begun to have money of our own, continue to feel powerless. And to throw away what little power we have!

The number of women functioning like credit card Cinderellas is in the millions. They see no connection between their fears of destitution and their underlying problems with dependency — their dreams of rescue.

One of the things that stops us from beginning the process of creating a healthy financial identity is our terror of being deprived — of ending up with even less than we have now. (And what we have doesn't mean what's in the bank; it means our *perceived* level of prosperity.) We believe that if we start to become more conscious about money, we'll have to make do with even less.

In fact, the opposite is true. You learn to put your own needs first — before your husband's, before your children's, before your creditors'. But at the same time, you look reality in the eye — document it day-to-day — and commit to a life without debt, all of which leads to both psychological security *and* actual abundance: that is, more money, better handled and effectively invested.

It leads to better relationships with our loved ones.

It leads to being able to operate from a true sense of choice.

Learning to deal with one's money brings about tremendous personal growth and change. Bank balances alone don't change, *lives* change. At first, the sense that this is going to happen is frightening. The feeling is: "I just want to get my finances under control, I don't want anything else changing." Impossible. While getting your finances under control, *you* change. You become a different person.

As I began to take hold of my affairs in the smallest, most basic ways, documenting what I was doing daily, I began to feel better about myself than I had ever felt.

I found that I needed to reach out, become less isolated — I needed to become *involved* with people, and let them become involved with me. I stopped judging. I developed compassion. And as I did so, I watched self-distrust peel away. I no longer felt compelled to compare myself to others — to do "one-up, one-down."

To unravel the web of untruths we've been told about ourselves requires a kind of deprogramming. We *have* been brainwashed, after all. And while much has changed in society, the brainwashing of females to be submissive, to flatten themselves, to fear standing on their own feet, goes on. But by facing that fear and taking money on as the next area of our own feminine development, we can gain a sense of power over our lives — perhaps for the first time. With money of our own we are free to live with whom we wish or live alone. We are free to pursue dreams we may have shelved earlier to raise children. We are free from undue fear of poverty and isolation in our old age.

It is my hope that *Maxing Out* will help women confront their financial self-destructiveness so that they can enjoy fuller, less compromised lives — so that they can live without the crutch of the Cinderella fantasy *or* the fear of ending up destitute!

Chapter 2

MAXING OUT IN A CULTURE OF DEBT

It used to be called "going into hock." Now it's called "maxing out." The very term has an aggressive ring, as if exceeding the maximum limit on one's credit balance is hip and bold — a sign of being one of the crowd — dauntless in your capacity to spend big. *Everyone* maxes out, is the attitude. The younger you are when you do it for the first time, the cooler.

"When my dog came down with lymphoma, I maxed out two credit cards on chemotherapy trying to save her," said Jeanne Hill, of San Francisco, who woke up one morning to find herself without enough money to live on.[1]

The two thousand dollars in veterinary bills she put on credit pushed Ms. Hill's total debt to twelve thousand. When she lost her job as a legal secretary and developed knee problems, her nine-hundred-dollar monthly card payment all but chewed up the $1,188 she was receiving from disability insurance.

Thus did Ms. Hill become, in the no-nonsense language of the credit card industry, "a bad" — someone who, for whatever reason, doesn't pay back what he or she borrows.

Americans ran up card balances by 19 percent in 1997, to $305 billion. And *that* after a 28 percent increase in card debt the previous year. People talk openly now about how much credit card debt they have, naming the thousands they owe as proudly as if they were citing money in the bank. Debt has become the signifier of a life being lived: trips taken, meals eaten, wines savored. People actually believe they are *worth* whatever credit's been extended them. It's amazing how quickly one gets sucked into a sense of limitlessness. I can do what I want, go where I want, wear what I want. Why not buy the Arche slings at two hundred a pop? I can afford it. The numbers on the bank statements bleed into meaninglessness, as evanescent as skywriting.

What's getting financed by the credit card companies is a culture of materialism: the right furnishings, the right shoes for every sport, monumental CD collections, cars, gym memberships, restaurant meals, bicycles that cost what a car used to cost. The whole notion of a middle class, with its paltry constraints, has been subsumed by the culture of debt. Anyone can do anything, so long as she meets the minimum payments. The longer you're in the game, the more credit is extended. You don't even have to ask for it. Notice that you've been given it will arrive in the mailbox. *God, they love me!* you think, as soon as you open the mail and find your latest credit extension of five thousand dollars. Immediately your sense of what's possible enlarges. Soon vacations become more elaborate, the clothes and gear for executing them more high-end. As your credit limit goes up, the more ridiculous it seems to stint. Those years of existing like a second-class citizen have almost faded from memory. Girl, you are *empowered*. Go *back* to school. *Buy* that house. *Lavish* gifts upon your loved ones. *Spend now, pay . . . whenever.*

Most women I know live this way. They do not think their

debting is a problem until the day comes when they can't juggle the minimum payments. Or they're denied a mortgage because their credit debt is too high. *Then* they look at the situation merely as something to be corrected. Money must be borrowed, say, to pay off the credit cards so the mortgage will go through. Or they shop around for a debt consolidation loan at lower interest. But they don't think they have a problem with running up debt. It's the crazy economy, the result of a lacuna, an expensive illness, perhaps, or even a misunderstanding — but it isn't, goddamn it, *them.*

"I'LL JUST PUT IT ON MY CREDIT CARD"

In her book *When Money Is the Drug,* financial counselor Donna Boundy shows the cultural background of the current dysfunctional attitude toward debt. "With the tone set at the level of federal government, money dysfunction during the 1970s and 1980s had huge reverberations in the corporate world as well. Ethics and long-term thinking were out of style. Highly leveraged deals (deals financed with borrowed funds) exploded in popularity. Corporations went on an unprecedented spending spree, assuming massive debt, selling assets, and failing to produce new capital."[2]

All the wild corporate spending and debt was made possible by the government's laxity in enforcing antitrust laws, and by changing corporate tax codes so that the interest paid on debt became tax deductible at a time when other corporate tax deductions were eliminated. "That gave companies a short term incentive to take on massive debt," Boundy explains. "Company A could buy Company B on borrowed money, and lower its tax bite."

Business decisions were increasingly based on short-term gain rather than what was best for the long-term growth and stability of the companies. "Immediate gratification reigned, just as it does with an individual addict," Boundy wrote, in *When Money Is the Drug.* "Get the high now; never mind the consequences later. Soon many corporations were up to their ears in debt, had no cash flow and few assets."

In some ways, pursuing money "highs" as a nation, over the past two decades, "represents the victory of addictive thinking over rationality, of denial over reality," says Boundy. "We seem to want to believe, like the individual addict, that we are collectively invulnerable, that we are always right and always in control."

More than any generation previously, those in today's younger generation are weighed down by debt before they leave their twenties — sometimes before they *enter* their twenties. The focus is no longer on starting from scratch. These kids debt from scratch.

The encouragement to spend rather than self-regulate gets serious as soon as a child is away from the monitoring parental eye but is still being funded by mom and dad's bank account. Solicitation begins the day the young person arrives at college to register for classes. Booths manned by credit card companies and long-distance phone companies are set up in the very hall where registration takes place. Requirements for the cards are ridiculously low. The effect of so much available credit has been quick and harrowing. In three years, said a *New York Times* report on student debt, student borrowing has almost doubled — from $18 billion in 1993 to $33 billion in 1996.[3]

Colleges themselves offer credit cards to students. The result of all this available money is debt so deep it forces kids to drop out of college. "As freshmen they get three or four cards, and they think they can duplicate their previous life style with parents, or can create a whole new life style," a counselor with the National Foundation for Consumer Credit told the *Times*. By the second year, their cards are maxed out and they get more. "Eventually, either their parents bail them out or they drop out of school to pay off their credit cards."

A survey at Iowa State University found that 76 percent of the students held three or more credit cards; 40 percent had six or more.

Financial aid officers say a growing number of young men and women are leaving college with huge debts and ruined credit ratings because of credit cards. They use credit cards like cash rather than regarding them as high-interest loans due now. " 'I was forewarned to get just one card and not go crazy, but I did go crazy,' " said Melissa, a sociology major at the University of California, in the *Times* report. " 'I didn't worry about working, because I thought, "Oh, I'll just put it on my credit card." It's unfortunate that it ruins your credit in the long run.' "

Credit counselors say young people know in the abstract that debt is not a great idea, but they have little sense of how much a ruined credit rating will affect them in the future. And, because of what was modeled by the families, they have little idea of what's required for staying *out* of debt. College isn't looked upon as a penny-pinching time, but as a good time. Kids learn little about the ins and outs of personal finance. They simply spend, with the vague idea that some windfall in the future will help them pay it all off.

Not surprisingly, the number of students working while going to school appears to be declining. Yet having a job is the only way many kids can get through college these days unless they want to face years of debt. Rather than fry herself with student loans, a psychology major at the University of Maryland is pushing herself through four years of college in three. But she's already a slave to MasterCard. Having put a part of her tuition on her charge card, she can't cough up more than the monthly minimum.

MARCY FIGHTS HER WAY FREE

We are sitting in my apartment on an August day so hot the air conditioner barely puts a dent in the humidity. Marcy is neatly dressed in a cotton skirt and sleeveless white blouse. I'm not surprised, somehow, when she tells me she's a perfectionist. "When I do something, I want to be the best."

She wants to be the best and she wants to get there instantly. "My problem in twelve-step programs has been that once I've worked through the steps, I think I'm recovered. That's just not how recovery works. Recovery comes in leaps and bounds. And also . . . I'm very critical of myself. I tend not to look at the recovery I've made. I can only think of how much money I still owe."

What she owes is nine thousand dollars in credit card debt. It haunts her that her spending has been out of control. Often, it's a daily struggle. "Today, for example. I finished this job that I was at for two and a half years, and I was sad. I started feeling a lot of anger, a lot of rage. I wanted to act out. I didn't want to drink; what I wanted was to pull out my credit card and go shopping. I think some people might not think that's a big deal, but it is a big deal."

Marcy, at thirty, has recently joined Debtors Anonymous. She grew up in a wealthy area of Westchester County, went away to college, then got a master's degree in social work. Today, she works as a family therapist in New York City. She owns her own co-op on the Upper West Side of Manhattan (with the aid of a family trust fund) and struggles enormously with issues of credit card debting and self-esteem. Early in her twenties she was in a substance abuse program, but dealing with compulsive debting, she says, is the hardest thing she's ever attempted.

"I've recovered from different things, including an eating disorder. Depression is something I've struggled with. But I think at the bottom of all my dis-eases is the money issue. Whenever I stopped acting out in some other way, the money thing was still there. For years it was something I never looked at."

To battle her tendency to be critical of herself, Marcy tries to acknowledge her successes whenever she can. "My progress today was that I didn't go home and pick up my credit card. I didn't overspend. I just let it go. And that is just a huge step for me."

Marcy's generation has been lured to debt the way it's been

lured to drugs. When I was in college, alcohol was the only drug, and big-time debting was impossible because no banker in his right mind would lend to someone eighteen or twenty. Not so today. In this generation both credit and drugs are equally available, and the struggle to avoid them can be enormous.

Marcy expresses, poignantly, the position of young people who've had credit thrown at them since they were teenagers. "I think credit card companies really exploit young people. When you feel deprived, or maybe you're not really connected emotionally to yourself, or you're in college or high school and it's hard to pay bills, having credit just makes you want to go crazy."

Also, she points out, it seems "to represent separation from your parents that you're making your own money, you have this credit card, and you can go out and get what you want without asking them for anything."

Easy credit is setting up those in their twenties and thirties to be in trouble for the rest of their lives. "It's an issue that's not even being touched, it's so loaded," says Marcy. "It involves banks and institutions that are much more powerful than I am. Credit card companies say you can get credit even though you've filed for bankruptcy. I was buying an apartment and the bank said I didn't have enough credit. And I said, 'Well, I had two credit cards that I canceled, and I owed money and I'm making my payments.' I thought it was a *good* thing not to have a lot of credit cards, but the bank thought that it *wasn't* a good thing. And I thought, 'This is crazy.' I mean, I don't want to be in debt. I don't want to *have* a lot of credit cards."

"What brought you to DA in the first place?" I asked.

"I felt out of control with money, I felt really powerless. I wasn't ready to deal with it. I'm not irresponsible with bills. I never have not paid my utility bill or my rent. But for some reason I just act it all out in credit cards."

Marcy says she got a lot of mixed messages about money when she was growing up. "Both of my parents came from working-class backgrounds but they became very affluent. They're both doctors, specialists. One minute they would say, 'You're going to have an allowance, and we're going to stick to that.' Next week, they would have forgotten about it. Mostly, they'd just give me money whenever I needed it. My dad didn't want me to have to get a job in college because he had to work so hard in college and was really poor."

"Have you gotten help from your parents since you've been out of college?"

"Yeah. And I have, a, I guess a trust, yeah, a trust fund."

"You're even having trouble saying it."

"It's not something that I feel very comfortable with. It was something my father controlled for a long time."

Three years ago Marcy finally began using her own accountant. "My parents had moved out west. My father said his accountant couldn't do my taxes because he wouldn't know the tax codes in New York. So he told me to get my own accountant and he'd pay him. I let him pay, that year, but since then I've paid the accountant myself. I think my father's very generous, but I think he's also very enabling."

"He's confused about how to be helpful."

"I think that's true. When I told him about being in Debtors Anonymous, the first thing he said was, 'How much do you owe?' And I said, 'That's not what it's about, Dad.' I said, 'I don't want your money.' He was ready to just pay off my debts. I said, 'You could pay off my debts and I'd be back in debt the next day.' My father had bailed me out of credit card debt once before."

Marcy says "the debting disease" runs throughout her family. "My brothers and my sister have all had trouble with credit cards. I don't know where they stand now. It's something we don't talk about. None of us talk about it. I think money is the one thing that people don't like to talk about."

What first got Marcy to consider doing something about her situation was reading *How to Get Out of Debt, Stay Out of Debt and Live Prosperously,* by Jerrold Mundis.[4] "It was like my bible. Still is. One thing I got from it was that nobody's going to go to debtors' prison these days. There *is* no debtors' prison. If I can only send a credit card company five dollars a month, that's okay. Even though I have money, and in a worst-case scenario my parents could help me, I still worry about money constantly. It's very destructive to have so much anxiety about money."

Maintaining solvency — which in DA terms means creating no new debt — is extremely difficult for the compulsive debtor. "I had sixty days of solvency, and then I broke it. I acted on my credit card. Now I have twenty-one days of solvency. I feel so frustrated. It's not easy. The whole one-day-at-a-time thing. I feel like I am an alcoholic with the credit card. I have a hard time delaying. It's instant gratification. I was into smoking pot. I was an overeater. It was about wanting things right away. And that's why having a credit card was like a stick of dynamite in my hand because I could get whatever I had to have that minute."

Marcy first became aware that her "money thing" was out of control after she had surgery for an ovarian cyst and the medical bills began flooding in. "Some things weren't covered by my insurance, and I started freaking out. I started really getting anxious and began feeling like, 'I can't deal with another bill coming in. What do I do? I have to take care of myself. I have to deal with this.' And I felt just so much anxiety. That still happens. I start freaking out about bills coming in, instead of being like, 'Okay, it's going to work itself out.' Anyway, with the hospital bills I felt really harassed and stuff, and I became completely hysterical, calling my mother and crying that I just couldn't take it. And my father was like, 'I'll just pay whatever you owe.' The hospital stuff was eventually taken care of by insurance. It was the other stuff, the doctors bill you separately, you have to figure out who gets what . . ."

"I gather that the main feeling was that you couldn't cope."

"I couldn't *deal* with it. I used to be afraid to open my mail or listen to my messages. I just wanted someone else to take care of it for me."

"Can we stop and talk about that? Where do you think that comes from?"

"Well, I think it's a feeling of powerlessness. It's a sense of, 'This is bigger than me. This is greater than me. It's so out of control, so big, I can't handle it. It's a monster.' "

"Was there anything in your upbringing as a female that might have contributed to this sense of 'I can't cope. I haven't had to deal with this before. I don't know the rules of this game. These guys are coming after me.' That freak-out feeling you describe."

"I know that my sister owed some money on taxes and she had a freak-out thing, too. She called my parents and they helped her. My brothers, I think, are just more internal. They just don't . . . I can't imagine them freaking out. I *can* imagine my sister freaking out, throwing up her hands and saying, 'I can't deal with this.' "

"Do you think some of the 'I can't cope' — the feeling that you didn't have what it took to sort out the medical bills — might be related to your having been reared as a girl?"

"My brothers wouldn't do that, I know. My sister and I were always treated a little differently . . ."

But here Marcy interrupts herself to reaffirm her feminist identification of herself. "I was always independent. Or I always *thought* that I was independent. I mean, yeah, I've definitely had *feelings* like, 'Oh, I just wish some guy would bail me out of this.' But now I really don't. Now I really wish I had some more money coming in. I *want* more money coming in."

"Do you think it's within your power to make that happen?"

"Well, I do, but I don't know how. I *think* I know how, but it's like, 'Do I want to start private practice? Is that something

I'm interested in? Do I want to write a book? What would I want to write a book on?' Or maybe it's even something more creative that I want to do. I think I have the skills and personality to do something beyond a nine-to-five job, but I don't know what it would be."

I have known and interviewed many Marcy's age who are floundering in the same way. They are bright, educated, privileged young women who, at thirty or so, have only the vaguest idea about what they want to do. Something in them has taken a serious detour from the goal of self-sufficiency.

"I want to earn more money. I don't want my parents giving me money. I want to get out of debt. That's what's frustrating. I want to be out of debt *today*. But I think the other thing is that I'm also scared to be *out* of debt."

"What would that mean to you?"

"I think I'm afraid of what it would be like to *not* be in debt. It's kind of like, if you're in a bad marriage you can't imagine not being in a bad marriage. What would it be like to *not* be married or *not* be in a relationship, to be alone."

"The unknown is frightening."

"Right. You don't know what that's going to be like. It could be actually wonderful, but it's also terrifying."

Marcy is circling in on the basis of her problem — her fear of financial independence. It is a fear that undermines women of various ages and backgrounds and levels of competence.

THE LURE OF THE BIG FIX

What would you do if you won several hundred thousand dollars in the form of a "genius" grant from the MacArthur Foundation? Build a house? Travel? Invest in a new business?

When Rebecca Goldstein won the coveted award for her novel writing, in 1996, she did with her $285,000 what most of us would do: used it to pay off debt. Sad but true; the juicy award ended up going not to new pleasures for Goldstein and her husband, but to cancel the effects of past indulgences — and not even the giddy indulgence of overspending so much as the expensive luxury of "not having to think about money."

Eleven years ago, when she was thirty-seven, Goldstein quit her teaching job at Barnard to devote herself full-time to writing. Her husband, Sheldon, makes a steady income as a math professor at Rutgers University, but the family finances began " 'spiraling down-ward' " when she quit her job, says Goldstein. They've never recovered. Yet they continue to spend liberally on their two daughters (ballet and music lessons and private school), and now the older girl is getting ready to enter Harvard, with a four-year tuition bill of $125,000. Their second car, a patched '78 Ford, is long overdue for replacement. The MacArthur award — which af-ter taxes boils down to a not so glittering $31,000 a year, paid out over five years — will offer them what Rebecca refers to as " 'undifferentiated relief.' "[5]

"Genius Grant Patches Up Family's Frayed Finances" was the headline on the article the *New York Times* ran. To create its story, the paper asked two financial planners to take a good look at the Goldstein's finances. Both said the couple should not be in such a shaky state. Their combined income is a little over $100,000. And they do not squander money. What was their main problem? They don't talk about money. If possible, they don't *think* about money.

Ms. Goldstein, whose novels are influenced by the philosophy she loves (and used to teach), notes that in *The Republic*, " 'Plato described a very socialist society where money was, as much as possible, to be avoided.' " Spinoza was another philosopher with " 'a high-minded disdain for worldly affairs.' " And Goldstein herself confesses to being bored by the subject. Whenever her husband talked about money, " 'my eyes would glaze over.' " And he often failed to discuss money matters with her, she says, because he knew she " 'felt bad' " about the irregularity of their income after she quit teaching.

But this is not a story about numbers or a fear of numbers. Professor Goldstein's field, after all, is mathematics. And anyone capable of understanding Spinoza has what it takes to plan tax payments wisely. *This is a story about resistance — resistance to responsibility, resistance to facing limitation, resistance, in spite of all the outward trappings of adulthood, to growing up.*

For how adult is this? The Goldsteins do no budgeting or tax planning. They've lived beyond their six-figure income for years. In the late eighties they took out an $80,000 home equity line of credit. It added $800 to their monthly expenses, on top of their $900 payment toward their original mortgage. The variable interest rate on the new loan has been as high as 10 percent. When Rebecca Goldstein got her first MacArthur check, she used $15,000 to shave off the $66,000 balance on the home equity loan. "I'm so desperate to be out of debt," she said. She was the daughter of a cantor; growing up, her family had been poor but solvent. But the Goldsteins, true to their generation, had been in debt ever since their eighteen-year-old daughter was born. And to be fair, nothing in their environment, from bank loan officers to TV commercials to what the Joneses down the street are doing with their money, has ever suggested that their way of life is anything but sensible.

But now, this sudden influx of money. The financial planners offered suggestions on what the Goldsteins would have to do to begin prying themselves out of their mess. Number one, they needed to start facing their finances in a conscious, consistent way. No more hiding. They needed to meet regularly, talk regularly. They needed to budget. They needed to create a plan for future large expenses. At an annual inflation rate of 4 percent, it was going to cost them about $140,000 to send their younger daughter to college in seven years. The only way the Goldsteins could possibly afford such a sum was by beginning *now* to set aside $865 a month and invest it at 8 percent.

Could a couple who had spent eighteen years borrowing instead of budgeting turn things around?

" 'Our family doesn't like to talk about money, but I'm much more receptive to the idea,' " Rebecca said. " 'I feel as though I've crossed a hurdle. Perhaps in the future my husband won't avoid talking to me about money, and I won't mind its details.' "

Perhaps. But usually it takes more than one crisis to institute the deep personal change required for turning around a lifetime of avoidance.

" 'I've always lived on a wing and a prayer,' " says choreographer Elizabeth Streb.[6] It is the artist's mantra. Often enough, it's the *woman's* mantra.

In the seventies, when she first came to New York, Streb supported herself washing dishes and working as a chef. To help pay for dance classes, she spent years living in a rat-infested, often unheated loft and renting it out to dance companies for rehearsals during the day. Then, in the early eighties, she began receiving grants — not huge ones, but enough, along with a sixty-thousand-dollar inheritance, to form her own company, Ringside. Today, with eight dancers, the company is known for its gravity-defying physicality, with dancers doing things like walking up seventeen-foot poles and flinging themselves against walls.

Supporting a company — paying dancers' salaries and the costs of producing performances — is an enormous challenge. Streb's inheritance ran out in three years, at which point she began relying on credit cards to finance everything. By 1989, she had fourteen credit cards and was thirty thousand dollars in debt.

Later that year, after the sale of some family property, she came into thirty thousand dollars. She paid off the credit cards and promptly locked them in a safe deposit box. But then, after " 'one desperate year' " of trying to keep herself afloat, out came the cards again.

Streb says she has never been a saver. Her bricklayer father, after all, had saved for years hoping to retire on a full pension. But at sixty-two, three years before his pension was due, he found himself too physically worn out to continue working. The rest of his life was less comfortable than he had hoped. " 'When you plan too fastidiously for your future, things fall apart' " was the lesson Streb took from her father's experience.

With her short, tousled hair, leather jacket, and aquiline profile, Streb is a serious-looking woman who gives the impression that putting together the kind of life she wants has been hugely challenging. But in 1997, when she was forty-seven, she too won a coveted MacArthur award. Will that $290,000 make it easier for her to live and pursue her artistic career?

Like Rebecca Goldstein, Streb will have to make serious changes in her financial functioning if she wants the money to be of any long-term help. First, there's the matter of her debt. When the award came through, Streb's dance company had a $12,000 credit card balance, which she was paying off at $200 a month. In addition, she owed $8,000 on her personal credit card. Then there was an old college loan that had come due in 1973, but which she'd managed to avoid until 1996, when the old alma mater caught up with her. Originally for $3,500, the loan now had a balance of $7,000.

Streb pays $50 a month on the college loan and the minimum payment on her personal credit card of $225. Her other monthly expenses include $700 for her loft (which she shares with a friend), $125 for telephone, $100 for electricity, and $400 a month for eating out. Recently, Ringside began doing well enough for her to be paid a salary for the first time. In 1996 it was $42,000. Streb's MacArthur payments will be about $45,000 a year after taxes — less if she continues getting that $42,000 salary.

Of course she has dreams. She would like to use the money to make dance more accessible, perhaps by having the company perform in shopping malls and parks. Her shower has long been unusable; maybe she could now have it tiled. Maybe she could even take a sabbatical and study physics. But two financial advisers think that debt is killing her and that the biggest chunk of her money should go to paying it off. Because of her credit history, she hasn't been able to consolidate her payments into one low-interest account. Her three credit cards are costing her an outrageous 18 or 19 percent.

Ideally, Streb should maintain a cash emergency fund of about $12,000. She should have health and disability insurance. (In spite of all her vigorous flying around, she's never had any kind of insurance.) And she should be investing for her future. The advisers recommended that $15,000 a year of her award go into a tax-deferred annuity. All of that would knock out about 75 percent of her first year's award.

Buying a home would be a way to lessen the tax bite on her award. If she were to put together $57,000 from her next several award payments, she'd have enough for a 20 percent down payment and closing costs on a $250,000 Manhattan co-op. With a thirty-year fixed-rate mortgage at 7 percent owning her home would cost her $1,400 a month. That's more than she pays now, but it would save her about $4,000 a year in income taxes. Still, she'd have to keep coming up with that $1,400 a month long after the MacArthur award dries up. Maybe, she thinks, she'd be better off staying in her rented loft.

All in all, what Goldstein and Streb are dealing with is the lure of the Big Fix. Like many windfalls, a MacArthur award is less than it first appears, especially when you consider that it's spread out over five years and taxes are removed. Nor does a windfall address the underlying question — which, in this case, is how to support oneself as an artist without going into big-time debt. Like so many women, Streb seems to have felt so overwhelmed by the odds stacked against her that she has never constructed a plan. And as for what will happen to her when she can no longer work, the prospect continues to be disconcerting. More and more, she thinks about which friends she might call upon to assist her in old age. Yet the idea of being dependent is repugnant to her. " 'Frankly, I don't want to act like a renegade nerd that's going to have to be supported.' "

Behavior patterns resulting from avoidance are difficult to break, for they are symptomatic of a whole host of destructive psychological attitudes. Being "bored" with the subject of one's own finances, for example, can be a sign of grandiosity. One has an inflated sense of one's own importance. One will survive, regardless of personal effort, because of one's specialness. One wants to remain above life's mundane chores.

People who are creative are particularly likely to suffer from grandiosity. It can even seem that a certain amount of self-inflation is necessary. How else can they begin with a blank slate and imagine a painting, a choreographed work, a novel? Who can make something out of nothing, if not a little god? And what god wants to bother with such petty distractions as bank statements and pie charts?

But the artist who understands her creative process will tell you it isn't, in fact, the vision of the finished project that keeps her going. What moves her, what fills her with pleasure, is the day-to-day *doing* of the thing. It's engagement with the process, the moment, that counts, not the future glory.

"*Real* fixes take place from within, not from without," writes debting expert Jerry Mundis. "Nothing external — from stardom to a winning lottery ticket — is going to make your *self* any better. The self is an internal image, who you perceive yourself to be, a composite of your thoughts and beliefs. If that self doesn't change, then you will continue to act and feel just as you did before."[7]

At some point in our lives — hopefully sooner rather than later, but with women, it seems, it often doesn't happen until later — we awake to the uneasy recognition that the story line we were expecting has taken a different turn. The white picket fence has fallen, the Prince is long gone, and we are now, and will continue to be, responsible for our own financial livelihood. There is no one to back us up when the rent comes due, no one to cover our expenses when we fall and break an ankle and can't work. We know this, and yet we still avoid doing what we need to do to create financial security for ourselves.

Today, nutrition experts advise against diets in favor of lifestyle changes. Changing the way you think about food. Changing the way you think about your body and yourself. Creating a new value system that will guide you in traveling comfortably and healthily forward, over the long haul of a productive life.

And so it is with money. As Jerry Mundis says, there are no quick fixes. A whole lifetime of attitudes and habits and techniques of denial are at issue here.

For reasons we'll explore, getting serious about earning, investing, and planning for retirement can make us very anxious. We are breaking taboos, acknowledging the truth of our lives.

But by facing that anxiety and taking money on as the next area of our own feminine development, we can gain a sense of power over our own lives — perhaps for the first time. With money of our own we are free to live with whom we wish; free to pursue dreams we shelved earlier to raise children; free from undue fear of poverty and isolation in our old age.

Chapter 3

THE WAY WE SPEND: WHEN
SHOPPING BECOMES COMPULSIVE

It was a fabulous Sunday in early fall, high crisp skies, humidity lower than it had been. My daughter Gabrielle, my friend Wilma, and I were going to "do SoHo." That meant shopping, of course; shopping with our eyes, shopping with our stomachs, shopping with our minds. I rolled back the sunroof, pumped up the volume, and we drove through the streets of lower Manhattan piqued by the female fever to see, to have, to take in.

"Do you remember where that store was we loved so much?" I asked Wilma. We had visited it months earlier, a spectacular environment filled with the most elegant objects: Giacometti-tall lamps of stretched copper topped by small beaded shades; long falls of filmy painted silk, silk meant not for the body for but the endlessly tall windows found in downtown lofts; a framed display of nothing but tassels — velvet tassels, shimmering metal tassels, tassels of roped silk. The store was cool and dark, with soft pools of light and a ceiling so high it was almost like heaven up there. No one shopped at Anthropologie for anything practical. They shopped there for dreams.

We noodled our way into a parking space, got out of the car, and discovered we were, of all places, in front of the store we'd been yearning for. What serendipity! Right next door, however, was a place we hadn't seen before, a store specializing in actual furnishings, sofas, primitive chairs, tableware that seemed to have been fired in Tuscany.

Wilma was wanting a sofa. She had been wanting one for years, but now she was really getting into it, thinking that just because the furnace was forty years old didn't necessarily mean they needed a new one. A friend, a genius friend, had said they probably only needed a new boiler. Or it might even have been just a part for the boiler, she wasn't sure. Anyhow, with Wilma's desires uppermost in our minds, we stepped right past the fantasy store and entered the inviting confines of Wolfman, Gold and Good Company. It was about eleven o'clock in the morning. A gorgeous down-cushioned sofa greeted us the moment we walked in. And imagine this! It was on sale. We walked around it, eyeing its perfect proportions, the thick, soft damask of its just-sloppy-enough slipcover. "Can I help?" said an extremely thin blond in a black sheath wearing necklaces loaded with ivory crosses. "Yes!" We pounced. "And *what* is that smell of cookies?"

"It's cookies," she said. "We bake them here."

She led us deeper into the comforting gloom, where soon, like Alice falling down the rabbit hole, we came upon a long slate-covered bar that sported a huge vase of bridal wreath and two pans of steaming cookies. "I guess they just came out of the oven," said the blond, as if taken by surprise. For the diet-conscious there were, in wine goblets bedded in ice, two flavors of Jell-O: lemon-lime and cappuccino. And of course there was the ubiquitous cappuccino itself. This was shopping at its most aesthetic, shopping as it had never been on Fifth Avenue, shopping as it could only occur in an enclave of artists and artist wannabes, people who knew color, who knew form, who had *taste* such as the rich had never even imagined. We felt something exciting could happen at any moment.

Wilma was wearing her usual. Pigtails, because she could never get her hair right, a rumpled black T-shirt, a long linen skirt with a slit up the front, clogs. She lounged in the middle of the wonderful couch that was on sale for only two thousand dollars and wondered what colors it came in. Only two, the Uma-look-alike saleswoman told her, Putty Swirl and Yellow Matelassé. She held out swatches. "God, it's beige," said Wilma, holding the Putty Swirl against the sofa. "I could never do beige. My mother did beige."

"Well, of course, you could do it custom, but the price goes up a thousand. This one's not only in stock, it's on sale. It's a really good deal if you can hang with the colors."

Wilma grabbed up the swatch again. "Well," she said, "it really isn't bad. It isn't bad at all. Anyway, my mother's dead."

Uma let slip a small smile. "Putty is not the same as beige," she said.

We exited the store with Xeroxed photographs of the couch, stapled with small swatches of Putty Swirl and Yellow Matelassé. I thought I might consider the Yellow Matelassé myself. This was a lifetime investment, after all. (We had not, I'm proud to say, indulged in the cookies or cappuccino-flavored Jell-O, but their presence helped consummate the sale. They definitely helped.)

We stepped out onto Mercer Street. It was by now high noon. We made a stop to look in the window of Steve Madden Shoes, where Gabrielle's eye fell on a pair of red patent ankle-strap platforms. She said, ruminatingly, "If I really wanted to do slut, I could wear them with my black rollerblading pants and midriff."

We were pretty sure she'd never really do slut, but the concept alone was enough. She slipped inside. They were having a fifteen-dollars-off sale. She came back out with her purchase. "Only thirty-five dollars," she said. "I knew, when I realized how happy I'd be just looking at them sitting on the floor in front of my closet, that I had to have them."

Next stop, Pottery Barn, to check out the sisal rugs. If Wilma was going to be happy with the Putty Swirl, she would have to mute the yellow tones of her pine living room floor. Uma had advised us that there was a particular shade of sisal at Pottery Barn that would do the trick. We stepped lightly, upliftedly, down the street. We were on a mission. With Wilma having shelled out two thousand dollars in only our first hour of shopping, we had to make that purchase *work*.

"Chaaarge it!" Betty and Wilma of *The Flintstones* used to bellow, with false feminine power, as they headed out of the house on a shopping spree.

Today, a little girl can get ready to be a big girl by playing with Melanie's Mall, from Cap Toys. At three and a half inches tall, Melanie is a mini-Barbie with long, silky hair and a series of stores that girls can collect to make — a mall! Among the shopping choices: Beauty World, Glamor Gowns, and Melanie's Makeup, each with its own shopping bag. For her purchases, Melanie has women's most powerful tool: a gold credit card.

The agenda, when women are feeling frustrated and powerless, is to swing into macho mode and go out and shop. "*I* know what I'll do, I'll create a new environment in the bedroom!" And *down* with the wallpaper, out with the carpet, days spent resurfacing the walls so that paint — more up to date than that dowdy wallpaper — will look good on them.

My friend Andrea hounds the stores for white sales so she can re-dress her bed, as she puts it, "for a song." Forget the expense of all the hours that go into searching out the sales. Andrea doesn't think that way. Sales are her métier. Shopping is her way of playing the market. But, of course, no earnings come from it, as they would if she were actually investing in a market. What comes from it is a new bedroom.

And the fleeting sense of having *acted*, of having done something transcendent. Each night, as she contemplates the calming eggplant walls, the airy panels at the window, the wonderful Ralph Lauren sheets she got for half off, she feels she has made something happen. And she has. But she rarely stops to think how her life might be different — more secure, more available for truly creative pursuits — if she were to take the same drive, and energy, and vision, and apply it to — managing her stocks.

Reducing her credit card debt.

Shopping around not for Armani knockoffs, but for a lower interest rate to hang all that debt on. What would happen if she spent her time learning what's involved in selecting mutual funds, investing in foreign markets, assessing utilities?

ENHANCING THE IMAGE

Often it's not easy for women to recognize problems with money and spending, or else they recognize the problems but not their own role in creating them. Instead, they focus on how hard they work — which is usually very hard indeed. And they are likely to spend on others' needs — a child's braces, school clothes, ballet lessons; a parent's wedding anniversary; a family vacation; the support of a lover. The married woman may see her salary as providing "extras" and take pride in being able to inflate the family's lifestyle. But the push to upgrade may be an acting out of her feelings of being second class.

I remember the pride I used to take, as I shopped at auctions and flea markets, in furnishing my house with "good stuff" — antique tables and velvet couches rather than the slightly cheesy-looking furniture from Sears and Montgomery Ward I grew up with. By haunting country auctions in search of nineteenth-century castaways, I was raising myself up from my lowly status.

Many women get a sense of power from being "makers" of the home. No matter that they have full-time jobs, what they do inside the home is create a world, an aesthetic environment that everyone in the family can rely on for identity and sense of self. It is the woman's job to do this, just as it is her job to make everyone feel good. And there's an emotional payoff. Her husband, if not her children, will be grateful to her, she feels sure. *He* couldn't do it, or wouldn't. He has bigger fish to fry. But he appreciates the safe harbor she has created for him to enjoy when he walks in the door at night. (No matter that she is walking in the door at the same time.)

Thus does the home, its "look" and its atmosphere, silkily suggest status to the woman, not only because it may exceed in grace and style the home she grew up in but also because her ability to transform flea market finds into something fabulous has become part of what she values about herself.

And is valued *for*, she believes. If and when the marriage breaks up, *she* will get to retain her aesthetic sensibility, while he, poor thing, will get to keep nothing but his bank account. Regarding as pathetic his inability to "make a home for himself," she may even feel a bit superior.

So much of women's shopping is driven by the need to flesh out the accoutrements of the Romance Myth: seductive bed linens, cushy towels for after the bath, candles, makeup, fragrances — domestica for the creation of a safe and womblike home. "But this is what women do so well," some would argue, "and it *is* important, and it *is* valuable, and what about the children? Are they supposed to grow up in the domestic equivalent of a concentration camp?"

The issue may be one of degree. How much time and money does a woman spend trying to scale up the domestic image? How much of her fantasy life is absorbed with images of what she *wants*? How much does she focus on getting things to appear better — either herself or the driveway or the kids' rooms or, God forbid, her husband's suits.

To what degree is she trying to make everyone in the family seem better than they are because she herself feels inferior?

My mother felt her survival depended on protecting, if not enhancing, my father's image. Her concern did not stop short of his armpits. For example, he refused to wear deodorant, considering it "prissy." My mother worried that my father might offend in his classrooms or at the faculty club where he lunched, so she devised ways of preserving his image (and thus, as well, hers). She bought enough white shirts so he could wear a clean one each morning and wangled from him an agreement to shower and wear clean underwear every day.

The rest she took into her own hands. She sewed "guards" into the armpits of every suit jacket he owned. Regularly, she removed them, washed them, and sewed them back in again. And my father, guileless in his reliance on my mother for holding his image together, stormed forth each morning fresh as a daisy to conquer the world.

In protecting her Prince, my mother was doing what women have always done to secure their livelihood: she was making sure he didn't lose it. People got fired for less than B.O. My mother couldn't afford to have my father offend people. If he got fired, who would provide for us?

My mother's fierce concern for my father's image, and for maintaining the domestic equilibrium, is but one example of the complexity of the female situation. Women live with the feeling of being trapped, because they have not been permitted to act directly on the world. Yet women today, increasingly, are responsible for *all* of their family's financial needs. They fear that if they were to go hell-bent-for-leather in providing these needs, they would end up — forever — alone, having to support themselves and their families with help from neither a man *nor* the government.

Trapped in the hopelessness of it all, women stalk the malls, keeping an eye out for the small, harmless comfort. And those tiny, insignificant-seeming tchotchkes add up and distract them, keeping them down. Junk-purchasing for the home is the opiate of the female masses.

It's long been known that people who feel hopeless about accumulating enough money to buy anything substantial — who essentially feel powerless to build capital — tend to spend continuously on small, compensatory items.[1] "It might be just a little drainer for the knives and forks. Or maybe a pair of pillowcases," says a woman I know who doesn't let a week go by without a quick tour through Marshalls, "but it makes me feel good."

Most women I know spend this way. We spend to reward ourselves, to offset feelings of deprivation and resentment. We tend to be overgenerous with our children, in misguided attempts to shape their lives, win their continued loyalty and love, or assuage our guilt. We spend as a declaration of our freedom, to prove we are different from our mothers.

Our mothers often knew how to make the family money stretch. But as children and young women observing them, we may have had a less than appreciative view of their restrictiveness.

As the women's movement got into full swing in the 1960s and 1970s, we began to exercise our right to spend — with a passion. As Annette Lieberman and Vicki Lindner put it, in *Unbalanced Accounts,* "We had crossed difficult barriers in order to achieve financial independence, sometimes at great cost; we did not want barriers around our ability to spend. We saw the things that money could buy as tangible proof of our success and as rewards for our struggles."[2]

No one was going to tell *us* we couldn't spend two hundred dollars on a pair of boots or two thousand on a skiing trip to Aspen.

"I tried to marry well," says writer Cynthia Kling. "Twice, even. I'm not saying that I sharkily set my sights on some Daddy Warbucks with bad teeth and a big back end. I invested in me — health clubs, haircuts, vacations — and fully expected that the man snagged would take care of the rest. Not the Saks bills, but the serious, long-term stuff — investments, taxes, retirement."[3]

We spend as freely as we do because we still expect that eventually someone else's money will protect us. That we're expecting to be rescued usually isn't obvious — at least not to us. After years of the women's movement we *know* better than to admit — even to ourselves — that we're waiting for a bailout. But we manage our finances as if we are. Most of us never really thought we were going to have to take care of ourselves up until the very end. "Well, I can do it for a while," we figured.

But then what? When it finally dawns on us that we're going to have to support ourselves for the last several decades of our lives, it's often too late. The Romance Myth has subsumed us. We are not only without savings, we are without the belief that we can keep on earning into our seventies and eighties.

BIG SPENDERS: GOING CRAZY

" 'As soon as she is solvent, it tends to be spend, spend, spend with her,' " said a member of the royal family, describing the over-the-top spending habits of the newly divorced duchess of York.

Lieberman and Lindner have found that divorced women often spend their divorce settlements on luxuries in order to compensate for the trials of the marriage and the further trials of the divorce.

"There is no question that her expenses are high," says the *New York Times* of Fergie. "Her house in Surrey reportedly costs $9,000 a month just to rent. Last year the Duchess was said to have spent $78,000 on food and drink, $120,000 on clothes and presents and $36,000 on laundry, plus hundreds of thousands on sundries, for a grand total of $81,000 a month."[4]

Nor does she stint on travel. When she took a six-week holiday in the south of France, British newspapers quoted servants who said that she stayed in a thirty-thousand-dollar villa and managed to rack up another $150,000 in " 'an orgy of consumption and late night partying.' " Meanwhile, back in Surrey, the electricity was almost turned off for nonpayment of bills.

Whether we're rich or poor, it always catches up. One of Fergie's benefactors, a society hostess who'd lent her the $150,000 for the French vacation, sued her in 1996, accusing her of paying back only $75,000.

It wasn't Fergie's first financial crisis. Two years earlier the queen reportedly came up with $750,000 after a bank demanded that the duchess pay up on another loan. When the suit over the vacation money followed, the royal in-laws had had it. They took the unprecedented step of announcing publicly that they would not help her. " 'The Queen has made a generous provision to the Duchess of York over a number of years,' " a palace spokesperson said. " 'Her business ventures are conducted quite separately from any royal duties, and any transactions resulting from them must be resolved between the Duchess and her creditors.' "

Those included a long line of clothing shops, credit card companies, and friends who had given her loans.

In America it's celebrities, not royalty, who go crazy with money. An example is the saga of yet another hardworking writer who almost blew it for good.

In early 1993 Patricia Cornwell had one crime thriller on the bestseller list and another on the way. Money was pouring in. The previous year she'd earned a million. "Not bad for a thirty-seven-year-old divorced former reporter who three years earlier had been working in a windowless office in the basement of the Richmond morgue, borrowing money from friends to pay the bills," commented the *New York Times*.[5]

Income from Cornwell's writing had jumped from almost nothing in 1989 to $560,000 in 1991 and $1.7 million in 1992. But like so many who become wealthy relatively suddenly, Cornwell was ill-prepared to manage her money. Instead of creating an investment plan, she spent like wild. " 'During my manic phases I would buy a $100,000 Mercedes and drive away in it, or I would buy $10,000 worth of jewelry,' " she said. One shopping trip resulted in the purchase of $27,000 worth of furniture.

Eventually, she cracked up. Driving home along the Pacific Coast highway after an afternoon of Bloody Marys and dinner with her agent, she bashed into a stalled empty van and rolled the Mercedes over three times. It took a Jaws of Life to pry her free.

Three years later, with six bestsellers under her belt, she says the brush with death is the best thing that could have happened to her. "Things were spiraling out of control. I took it as a wake-up call."

Cornwell was diagnosed with bipolar, or manic depressive, disorder, a type of depression in which lows alternate with highs that manifest themselves in frantic spending sprees and episodes of out-of-control behavior. Flamboyance is typical of anyone with this illness, but those with a lot of money get media coverage for throwing it around. Cornwell told the *New York Times* that once, a hospital nurse who'd taken out some stitches after an accident " 'looked at me in my Escada jeans and said, "Oh my God, sweet Jesus, is that Escada you have on?" ' " Cornwell was troubled. She rushed to Escada and spent two thousand dollars on a jacket for the nurse.

Feeling overwhelmed and out of control, Cornwell put more and more money into hiring people she hoped could help her. A lawyer was retained at seventy-five dollars an hour to handle her personal affairs. She had her phone lines switched to the law firm so a paralegal could take her calls. " 'If I were to sit down and spend all my time talking to lawyers and accountants, I would never write books. I don't pretend to be a business person. I am just a person who has business who is an artist.' "

Creative people often try to avoid the details involved in managing their finances, claiming a kind of special entitlement because of their artistic gifts. It's a claim that *always* backfires.

MILDER FORMS OF MANIC SPENDING

Manic depression is on a spectrum of mood disorders. There are milder forms of it that often go unidentified. A feeling of grandiose inflation when shopping is a clue that spending might be symptomatic of an illness. And yet how many women experience the giddiness of shopping mania and simply assume it's a good way to get through the day? First-person accounts of shopping mania are seen increasingly in magazines and newspapers.

Martha McPhee describes the exhilaration of shopping at her favorite store in Manhattan, agnes b. " 'There was a small selection but I wanted everything. Everything looked good on me.' "[6] How tempting, then, to buy everything.

The store was beyond Martha's means, a simple T-shirt costing more than she ordinarily spent on a winter coat. Usually she went in only to have the experience of fantasy. " 'Walking in there was like stepping into possibility.' " She could spend hours trying on clothes, imagining what it would be like to wear them.

Then one day she saw the writer Tama Janowitz come in, try on a huge pile of beautiful things, and purchase every last one. Martha was crushed, feeling suddenly impoverished because she could only dream. But then, *mirabile dictu,* in the mail came a new credit card! " 'Huge limit. No questions asked. Buy now, pay later — the American dream.' " She took the card and ran. Ran to agnes b., where she " 'went crazy' " — dresses, coats, suits, a leather jacket, " 'even underwear.' " (And underwear, at agnes b., is no trifle.)

Today, like an aging film diva looking back on marriage to a handsome cad, Martha says she has no regrets. " 'The clothes, after all these years, they're still perfect. And I'm still paying them off.' "

Another woman, Meghan Daum, describes falling in love with

a suede shirt. It was, she says, "a maiden voyage into the world of clothing infatuation."[7]

There's nothing like the first time. Daum snatched up the shirt, recently marked down from $300 to $129.99, and instantly lost her love for generic Gap pants and misty, mossy woolens. This was clothing as magic. "The shirt itself was simple, the material equivalent of a lover whose attributes no one else quite understands."

To Meghan, it was more than a shirt. "It was everything I wanted to be, every hip and exclusive place I imagined I was going."

Finally, she gets down to the nitty-gritty, describing how good it made her feel to "look expensive." She could even attend a friend's bridal shower without envying the gifts or the groom because of the insulating effects of wearing — the Shirt.

Entirely another type of superiority gets exercised by those who shop from catalogues. "The shopper is always the hero, the Star. Every caption, photo, and tableau bends toward her cool, appraising eyes. Only she has freedom of movement. Only she can choose," explains Walter Kirn, writing, of all places, in the pages of *Vogue*.

In stores you've got to *hunt*, scavenge. "With catalogues you sit back and spin a globe. It's all about control."[8] Control and easy credit.

It's a provocative theory, given how much of women's time is spent feeling *out* of control. The theme of most catalogue writing, Kirn claims, is "overcoming chaos." First the catalogue creates a problem (as in "It's frustrating to eat half of a grapefruit as it slips and slides and otherwise misbehaves"), then the catalogue solves the problem (by offering the help of a nifty little grapefruit spoon).

Why should flipping through the pages, selecting, dialing up the order operator, spitting out our credit card number, thrill us so? Because women don't experience enough power in their day-to-day lives.

Buying things can produce a feeling of power, offering women a sense of being in charge of their world. Masters nowhere else, they become masters in the domestic arena, and the arena of personal appearance. I can change this, they feel — with makeup, a new dress, tights with a higher Lycra content. I can get my legs to look different, my living room to look different. I can, by making this purchase, get people to look at me differently, and in this way affect my fate.

CONFESSIONS OF A SECRET SHOPPER

I am in the sauna at Equinox, a New York health club. Stretched out full length on the cedar benches beneath me are two women, naked but for their fingers, which are loaded with antique rings. Every so often one of them gets up and pours water on the rocks, releasing a eucalyptus-scented cloud of steam. In New York saunas tend to be single sex. I don't know what men's saunas are like, but women's, as at the hairdresser's, can be remarkably confessional.

These women, I notice, are well moisturized, with perfectly depilated bikini lines. They are "women who take care of themselves."

At least on the surface.

Woman Number One yawns. "Have you ever had a budget?"

"It's kind of an abstract thought to me," Woman Number Two replies. "Would I ever do it? I doubt it, though it would probably be very practical to put down in black and white what's there and what's not there. Put it all down. I used to do that with what I ate. Still, I have an idea of the disproportionate amount of money I spend on frivolity and clothes."

"What's the difference?" says Woman Number One. In conversations between two women, I've noticed, one often does the revealing while the other plays inquisitor.

"That's it. Frivolity *is* clothes," shrieks Woman Number Two. "I used to go to a therapist who told me that what I was spending wasn't so awful. He said that considering my income was combined with Peter's income, it was perfectly okay for me to spend X number of dollars on clothes. Like ten or twelve thousand a year."

"That's a lot of money to spend on clothes."

"Yeah. And the fact is, my income is *not* my income plus Peter's, it's really only *my* income. We don't combine things. So my clothes and other expenses need to be based on what I make."

It's interesting, I think, how male therapists continue to view their women patients as traditional wives.

"So how much do you think you spend on clothes?" says Woman Number One, pressing for a bottom line.

The request for an actual figure changes the tone of things, as Woman Number Two begins to reveal how lost she is. "For last year, you mean? Well, I suppose I could look it up. I wonder how much I did spend? Seven thousand? I've really been making an effort to cut back. I do a lot of BCBG. I just spent seven hundred dollars there. I don't even think that's so much money because I got two outfits, spring/summer. And I've been thinking of going back and getting more. What really messes me up is the jewelry store nearby where I can walk in and spend . . . Two months ago I walked in and I got a necklace for two hundred dollars, earrings for a hundred dollars, and another pair of earrings for a hundred and sixty dollars. And then I have a bracelet on layaway. And of course Peter doesn't know that any of this goes on. And *that* was on impulse."

"I never quite get what 'impulse spending' means."

"To me it means spending money that I don't have. I think it's like eating, and I get the same kind of feelings that I do when I eat compulsively. There's kind of a rush and an anxiety at the same time."

"Do you think of it as bingeing?"

"Yes."

"Do you do it to change your mood?"

"I've been wondering about that lately. Do I do it when I'm

depressed or when I'm not getting something that I need, prob-ably particularly in relation to Peter, or if there's a lot of stress and anxiety going on? Sometimes I think to myself, Am I doing this right before I think we're going to split up, so I can get it while I still can?"

It's getting hot in the sauna, very hot. I wish I'd picked a lower bench where the heat is not as intense, but I don't want to get up now and disturb the flow.

"How do you feel before you do it? Do you *know* you're going to do it?"

"No, not all the time. Sometimes I think, All right, you want to go in there and buy something that you shouldn't, so get a grip. But mostly it just hits once I'm already in the store. I just say, 'OK, go ahead, *do* it.' "

"How often do you do it, impulse spend?"

"I would say . . . let's see. I did it in October when I was in Italy. *That* I don't even put in the same category because I was in Florence and I had opportunity that I don't normally have. And I don't regret that at all.

"What I did in the neighborhood jewelry store, I'd say I do around once a year. The earrings that cost a hundred and sixty dollars I had to get for my daughter's birthday present. So there was one for her and one for me. Then I stepped on my earring and broke the back off, so I took it back to have it fixed and then saw all these other things I had to have."

"How do you feel *while* you're doing it?"

"Giddy."

"And afterward?"

"Afterward I have a conversation with myself. Not so much, 'You shouldn't have done it,' but 'What are people going to think when you die?' "

Woman Number One guffaws. So do I. The mood in the sauna changes to one of hilarity, group-confessional style, women acknowledging their naughty secrets.

"And when you die they open your drawer," Number One says. Her aunt Zoe died with fourteen boxes of jewelry and a hundred and forty disposable razors.

"Did you get the jewelry?" Woman Number Two asks.

"Yes. Actually, my mother got some and sold it for far less than it was worth."

"All my credit cards have gotten really high," sighs Woman Number Two. "I had to get a low-interest loan so I could pay them off at a lower rate. I decided to get things a little more under control, but then Christmas came and I had a relapse."

"How long did it take to accumulate the debt?"

"I'm trying to remember. My Visa had like six or seven thousand on it. Then my Optima had four thousand, so that was ten thousand. Then I paid off some of the MasterCard, but I used it right up again. The other cards I cut up, so now I have one card that I can have a carryover debt on."

"How much did you relapse at Christmas?"

"About six thousand."

Clearly, this was a spiritual sweat as well as a physical one. "Six *thousand?*"

"I'm trying to remember why I spent so much. Some was gifts. Maybe I should go back and look at my bills. What did I get that was so expensive at Christmas? Then there's this woman that used to sell out of her house. And she was part of my problem also. She had these incredible things. I mean you don't see them in most stores. She moved out of New York and she was coming back for a final visit. She called me to see her stuff, and I went and bought some things, but still not as much as I used to spend. I'm trying to remember what I *spent* it on at Christmas."

"Well, some of it must have gone on presents."

"Some on presents and some on me. I'm having a hard time remembering. I'm trying to go through my closets . . . (brightening) oh, *I* know! We had a fancy wedding to go to in California, in February. And I got some really terrific things. So that was part of it.

I got a suit to wear to work and a suit to wear to the wedding. They probably came to over a thousand dollars, easy."

"God, and you racked up the six thousand right after you consolidated your earlier debt? How did that make you feel?"

"Nervous. Very nervous."

"You knew you were doing it while you were doing it?"

"Yes. But you have to understand how I get reinforced. The problem is, I never used to feel like I was attractive. I felt that I was fat and ugly and awkward. Actually I weighed more, in my twenties. Then I got thin, but I still used to go into the stores and ask for large. Then I found this BCBG store in my neighborhood that actually wasn't super expensive. I began shopping there, and they were really very, very nice people. They were always so complimentary to me. They began to make me realize that maybe I wasn't fat and awkward. I used to be so concerned about my appearance, that it had to be perfect to compensate for the inadequacy. Plus, I used to get reinforced. Because the salespeople used to tell me that I looked good."

Woman Number One decides to lighten up. "So you're going to die. Next week you're going to get run over by a taxi. Do you want me to go in and hide your stuff?"

Number Two laughs. "Get in fast and take what you want."

"Do you not feel entitled to what you buy, or what?"

"It's a mix. I think some of it *is* excessive. But a part of me says I don't want to die with an accumulation of money I haven't spent. We don't know when we're going to die. I don't walk around maudlin or anything like that, but I don't want to live the way my mother lived. Maybe part of my spending comes from that."

"How did she live?"

"Essentially she was penurious. She inherited money. She spent on certain things; she would take trips. But absolutely not extravagant. She would be more likely to spend money on me, to take me to a really expensive restaurant. She would never think of doing that for herself. Never spent money on taxis. That psychology I don't agree with."

"You said that Peter doesn't know about your spending."

"What he doesn't notice I don't discuss with him. I have a leather jacket I got two or three years ago. I haven't put it on yet. I bought it on sale in San Francisco for six hundred dollars. It was a complete bargain. But I'm so self-conscious about how wonderful this coat is, and that I didn't really need it, that I haven't taken it out of the closet."

"So Peter doesn't know about your binges. What would his reaction be?"

"He has an idea of my spending because when I got the loan he had to countersign it, and he said, 'What's all this about?' When I told him I'd gotten behind in my credit card bills, he said, 'Is there anything else I don't know about you?'

"He has seen me do *some* impulse spending on his credit card. When we were having some people for dinner, I went to Balducci's and bought four crown roasts of veal. I wanted to be sure we had enough. They cost almost three hundred dollars. He said, "What *is* this?" when he saw the bill. I took them back and bought steak."

With that I left the sauna. Number One and Number Two stayed on, sweating it out.

A feedback loop shapes up early in life in which shopping for things becomes a way of creating stimulation. Buying, itself, studies have shown, can act as a stimulant on the brain. But once the shopping binge is completed, the woman feels depressed again and is soon out stalking the stores in search of another lift.

As the shopping syndrome progresses, behavior begins to resemble an addict's methods of defending her habit: hiding, covering up, avoiding, even "isolating" (preferring, for example, to go shopping alone rather than spend time with one's friends). The particulars depend upon the individual's personality and circumstances. She may hide her purchases to avoid the scrutiny of loved ones (the way the boozer hides her bottle). She may return much of what she buys, so that she can guiltlessly go out and buy again. (It is the actual purchasing that stimulates the brain, not the owning of the object.) She may give her excess clothing to her children, having worn it once or twice or not at all, thus seeming to negate the compulsiveness of her clothes buying. She may become a lavish gift giver so that she can have the thrill of buying the stuff without the guilt (although many compulsive gift givers end up buying "a little something" for themselves every time they buy for someone else). She may stash her purchases in a special closet so that she can forget them. All of these behaviors are aimed at the goal of denying that she has a problem — maintaining the illusion that she is still in control. Thus, the behavior helps to reinforce the problem. The compulsive spender may "get by" for a long time. She doesn't *quite* crash. But she is in a constant state of tension trying to stay on top of her addiction.

Tension also comes from avoiding the fact that managing an addiction is actually what she is doing.

New York psychologist Oriole Peterfreund says shopaholics — 80 percent of whom are reported to be women — often suffer depression and low self-esteem and acquire material goods in an attempt to make themselves feel better.

According to a study by the University of Minnesota, the typical compulsive buyer started as a teenager but didn't recognize the full magnitude of the problem for another ten years. "Psychologists have long pointed to women as the chief sufferers. And recent studies — the one from Minnesota and one by the University of Iowa School of Medicine released in 1995 — have identified the typical compulsive buyer to be a college-educated woman in her thirties," reports the *New York Times*.[9]

The article tells the story of Barbara, a forty-seven-year-old management consultant, author, and speaker, in Los Angeles, who, though she earns over a hundred thousand dollars, has to borrow money to pay her bills every few years because she can't stop spending. The incidents she recounts are characteristic of compulsive shopping. On a trip to a small novelty shop to pick up a holiday present for a friend, she'd allowed herself a thirty-dollar cap on the gift. She stuck to her plan but picked up two vests made from men's ties, a sculpture, three skirts, and a pair of earrings, as well as the thirty-dollar picture frame, for a total of four hundred fifty dollars.

" 'Most compulsive spenders are people pleasers,' " says Janet Damon, a Manhattan psychoanalyst. " 'When a compulsive spender buys gifts, he's trying to buy love and power. This isn't really about money. It's about the feelings of anxiety they are trying to relieve through spending.' "

Holiday buying sprees are only exaggerated behaviors of people who spend compulsively to begin with — the holidays just create an aura of It's okay. Barbara told the *Times* she had recently succumbed to an urge to go Christmas shopping and spent fifteen times more than she had planned. " 'When I buy these presents I feel so powerful and generous,' " she said. A member of Debtors Anonymous, Barbara had agreed to be interviewed on the condition that she not be fully identified.

At home she stuffs the presents into a closet just for gifts, rarely recalling what she bought for whom. Over the course of a year she may buy five gifts for the same person for the same occasion.

Barbara has ten credit cards, on which she now owes sixty thousand dollars. (In addition, she has a two-hundred-thousand-dollar mortgage.) She says she's been getting loans from her mother, averaging six thousand a year, to help pay her bills. Asked about the interest rates on her credit cards, she said, " 'I can't tell you what they are.' " She hasn't yet filed her taxes for the previous year. " 'I bank in the fog bank,' " she said, using a Debtors Anonymous phrase.

She's not the only Phi Beta Kappa to do so.

It's in the very nature of compulsive spending to *know* what you're doing, even as you feel helpless to stop. Woman Number Two in the sauna *knew* she was buying to boost her self-esteem, but even after she'd gained the insight, it was hard to stop. A reinforcement mechanism gets set up. You try on the dress; the shopkeeper tells you how great you look; you buy, sailing out the door on wings of hope.

COMPULSIVITY AND THE BRAIN

Neuroscientists think the shopping syndrome — not unlike what happens in an addiction — actually has a physiological basis. Some I have interviewed believe shopaholics suffer from a form of obsessive/compulsive disorder resulting from an imbalance of certain brain chemicals. People who are destroying their lives with shopping over which they have no control can be treated with serotonin-boosting medications and actually lose the urge to shop. The drugs are chemically no different than antidepressants, which are helpful in treating a number of compulsive disorders, including binge-eating disorder, binge eating and purging (bulimia), compulsive starving (anorexia), gambling, and binge drinking.[10]

One of the first scientists to specialize in medical treatment of shopaholics is Dr. Susan McElroy, head of biological psychiatry at the University of Cincinnati School of Medicine. McElroy was on the Harvard team that conducted the first studies showing that antidepressants are helpful not only in the treatment of compulsive shopping, but of kleptomania, or compulsive stealing.

McElroy says the uncontrollable urge to buy affects about 1 percent of the population, mostly women. Usually the person feels a mounting tension that is relieved only when she or he hits the stores and experiences "a rush, a thrill, a high" from shopping.[11]

McElroy told the 1995 meeting of the American Psychiatric Association that 90 percent of compulsive shoppers she has worked with also had a serious mood disorder, such as depression alone, or mood shifts from depression to mania. Shopping stopped for nearly three in four after they took prescribed mood-stabilizing medication.

Many women who suffer from bulimia also report feeling compelled by an irresistible urge to steal stuff they don't want or need. Drs. Harrison Pope and James Hudson, of Harvard, describe such behavior as a "breakdown in the voluntary control mechanism." Most of us turn off urges to do things that are inappropriate or harmful dozens of times a day. "The process is so rapid and automatic that we are hardly aware of it — we take our voluntary impulse control for granted," they told me in their office at McLean Hospital, outside Boston.[12] "People are invariably shocked when we report that about one-third of our bulimic patients — many of them affluent, law-abiding people with sterling reputations in their communities — regularly engage in thousands of dollars' worth of compulsive shoplifting."

Hudson and Pope, who pioneered the use of antidepressants in the treatment of bulimia, were struck by the discovery that shoplifting bulimics, when treated with antidepressants, stopped their stealing as well as their bingeing. Locating ten large studies of shoplifters, the scientists found that in eight, subjects had shown elevated levels of depression. It is notable, they reported in the *Journal of Clinical Psychopharmacology,* that both bulimic and shoplifting women "responded to drugs that affect serotonin neurotransmission, and serotonin has been associated with effects on mood, appetite, and impulsivity."[13]

Though McElroy, Hudson, and Pope have studied mainly women with extreme compulsive behavior (namely, bulimia and kleptomania), their work has important implications for understanding less severe forms of compulsivity. The behavior causes a "rush," or giddiness, *because* it raises serotonin levels. This suggests that women may be unwittingly self-medicating. Their depressed serotonin levels get a momentary boost when they shop, producing a temporary high that feels a lot better than depression. As with any serious addiction, the reinforcement they're getting is not only psychological but physical. Their very brain chemicals are kicking in, giving an extra pow! to the experience. Whether it's food or drink or drugs or shopping the individual's addicted to, the devilish combination of psychological and physical reinforcement makes the behavior difficult to give up.

The precariousness of our lives when we are not paying attention to money eats away at self-confidence and joy. It puts us in thrall to our terrors. We may not recognize this — usually we don't — but the fear of abandonment is always there. This, ultimately, is the fear that keeps us down.

Chapter 4

BAG LADY DREAMS: WHY WOMEN ARE AFRAID OF ENDING UP DESTITUTE

In the summer of 1996 this small item ran in the *New York Times*'s "Dance Notes": "A plea has gone out for funds to provide electricity and gas to Katherine Dunham's home, school and museum in East St. Louis, Illinois, the poverty-stricken city where Ms. Dunham, who is 83 and in poor health, has lived and worked since 1971."[1] Contributions were requested. They could be mailed straight to Ms. Dunham's bank, in East St. Louis.

The gut-clench of recognition. Katherine Dunham, choreographer and grand lady of American dance, unable to pay for her heat and light, at eighty-three? Horrifying.

"I have this recurring fantasy that haunts my blackest nights," writes Barbara Kerbel in her newspaper column, "Working Woman."

Rather than living out my grandma days clipping coupons and sending freshly baked cookies to my adoring grandchil-

dren, I will be featured on the 11 o'clock news poking around in the garbage cans that line Fifth Avenue.

"Do you recognize this woman?" the voiceover will intone as the camera pans in close to my weatherbeaten face. "Once a syndicated columnist and publishing executive who raised two daughters in a suburb minutes from Midtown, she now makes her home on benches and alleyways." [2] (Emphasis added.)

I've met Kerbel, and she's a sharply dressed, bright, funny, and accomplished woman who works and writes in a lovely community on Long Island. But she's not kidding about her fear of ending up destitute.

Women's fear of destitution, as we shall see, has to do with financial reality; but I believe it is also a result of the head-on collision between traditional cultural norms and the relatively new expectation that women be self-sufficient. How this all comes to affect the individual, sometimes paralyzingly, is what I hoped to unravel during my research. I found this: while our nightmares are caused by the economic precariousness of women's lives, they are also caused by the vague but persistent sense that we are out of control with the money we do have. Many of us haven't accepted the fact that we, and no one else, are responsible for our financial support — and that we not only need to earn money, we need to manage it.

Fear of ending up destitute is a preoccupation of one in two educated, middle-class women, one survey found. For women, the bag lady has become the visible representation of a terror that has been with us since the millennium — the fear of being abandoned, of having no one to take care of us.

For contemporary women the bag lady is a compelling, even archetypal image — the symbol for a host of vague, ill-confronted anxieties that relate not only to the economic biases against us but also to our resistance to taking financial responsibility for ourselves.

To understand the tenacity of women's psychological resistance to dealing with money, the first thing we have to look at is how we've been affected by the economic system's being stacked against us. That age-old discrimination has made it hard for us to have any confidence in our ability to make it on our own for the long term.

Few recognize the extent to which women continue to be financially discriminated against. In the thirty years since the Equal Pay Act was passed, progress has been excruciatingly slow. "There is overwhelming evidence of the persistence of sex discrimination in wages," reports Rosalind Barnett, from the Wellesley Center for Research on Women.[3]

Between 1985 and 1990 women's wages crept up a penny a year, Maggie Mahar reported in *Working Woman*.[4] In 1991 they slipped back two cents. The best-educated men, by contrast (those with a college degree plus two years postgraduate education), were able to keep up with inflation. Between 1973 and 1991 their pay held steady at about $21 an hour. Women with two years of postgraduate education saw their real, or inflation-adjusted, wages slide from $18.01 an hour in 1973 to $16.57 in 1991.

In 1996, the median pay of full-time working women was 75 percent of men's median pay. *Yet, in spite of their lower pay, women are contributing as much or more than men to the family income.*

This is a historical turning of the tide — one, I should note, that was buried on page 20 of the *New York Times*. A nationwide survey published in the fall of 1997 found that almost two-thirds of working women earn *half or more* of their family income! Even among women living with husbands, 52 percent are now contributing half or more to the household income.[5]

"Women are feeling increasingly responsible for their family's well-being," Karen Nussbaum, director of the A.F.L.-C.I.O. Working Women's Department told the newspaper.

They're not just feeling responsible, they *are* responsible; responsible by more than half!

THE FANTASY OF FINANCIAL SECURITY IN MARRIAGE

"I was freaking," said Roxanne, a woman in her early forties, of the "almost breakdown" she experienced after leaving her marriage and having her former husband cut off everything, even when it meant spiting himself. "He was a successful doctor. He had investments in real estate. We owned seven houses which generated income. And suddenly the mortgages were being foreclosed so I wouldn't be able to get any income from them. Of course, neither would he, but he was so angry at me he didn't care."

As often happens, dad's anger at mom created financial havoc in the lives of Roxanne's children. "For six years I got no child support at all."

Roxanne feels that her identity has been assaulted, as well as her bank account. "I used to think of myself as a rich woman." Now she buys her teenage son's boxer shorts at Daffy's for $1.33 a pair and lives in an apartment in a housing project on the West Side of Manhattan.

"How did you qualify to get into the projects?" I asked her, knowing that income limitations were strict.

"Easy," she said. "I'm poor."

"Some would say that marriage isn't forever and women should be economically prepared," observes journalist Charlotte Kintslinger-

Bruhn, who reported on the poverty of Ulster County's single mothers. "But many women of my generation, raised postliberation movement, have somehow been unable to escape the deeply ingrained patterns of mothers who've gone before us: A career is nice, marriage and children are better; that is still the unspoken gospel — educated, uneducated, rich or poor."[6]

It is total illusion, this idea that society takes care of women and children. It doesn't. Women and children are the most vulnerable. When the fabric of family tears, when the breakup of marriages is the *rule,* as it has been for the past two decades, the illusion of protection at the very heart of the system becomes manifest as the rot at the core of a late-falling apple. The family doesn't protect us; the system doesn't protect us. No one protects us. This is something we have only begun to face.

We're not talking, here, about women who've never worked outside the home. Most wives work, but they don't get paid enough, they don't save enough, and they don't end up with enough in Social Security and/or pensions. Namkee G. Choi reports in the *Journal of Family Issues* that despite an average work history of more than twenty-three years, *over a third of divorced women are poor or near poor after retirement.*[7]

"Divorce is often a financial disaster for women," write Sharon Hicks and Carol M. Anderson.[8]

Experts have been telling women this for years, but we continue keeping our heads in the sand, preferring, apparently, the fiction that marriage offers women and children a safe haven.

"Instead of starting a career for myself, I helped my husband get his business started," says Christine Durth, of suburban Detroit. But with divorce, she and her children experienced the usual plunge downward in their standard of living.[9]

During her marriage, Durth had done women's typical double duty: work at the office and work at home. "I had four children. I made the beds. I cooked the meals. I cleaned the house. I kept my marriage vows. Now I find myself divorced in midlife with no career." Her former husband earns a hundred thousand a year, while she and the children struggle to get by on a quarter of that.

From this dispiriting story women can distill at least one moral: Don't count on laws to protect you. And don't "help" your husband start his career. If he needs assistance, let him hire someone else. Start your own career, and keep building your skills — *and* a separate bank account.

In 1996, Dirk Johnson wrote a shocking report, published in the *New York Times,* on the effects of "no fault" divorce on single mothers. The incidence of divorce has jumped 30 percent in the last twenty-five years. Some fault no-fault divorce as contributing to half the jump. It's women and children who suffer. In 1994 the median wage for a married couple with children was about forty-seven thousand dollars, but for a family headed by a single mother, the median income was less than fifteen thousand. After divorce, writes Barbara Ehrenreich, in *Time,* it's the man who gets the bachelor pad and the woman who gets the playpen and potty seat. "More than at any other time in the past 25 years, men are living in a state of radical disconnection from the women-and-children part of the human race."[10]

Only 20 percent of men comply fully with child support orders; another 15 percent comply only partially.[11] According to the federal Office of Child Support Enforcement, within six months after a divorce is final, 80 percent of noncustodial parents are behind in payments.[12] That euphonious phrase "noncustodial parents" means men, essentially, since 90 percent of parents with custody are women.[13]

The shocking fact is that 59 percent of single mothers are the sole support of their children![14] About one in ten heads of household live in poverty, but with single mothers and displaced homemakers who are heads of household, the figure jumps to four times that.

Almost half of single women and their children live below the poverty line.

Single black mothers are at the bottom of the totem pole. The 1985 median income for white male heads of family was $16,322, as compared to $13,551 for black male heads of household. The median income of white female heads of family for the same year was only $5,561, and for black female heads of family it was a terrifying $3,917.[15]

LOOKING AT THE OLDER WOMAN

Even though they have significantly more education and longer work histories, divorced women who retire do not have significantly higher income than women — widows — who never worked outside the home. This is a shocking revelation. *Females with the most substantial work histories — women who are better educated, healthier, and more likely to still be working when they are older — are still more likely to be poor than are widows, who as a group have less substantial work histories by far.*[16]

As its effects accumulate over the course of a lifetime, the significance of the "earnings gap" becomes painfully apparent for the older woman. A full-time working woman who earns the median wage and retires at sixty-five, after forty years of uninterrupted work, will have earned, pre-tax, $818,840. A male worker, earning *his* median wage for the same length of time, will gross $1,289,840. That's a lifetime difference of almost half a million dollars![17]

Discrimination deals its final blow at Social Security time. Benefits are based on earnings, but since earnings are sex-biased to begin with, women lose out again, receiving about 60 percent less than men — or, on average, $4,226 annually, as compared to men's $7,342.[18]

As they age, women find themselves with one foot on shore and the other on the boat as the gender gap widens. Those fifty and older

earn only 64 percent of what men get.[19] And, often, they have less
time available in which to do the earning. At midlife women are
called upon to start spending a lot of time caring for elderly parents.
Over 75 percent of those who do the day-to-day care of the elderly
are women. And it takes its toll. The hours required to assist ailing
parents mount frighteningly from one year to the next, absorbing
time daughters could otherwise spend at the workplace. "Caring for
these elderly parents causes [women] enormous financial strain,"
reports Anita Jones-Lee.[20]

As they grow older and watch their incomes dwindle, women
find the specter of the bag lady looming larger. Actually, they need
far more money for their old age than men do (those who reach
the age of sixty-five will live an average of twelve years longer than
men) and are haunted by the prospect of not having enough. A
survey by the American Council of Life Insurance found that 67
percent of women fear their savings will run out before they die.[21]

They have reason to be afraid. Almost half of older women in
our society have median incomes of less than five thousand dollars
(as compared to one in five men).[22]

The *AARP Bulletin* tells of a sixty-four-year-old female college
professor who was earning two-thirds the average salary of male
colleagues. Another woman, at fifty-seven, was earning half as
much as she would have had she not made the tragic error of
quitting for twelve years to raise a family. Now, she said, she was
"day-old goods." By the time women reach fifty, this woman told
AARP, "they are considered over the hill. Companies don't believe
it's worth making career investments in older women."[23]

But even women who work uninterruptedly over the years often
have to rely heavily in old age on gender-biased Social Security
payments. Corporations, after all, aren't noted for being interested
in the financial security of women — whether employees or wives
of employees — in their later years. Sixty-one percent of women
working today do not have pension plans, reports *Money* magazine.

And 76 percent of women who are now retired receive no pension benefits.[24]

"For most widowed old women, their dead husband's Social Security check is their primary, if not the only, source of old age income," writes Beth B. Hess, an expert on how social policies affect aging women.[25]

A frightened subtext rumbles beneath the conversations of baby boomer women who are now hitting midlife: "My mother, my mother." The fear is that their mother's money is going to run out. Not enough has been provided for these women in their longer and longer old age. Their husbands took Social Security early. Or, God forbid, their husbands left them. They themselves may have worked all their lives but never made enough to save anything. Younger women — daughters, granddaughters — look at this generation of women living out their last days in fear and trepidation, and suspect their plight will be no better.

A woman feels at the mercy of the system, though she may go for quite some time hoping that Big Daddy will protect her. At night she dreams of trying to get somewhere and not being able to keep her shoes on her feet. She is supposed to go off on a big trip, but she can't get her bags packed. Her clothes are sprawled on the sidewalk, and she squats there, trying to shove all her belongings into a few suitcases. The task defeats her. The bus to the airport arrives, but she misses it. The dream ends with the feeling "I am alone and still struggling."

The dreamer of that dream was me, a fifty-eight-year-old woman, successful at writing for thirty years, a mother of three, grandmother of one. As with other women I interviewed, seeing my mother die not long before her money would have run out attuned me exquisitely to the danger of my own position. For years before she died, fear of destitution assailed *her* dreams as well.

During the day she went over and over her figures, trying to maintain a semblance of control as medical bills ate her pittance away. At night she dreamed of being caught "in a bad part of town" and of not being able to find her way home. The dream came to her again and again, worrying her during the day as well as waking her at night. Why was she in that bad (read "unsafe") part of town? She was lost, confused, alone — essentially abandoned.

My father, a university professor, had a pension, but he was convinced he would outlive my mother and had planned his payouts accordingly. She ended up outliving him by four years, and during those years she wondered daily who would get her first, the Grim Reaper or the bag lady.

The truth of women's economic vulnerability comes to light in our dreams. And what our dreams tell us is this: *On our own, we don't make it. We are not being supported. Our kids are not being adequately provided for. We are up against the wall.*

AFTER THE BALL IS OVER

In a research project supported by the University of Pittsburgh Medical Center, psychologist Carol Anderson interviewed ninety subjects — women who'd never been married or who were divorced or widowed, but all of them living on their own. Those who'd been divorced described the experience as "nightmarish" and could barely grasp — so stunned were they, at first — that living as a single person was a viable alternative. Initially, they could only think of remarrying. "Marriage and feeling worthwhile as a woman are so linked in women's consciousness that, once the initial period of paralysis has lifted, it is natural to search for another 'prince' who can rescue them from the humiliation of defeat and help them reconstruct The Dream."[26] It was as if their very lives had been taken from them. "These women had achieved The Dream and now they had to survive its obliteration."[27]

Women who don't instigate the divorce themselves seem to have it hardest of all, for theirs is the loss not only of a marriage but of an illusion. Most of the women studied by Carol Anderson described a feeling of "spinning out of control" after their husbands left them. "They found themselves traumatized by the complete destruction of their life plans, unable to function as the women they had always been brought up to be."

Yet these women, "having been left by or forced to leave one 'prince,' " were quite aware that looking for another man to rescue them would be foolish. Now the point was to get their lives back on track. More often than not, as Roxanne, the former doctor's wife now forced by poverty to live in a Manhattan housing project, discovered, that meant a major effort, as they took on all or most of their own and their children's support.

Many of the women in Anderson's study said coming to grips with money was one of the most formidable challenges they'd encountered. "Dealing with their own financial issues can feel like flying into the heart of a treacherous storm," the psychologists wrote. Money became "the final frontier of their independence."[28]

Yet, sympathetic as they were to the divorced women's economic reality, Anderson and her colleagues made an important observation. Among the women they interviewed, *the threat of being alone and poor seemed to generate an atmosphere of insecurity and vulnerability far beyond the actual issue of having enough money.*

The mere idea of being alone, that is, conjured visions of destitution.

A surprising number of women use the dreaded image of the bag lady to express their fears of ending up destitute. Yet the desperate financial picture for women — in which they earn less, save less, invest less, and are poor in old age if not before — has to do, in part, with problems they continue to have in dealing with money. On some level, women still don't get it. An if-I-do-the-right-thing-I'll-be-taken-care-of mentality persists.

Women fear destitution because destitution is actually the omega point for many females in our society. But they also fear it because they know they aren't protecting themselves. Of sixty-five women I interviewed for my previous book, *Red Hot Mamas*, a report on the new midlife of baby boomer women, only two had adequate savings or investments — even though some were earning over one hundred thousand dollars a year! These women all nurtured the fantasy that when they were older they'd get bailed out — by friends, by children, by the government, by the sudden appearance of a knight in armor, no matter how rusted by disuse his lance and shield.

Asked what she thought her pension would provide when she retired, Linda, a part-time addiction counselor and divorced mother, told me, "I haven't thought about it that much. I never thought I would *have* to think about it. I guess I thought a man would be taking care of me at this point. Instead, I'm taking care of myself, my mother, *and* my kids."

Some of the women I interviewed for *Maxing Out* described a debilitating fogginess that washes over them whenever talk turns to zero coupon bonds. Sixty-seven-year-old Marcia, divorced, widowed, and working "probably forever," calls it her dumb act. "I glaze over, forget important details, become strangely inarticulate. I think I'm trying to reassure people that I'm not really in control. It's like, 'Don't worry, I don't *really* know what I'm doing. I'm not *really* a powerful woman.' "

Beneath the improved salaries, the M.A.'s and M.B.A.'s and Ph.D.'s, the external savvy and enjoyment of being in the world, there's a pernicious vein of self-destructiveness undermining women's security. Many of us are *not* in control. Money runs through our accounts like water through a sieve. We don't hold on to anything. We don't invest. And *the fact of our financial irresponsibility is directly related to our fear of ending up destitute.*

LADIES-IN-WAITING: WHY WOMEN SABOTAGE THEIR FINANCIAL INDEPENDENCE

Not unlike our mothers, many of us don't have faith in ourselves — not fully, not wholeheartedly, not for the long haul. We have what you might call episodic confidence, confidence that is related to particular events, special achievements, momentary triumphs. That is different from confidence related to *us*, to enduring faith in our own skills and intelligence. We rely heavily on the illusion of control, the tenuous hope that we might be able to hold things together through willpower, scheduling, nose-to-the-grindstone perseverance. Give up that control for one minute, one second, and there we'll be, flat-out destitute, with nothing more we can do for ourselves than fix that wobble in the right wheel of the shopping cart before all our earthly belongings tumble into the gutter.

Even among never-married women — who, notably, have fewer financial problems than women who are widowed and fewer still than divorced women — a belief that the unmarried state is temporary wreaks havoc with financial stability.

Too often, a never-married single woman has adopted the view that she will someday marry a man who will provide for her financially, write Sharon Hicks and Carol Anderson, of Western Psychiatric Institute, in *Women and Families*. "Given this assumption, she may work on her career, but she probably will not concentrate on managing her finances in the way her male counterparts do; she is less likely to consider investing her money, signing up for retirement benefits, or buying a home. When the realization dawns that she must permanently depend on herself for support, she may be faced with very real financial problems and little time to come to grips with them."[29]

In their study of Pittsburgh women living on their own, Hicks and Anderson found the lack of what they call "financial health" to be a major problem. "Despite professional success, a surprisingly high number of otherwise intelligent women do not manage their finances well. Checkbooks do not balance, investments are not scrutinized, savings are a myth."[30]

In what came to be viewed among family therapists as a breakthrough in treating single women, Hicks and Anderson began training a beam on the effects of finances on the lives of their unmarried women clients. What they found caused these family therapists to make a paradigm shift. They stopped viewing women's incapacities with money as symptoms and started looking at them as *cause* — of anxiety, of loss of self-esteem, even of loss of identity.

"Unfortunately," write Hicks and Anderson, "a substantial proportion of these women remain 'ladies in waiting,' thinking that sooner or later a man will come along to rescue them."[31]

Waiting, they never adjust to the reality of the present, much less plan for the possibilities of the future.

An organization called An Income of Her Own (AIOHO) began in Santa Barbara in 1992 as a grassroots effort to "introduce teen women to economic literacy."[32] Now nationwide in outreach, AIOHO has identified 123 million teen women in the U.S. as being "economically at risk." In large part this is due to living with mothers who themselves are poor, mostly because of death of or divorce from husbands. AIOHO has persuaded both Girl Scouts and Girls Inc. to make its financial awareness and skill-building programs available to girls. "It's not unreasonable to expect," say the founders of AIOHO, "that young women, more economically literate, will in fact be better prepared to attend to their own economic well-being."

Not unreasonable at all.

About a year before my mother died, I sat down with her, went through her checkbook, and figured out what it was costing her to live each month. I determined that if her rent were lower, she would have money enough to last another five years. I went to the manager of her retirement community and presented my mother's situation. For $1,350 a month she was getting, in addition to her apartment, two meals a day and maid service once a week. It wasn't a bad deal, but that rent figure was the only item in my mother's medically assaulted budget that could possibly be changed.

Remarkably, the manager, upon listening to my mother's story, agreed to cut her rent by four hundred dollars. When I told my mother this, she was ecstatic with gratitude and relief. I was triumphant with pride. I had been able, at last, to really help my mother. Her dream about ending up alone, lost at night in a bad part of town, would come less frequently.

But there was another effect. The dive into my mother's finances brought me up against the perilousness of my own situation. I had never made an adequate plan for my own financial future. What would have been the point? I knew I didn't have enough money, should I become sick or disabled, to last more than a couple of months. It was too horrible to contemplate, and so I avoided it, focusing instead on others' problems. I gave money to my kids when they needed it. I didn't want them to feel as abandoned, in their twenties, as I had felt.

My biggest problem with money was gaining the sense that I was responsible for my own welfare. This was somehow a missing concept, an idea toward which no bridge had been built. After all, what was graduation for a female leaving college in the fifties but a passage into a waiting time, a limbo of expectation? New York, apartment roommates who came along with me to the city from school, a job that paid me forty-five dollars a week to start — it all seemed like an extension of college life. Kids got together in beer halls and chugged the weekends away. We cadged cigarettes and borrowed from one another — clothes, money, old boyfriends. This was the great paradise of irresponsibility in which we thought we could lounge until reality took over — meaning, for girls certainly, marriage.

Our generation of females wasn't the only one to feel we had time to kill before entering the safety of wedded bliss. Our mothers' generation also viewed their early twenties as a kind of last fling with the fun and freedom of being a girl. They were ladies-in-waiting; waiting for life to begin in earnest, waiting for the Prince to arrive at their doors.

It wasn't until she was in her eighties that my mother told me about this time of blissful innocence in her own life. I had never really pictured her as a working girl in Washington, buying new dresses, canoeing on the Potomac, attending "tea dances" on weekend afternoons. At one such, she met my father, and they eventually married — but before then, oh, the freedom! She joined a chorus because she loved to sing. She took courses at night, working toward her bachelor's degree. She lived in an apartment with girlfriends — just as I had! She took vacations.

Somehow I'd never known this about her, that she'd had a time of freedom and gaiety in her life. I think she married the graduate-student-on-his-way-to-becoming-a-university-professor to escape a future of want. Being a secretary, as my mother had, was about as far as any woman could expect to go in the thirties. But no one could survive over the long haul on a secretary's salary, not if she wanted to have a family.

So my mother bargained for security — and lost her freedom. I *felt* that somehow — felt it as a very young girl. *It has been the message, I think, for the daughters of women of my mother's generation: You can have your freedom or you can have security, but you can't have both.*

I was never given to understand that I would one day have to assume such responsibility. Girls weren't. I ended up thriving on chaos. As I grew into adulthood, I liked the idea, if not the reality, of putting myself on the edge. I liked the presumed freedom, if not the day-to-day turmoil, of acting on impulse. I married a man who was impulse personified and for nine long years we hung by our fingernails getting by, until I couldn't stand the strain anymore — and left.

I tried creating a more stable life on my own. I knew that my children needed it. *I* needed it. But money was always an issue. There was very little of it and for reasons I never explored, I couldn't contemplate the idea of budgeting, much less saving. I paid the bills whenever I could and managed to keep the wolf from the door.

But not the bag lady. I lived in fear of not having enough for next month's rent.

Still, I took pride in the fact that I was supporting my children as a writer, and without any help. I didn't think I could *do* any better than I was doing. Most of my friends — women who'd left their marriages to go it alone, in the freedom of the feminist seventies — were living as close to the bone as I was. We loved the idea of being on our own, but at night we dreamt bag lady dreams. We might not have admitted it while the sun was shining, but in our deepest being we were scared.

Twenty years later that fear persists. Oh, we've grown more accustomed to financial instability. It's remarkable how easily we become acclimated to anxiety. We even laugh about it. ("It's ridiculous! Look at the money I'm making, and I'm still having these dreams.") But we don't *feel* secure. Our old age is in jeopardy. Even next month is in jeopardy.

"Women don't only wonder about their future, they worry about it — a lot," reports *Money* magazine. In a Phoenix-Hecht/Gallup poll, 20 percent more women than men believed they weren't saving enough for the family's needs or for their retirement. " 'We call it the Bag Lady Nightmare,' " Olivia Mellan, a Washington, D.C., psychotherapist told *Money*. " 'Even wealthy women worry that one day they'll end up homeless.' "[33]

Some women look for answers to their money fears on a web

site called Bag Lady Syndrome (http:gnn/meta/finance/feat/bag). "It's working women who visit this site," says financial planner Suze Orman, who runs the site. "But they still have this fear at the pit of their stomachs."

"I know saving is important, but I just can't seem to do it. It's really like a denial; I get a sense of panic. It's almost like being a child forever, which I'm angry at myself for."

The woman speaking is no child. She is a forty-four-year-old travel industry publicist who is admitting the chaos of her financial situation. Just last year her father had to help her when she couldn't come up with the money to pay her $2,300 tax bill.[34]

A surprising number of women interviewed by Leslie Brenner were "terrified of money." They let their bill-paying slide and their credit card debt soar. They found it hard to ask for raises. They couldn't bring themselves to balance their bank statements. "Though they may consciously want to earn more money, and even derive a sense of excitement from it, they also feel guilty and anxious about wielding the power that earning represents," writes Brenner, in *New Woman* magazine.

This is true even of women in their twenties. Faye Girsh, a San Diego psychologist specializing in money issues, told Brenner, " 'Younger single women who fear taking care of their own finances are also afraid of remaining alone and having to fend for themselves financially and emotionally.' " Moving out of their parents' homes, they become terrified of having to support themselves for the first time, and of having to handle bills and credit cards responsibly. Many decide they can't make their way by themselves. Says Girsh, " 'They indulge in a kind of magical thinking that someone will provide. Or something will happen, and they won't be destitute.' "[35]

For many, the deep wish to be taken care of by someone else continues indefinitely. Sharon Greenburg, Ph.D., a Chicago psychologist, says, " 'With women there's ambivalence about being taken care of.' " That ambivalence affects the way they deal with money. " 'You can't be truly financially independent when you're emotionally depending on parents or someone else.' "[36]

"Women must be helped to get control over financial matters," wrote Hicks and Anderson. "Without this control they will never fully experience their own power, self-esteem, pride and autonomy."[37]

Dependency is at the heart of women's difficulty in creating security for themselves. As long as a part of us is involved in the idea of romantic rescue, we will continue jeopardizing our financial independence.

But why, we may wonder, are women still compelled to believe that romance is where their security lies? The most powerful message young females today receive is that they can't make it on their own. This, even, in spite of feminism, and the fact that many of the women teaching and rearing them believe themselves to be emancipated.

As we shall see in the following chapters, girls and young women, today, continue to give up on independence, fearing that autonomy will lead to lives in which they are isolated, loveless, and alone. Better poverty than that!

And with those two poles as the armature, they begin to spin out the web of their own self-fulfilling prophecies.

Chapter 5

BECOMING "COOL": HOW WE LEARN TO BETRAY OURSELVES

At six I bought my mother a nest of brightly colored mixing bowls for Christmas, pleased that I could afford such largesse. It was my father, of course, who gave me the money.

By seven, I had entered a more complicated realm of gift giving. I had begun to see my mother as overworked and undervalued. The electric mixer I gave her that Christmas was intended to make her life easier, but also, I see now, to lift her up, increase her value, make her the owner of a hot new technological product. I wanted my mother to feel like a first-class citizen.

I thought for the longest time that I didn't have a particular money story, a reason, or set of reasons, that might explain how I ended up so deeply afraid of the challenge of providing for myself. Years of psychotherapy had produced no major insights. Money, per se, is often not dealt with directly in therapy. Problems earning and managing it are considered symptomatic. Cure the woman (or man), and insolvency will take care of itself.

In my case a pattern of debting was never identified during the course of a sixteen-year psychoanalysis. In part, that happened because the longer I stayed in therapy, the more money I made. It had been seductive for us to believe, the analyst and I, that any financial problems connected with my tendency to be overly dependent on others had been conquered.

But, in fact, the most dramatic shift in my financial situation had been due to a windfall publishing event. Ironically, the book that made me so much money was about the very problem with which, unaware, I was still enmeshed. I thought that *The Cinderella Complex* went to the core of women's difficulties with self-support. What I didn't then understand was how deeply layered the problem is, how on the surface one can appear to be long past destructive problems with dependency — and yet still be in conflict with one's deepest fears about surviving as a woman.

FEELING THE LACK

Although money was tight growing up, we weren't poor. My father was a college teacher, my mother a stay-at-home mom. To the eye of an outsider, ours was a "normal" family — no addictions, no flagrant abuse, merely the usual power structure of a traditional family in the fifties. But yes, there was a story. There is always a story.

I remember myself in a second-grade school picture, thin, sandy-blond hair, and a space between my front teeth. The eyes were curious, the smile shy. Here was a female in embryo, wearing a blouse made by her mother.

She sewed beautifully, my beautiful mother, carefully, painstakingly, making me outfits to go with hers, lined woollen suits, little pillbox hats. Employing thrift the way a man might wield a machete, she looked for good fabrics on discount and had an eye for fanciful trimmings. I acknowledged the elegance of the stuff she sewed for me: I understood as she taught me about properly made darts and silk thread and finely wrought buttonholes. But

I didn't feel like myself in these clothes. My mother had had to labor too greatly over them. They were too fancy, just as my hair was too fancy. When I was seven, my mother had tortured it into an artificial fluff, administering a smelly Toni Home Permanent at the Formica kitchen table.

Something was off. My mother was trying too hard, and I was both witness to her trying and unworthy of the effort. But what was her effort about? To have us be attractive, yes, but also to wreak a change in status. To know, and wear, what was good, to dismiss, or rise above, what was shoddy and poorly constructed. Neatness also counted. I think my mother may have permed my lank hair because she couldn't stand the way it looked falling in my eyes.

Even at eighty-eight, the year she died, my mother was careful with her dress. The shoes always went with the outfit. The scarf always went with the blouse. I was happy for her, as I helped ease her old feet into the little red ballerina flats. Her hose were without runs, her eye shadow smoothly applied. I was happy because she took pride, still, in her appearance and carried herself with dignity. Often, over the years, I had felt diminished by comparison. Sometimes my mother would admire the cut of my pant leg or the quality of silk in my shirt, but in general, she took a resigned view of me. I "dressed," in her sense of the word, only when the occasion insisted upon it, and even then I couldn't bother matching things up.

There was between us, of course, a generational difference. Middle-class women in the years my mother came of age "put themselves together," attempting a kind of completeness, a balancing of costume jewelry with the shape of a collar, the size of a buckle on a shoe. Women of my generation are interested in comfort and simplicity, one smashing color, or else black. My mother hated black. When I went to visit her, I always felt as if, in her eyes, I was slightly lacking.

Lacking is the operative word here, as it is in most money stories. In fact, as I was to discover, it is possible to have quite a lot of money and still feel lacking.

My parents didn't come from families with money. My mother, the fourteenth of sixteen children, lacked most everything growing up. Her parents were German immigrants trying to pry a living from the land. My father, the oldest of seven in an Irish working-class family in the South, also grew up with little money. He was the only one of his brothers and sisters to go to college. After that he went immediately for a master's degree, in Washington (where he met my mother), and then nine years after I was born, he received a doctorate from Columbia University. My father's upward mobility took the form of intellectualism. My mother's took the form of marrying my father.

In photographs of him as a young man, my father looked debonair in his black coat and white silk scarf. On their first date he got my mother's attention by taking her to the theater. Later in their relationship he would court her in a canoe on the Potomac River. When they capsized one night, she emerged from the water dripping in a white lace dress. They took a cab back to Georgetown.

This was a far cry from the marginal farm life of her Nebraska childhood, and of my father's early days in Charleston, where he and the other skinny boys who swam in the harbor were called wharf rats. The most wonderful gift my father ever received was a donkey his father had won in a bet. He named it Moses and rode it around downtown Charleston, never suspecting that one day he would leave his family and move north, to meet and marry a girl from Nebraska, and eventually to become isolated in a field of academic endeavor that neither she nor his children would ever comprehend.

Everyone's money story has its details. They are poignant, and they mean something. At first, though, and for a long time, the details may appear to have little to do with money. Money is the last sin, the secret vice. Like sex, the indulgences and distortions with which we approach it are almost universal and shameful enough to keep buried. Most people don't even know how convoluted are their attitudes toward money, how, like a noose, these constrict their very breath.

Until I was nine, my father worked at the Brooklyn Naval Yard during the day and went to Columbia at night, where he was getting his doctoral degree. Money itself was never my parents' goal, but stability was, stability and a certain improved status. My parents valued their ability to provide and to maintain a consistent standard of living. But beneath their apparent contentment with having edged into the middle class, there was striving — striving to be recognized, to be accepted as valuable, to be first-class citizens.

My own sense of what was needed for recognition as a female was influenced by my mother and became increasingly apparent as I approached adolescence. Those crisp cotton dresses hanging in the closet were what she created to make her — and me — feel acceptable. On Friday afternoons, after the maid had gone home (she was black, came once a week to do the ironing, and was expected to change out of and into her street clothes in a tiny basement bathroom), I would open my closet and think how lucky I was. My bedroom reeked pleasantly of starch. The dresses were pretty. I had a feeling of abundance. If things kept up, maybe I would grow up having the things I needed to make a life.

Of course I wasn't sure what I needed. Nor did I have even the vaguest sense of what would be involved in making a life. The starched and ironed dresses made me presentable; they made me feel, when I chose one to put on, "turned out."

That was in the summer. In winter, in the private girls' high school whose tuition payments were a struggle for my parents, I felt second class. Most of my friends came from families with more money, and while our hideous brown uniforms would seem to level financial differences during the school week, on weekends the cashmere sweaters other girls wore filled me with discomfort. It wasn't that I wanted a cashmere sweater so much as that I thought the others would find me lacking because I didn't have one. Their houses, when I visited, were bigger than mine and more elaborately furnished. There was an atmosphere of expansiveness, of plenty. I began feeling cramped in our small row house, with its fenced-in backyard and proximity to neighbors. I hated the closeness of the rooms, with opera and baseball games blaring at the same time. When my girlfriends picked me up in their fathers' cars, I felt I was escaping to a better world, a world where people not only *had* cars (my father refused to own one), but where daughters were entrusted with driving them.

I wouldn't have been so entrusted, I felt quite sure.

FORCED PASSAGE

I remember my mother as earnest, always trying to do the right thing, rarely laughing. I don't remember sharing moments of pleasure, where her guard came down. In fact I have a hard time remembering much about her at all from my childhood. As an adult I was angry with her up until the last few years of her life. I think the sense of betrayal and abandonment I felt was enormous. She allowed us to be emotionally injured by my father because she was afraid of him herself. He was irascible and unpredictable and would lash out meanly when something angered him. We never knew what that something would be. Everything had to be done on his schedule. If he said we were going to leave the house at a certain time, we had to be ready to leave at precisely that time. He never doubted his right to command.

Nor did he doubt his right to punish, if he thought the occasion demanded it. He hit me twice, once when I was ten or eleven and came in five minutes late on a summer evening. The other time I was fifteen, and he'd caught me smoking in the drugstore one April evening, after a Lenten service at church. As we left the drugstore and were walking down the street, he struck me several times on the buttocks, and I felt utterly humiliated.

For weeks after the smoking episode I was not allowed to go anywhere, but I do remember my mother intervening to persuade my father to allow me to go to a dance I'd been awaiting for a long time.

She intervened, as well, about an earlier dance, when I was twelve and a freshman in high school. My father had said I was too young to go. She told him if I was old enough to be in high school, I was old enough to participate in the social activities.

Looking back, though, I *was* incredibly young. The dance was held in a hotel in downtown Baltimore. I had to call a boy and ask him to accompany me. It was awful for me do that. The dance was something I felt I had to do — a terrifying rite of passage — and I didn't look forward to it. I remember the dress, turquoise taffeta, store-bought, with what was called a keyhole neckline. I stuffed my bra with nylon stockings and at some point during the dance went to the ladies' room and discovered to my horror that a stocking had edged up above the bra and was peeking through the keyhole.

Imagine being twelve and feeling that the only way you could pass, at this hotel dance with a live band and streamers and balloons, was with nylon stockings stuck inside your bra. I don't know if the boy ever noticed. But I remember the occasion of that dance as my first experience of playacting as a girl about to enter adolescence. None of it felt natural, only forced. Leaving childhood was *not* about passage. It was about one day being outside skinning my knees playing tag and the next wearing makeup and hosiery and shoes with little heels and dancing like a robot with a boy in a hotel ballroom. I was glad when the date was over, glad, glad, glad. No exam had ever made me more anxious. But I did it, I got through it.

I think my mother was right on the position she took with my father about these dances. I think she knew that if he had his druthers, I'd grow up without a normal social life. He was too anxious, too scared of life himself. But I never felt I could confide my own fears to my mother. She was an ally against my father's rigidity, but not really an ally *with me*.

At the times when a girl needs her mother to help create a passage, my mother could not make herself available to me. Sex education was a church-authorized book of euphemisms. Nor could I talk to my mother about relationships with girlfriends because she was envious of them. They were trying to take over my life, she warned. "That Gerry doesn't want you to make a move without her knowing about it." This was true, a part of me had to acknowledge, but I couldn't really talk about the dilemmas of intimacy without providing fodder for my mother's unstated agenda, which was: Break off with these girls; stay home with me. As I grew older, she broadened her critique. My girlfriends weren't good enough, smart enough, their families didn't listen to the opera.

And so my real life, of necessity, became a secret life. Oh the freedom, the lightness, the buoyancy I felt, running down the front steps and into my friend's father's big green Buick, the joy of getting out, of taking off. It was such a prison, that house, of unstated fears and unexpressed love. It was so joyless.

WHERE WAS MY VISION OF A FUTURE?

Getting out, of course, is never enough, for as soon as you do, the second half of the problem raises its hydra head. Where do you go? How do you proceed with your life?

Ordinarily, one looks to one's parents for guidance and for modeling. My mother's role in the family was that of minder and mender and oft-disgruntled appeaser. My father took up so much air that it was hard for anyone else in the family to breathe. I didn't want a life like my mother's, but I couldn't imagine a life like his, either.

We were only four in our family, my brother five years younger than I, but to me the house often seemed crowded and noisy. My father got to leave every morning and go off to the university, where he earned the family living teaching and doing research. Engineering wasn't for girls in those days, and in any event I wanted nothing to do with the theorems my father was always scratching down on sheets of lined yellow paper. But I wouldn't have minded getting to leave our crowded little house in the mornings and going to a campus full of interesting people and having lunch at the faculty club.

I once spent a summer typing for my father in his office and decided his life at the university was pretty sterile after all. I took my lunch in a nearby drugstore, one he didn't know about. There, hunched in a back booth, I smoked cigarettes and read romance magazines to learn more about men and women and about sex.

Had I chosen my mother's life I would have felt stifled and depressed. Had I chosen the dominant life, my father's life — well, that, too, was out of the question. Yet those were the only possibilities that seemed available to me. My relatives lived far away, in South Carolina and Nebraska. There were no aunts to spend afternoons with, no models for another way of life, only a sense of being cut off from everyone and of my parents preferring it that way. Ours was a typical isolated family, called, in reference to the tightly knit parts of an atom, nuclear. But I thought for the longest time the reference was to the type of war we were all worried about: nuclear, in my mind, meant small, contained, and highly explosive.

BEGINNING TO DOUBT, BEGINNING TO DEBT

By the time I was midway through adolescence, I had lost all sense of agency. In college I began to debt — cadging cigarettes, bumming money for a Coke or a cup of coffee, an occasional dinner with friends in downtown Washington. It seemed I always owed someone a little something.

Once my roommate, a girl from a well-to-do family in Trinidad, expressed anger at me for always bumming her Chesterfields. I was shocked. I didn't think of my cigarette bumming as being quite so habitual as she did. Besides, her allowance was seventy dollars a month — over three times mine. What could a few Chesterfields possibly mean to her? I began to think of her as withholding and stingy, and from then on, when I borrowed from her — money, cigarettes, clothes — I did it with a paralyzing mix of feelings. I feared she would turn me down. I resented her for her power over me. And I felt humiliated.

Still, I had to ask. There were events I just didn't have the right clothes for. There were places I felt I had to go if I wanted to be a part of things. And there were those damnable cigarettes. I certainly had to have *them*. The trouble was, five dollars a week wasn't enough. That, at least, was how I framed the problem: I don't have enough. *It never occurred to me that I might find a way to earn more money, or reassess my needs, or in some other way take control of my situation.*

I felt, at the core of my being, powerless. I needed someone else to take the brunt of my support, and who more likely than my richer and thus more powerful roommate? (Not surprisingly, she lined up another roommate for the following year.)

For a long time I interpreted those college years with the depressive poignancy of someone who feels one-down, trapped relentlessly in the second class: not a bad person, but not an okay person, either. Someone who, through no fault of her own, didn't have what she needed and couldn't *get* what she needed, except by borrowing. I never acknowledged my lifetime pattern of debting and probably never would have had I not finally entered a financial recovery program. For decades the debting continued and, like a progressive illness whose symptoms are barely visible, quietly worsened. And that same mix of feelings I'd experienced when bumming from my college roommate kept returning again and again in my adult dealings with money. The more they recurred, the more they paralyzed me as I developed increasingly sophisticated denial strategies to help me ignore my money troubles.

In the beginning, it seemed a perfectly ordinary scenario: young woman tries out her wings in the big city. If she has trouble with money, well, don't all kids out in the world for the first time have trouble with money? I lived with three women I'd gone to school with. My job as assistant editor at a fashion magazine was considered by all of us to be a prestige position, but it paid very little. Working at *Mademoiselle*, it turned out, would provide a perfect environment for supporting the split that had begun in childhood. Here were all these editors running around in chic wool dresses and good shoes. My job wasn't in the fashion department, but that hardly mattered. We were *all* expected to hew to the values being marketed by the magazine's editorial position, which was, in a phrase: Style is everything. High in Condé Nast's aerie on Madison Avenue, properly constructed buttonholes counted for as much as they ever had in my mother's sewing room.

The people who worked in my department, which produced articles about careers and education, considered themselves the staff intellectuals. We wore stockings with runs, scoffed at those who obsessed about skirt lengths, and at the same time coveted the sophisticated looks of the fashion savants, who thought we were naive and not a little nerdy (and certainly, from a fashion point of view, we were). We prided ourselves on our brains and looked down our noses at the know-nothings whose dreams, we imagined, were filled with Erwin Pearl earrings.

The envy I felt, and my arrogant defense against it, was a perfect replica of the way my father related to the world. He dealt with his desires by denying they existed, by rising above them, compensating with what he believed to be his mental superiority.

My mother dealt with her desires by trying to catch up — by becoming an expert tailor, and eventually by going back to college and getting A's in history. There was definite upward striving in my family, but it wasn't talked about. You weren't supposed to want. Wanting was for plebeians. When I had my first "pressure relief meeting," after joining Debtors Anonymous, I was assigned the task of making a wish list. I looked at the man and woman giving the meeting as if they were crazy. Okay, so I coveted the clothes in *Vogue,* the furniture in *House & Garden,* the flowering pears in the Gardener's Eden catalogue. I spent every free minute in a swivet of wanting. But cop to it? Write things down on a list? Own up to my desires? Never. To want things would mean that I didn't feel complete unto myself.

I didn't, of course, but that was not something I could even think about for years. Keeping desire under wraps was central to my psychological defense as a female. Desire is power. Without it — that is, without conscious recognition of it, for desire itself is never entirely squashed — we remain stuck.

I would spend half a lifetime playing games with desire, acting out my wants rather than relating to them and getting what I needed directly.

According to an increasingly compelling body of research, my trouble holding on to my self, in relation to others, was in no way unique. It started with the stifling, beginning in late childhood, of my true thoughts and feelings.

This was the very loss of "voice" that researchers in the eighties came to see as a central problem in the development of girls. What I would come to understand is that stifling their own voices affects girls' ability to grow into self-sustaining women able to deal powerfully with money. As I delved into the current studies of girls, I would reassess my own childhood. What the new research documented, for the first time, is just how systematic is girls' training in self-abnegation. What surprised me was how totally identified I felt with girls who were coming of age in the nineties. It could have been me, my childhood, that these contemporary social scientists were describing.

ENTERING THE FEMININE UNDERGROUND

In the fall of 1981 a young woman on the faculty of the Harvard Graduate School of Education drove from Cambridge to Troy, New York, to Emma Willard School, a day and boarding high school for girls. She was about to spend four years studying the students in this privileged but oddly sequestered environment. "The school is surrounded by walls, set up on a hill, apart from the town, from Rensselaer Polytechnic Institute which is down and across the road, from the river, from the valley, from boys," she would later write. "The buildings extend the atmosphere of seclusion; they are mostly gothic — elegant against the late September sky, a cloister enclosing a greensward, grass carefully tended and crossed diagonally by paths."[1]

The woman who wrote those words was Carol Gilligan, a groundbreaking psychologist about to embark on a study of what "development" actually means for girls coming of age in the late twentieth century. Up until then, psychological development in females had always been assumed to be the same as in males. Gilligan's project, which soon would be recognized as a landmark study, was sponsored jointly by Emma Willard School, the Harvard Graduate School of Education, and the Geraldine Rockefeller Dodge Foundation. But as Gilligan told the girls assembled before her on that first crisp morning in autumn, she hoped her true collaboration would be with *them*, that they would "labor together to begin to fill in a startling omission: the absence of girls from the major studies of adolescence."

This omission, to at least one girl in the auditorium, was not all that startling. Raising her hand, she crystallized, in one question, the effects of that long oversight: " 'What could you possibly learn by studying us?' "

Gilligan, of course, was aware of the mental health problems of female adolescents. Teenage girls are more disparaging of themselves than are boys. They have more disturbances in body image. From puberty onward, episodes of depression are more than twice as likely to occur in girls as in boys. Since Freud, the "flight from self" had been considered predictable — and inevitable — for female adolescents. Yet, until the 1980s, no one had ever studied what actually happens to girls as they go from prepubescence into their teenage years. What had so long been recognized as a falling-apart time for girls was glanced at, taken note of, but never studied in any systematic way. It was simply considered predictable.

Harvard's interest in sponsoring research on girls came on the heels of extraordinary popular and academic acclaim given Carol Gilligan for her earlier work on "voice differences" in males and females. Men think that if they know themselves they'll have no trouble knowing women. Women imagine that only if they know others will they come to know themselves.[2] Most women, Gilligan wrote, in *In a Different Voice,* feel that in order to be in relationships, they have to choke off their true thoughts and feelings. Relationships are so important to them that they fear doing anything they think might put their connections with others at risk.

This was certainly true of women I interviewed. A singer-songwriter in her early sixties described a relationship with her thirty-five-year-old son in which she felt utterly constricted. "I just can't be myself around him," she said, sadly.

She couldn't disagree with her son in any vehement way, couldn't prance in his presence, carry on, flaunt her intelligence, for fear that her strength would make him crumble — or that he would walk out on her in impotent rage. Her therapist suggested that she had transferred to her son the same feelings she'd once held toward his father, from whom she was long divorced.

"What is it that you equate with becoming more aggressive?" the therapist asked her.

"Loss," she replied.

At its best, family life offers children a sense of possibility, hope, a belief in their ability to make things happen. At its worst, the nuclear family explodes, and whether loudly or quietly, extinguishes a child's sense of self-worth and future. I believe this can happen even in so-called normal families. It happened in mine.

My parents' greatest sin was in giving in to their anxiety. My brother and I were taught to avoid risks. My father told us the danger was outside, in the world. But the danger we experienced was inside, in the family.

Nor was there any bridge, as I was growing up, between the family and the outer world, a sense that I was being prepared to go forth into a life of my own. It couldn't have been any clearer if they'd said it aloud: "We are teaching you how to behave, right now, in a way that keeps us from having to deal with you. We aren't even thinking about tomorrow."

My rebellion occurred in high school; I was afraid to rebel at home. At school, the nuns exhibited a powerlessness that both annoyed and encouraged me. Compared to my father, they were pushovers. I quickly fell to mocking them and breaking the rules. I smoked in uniform whenever I got the chance, a cardinal crime punishable by expulsion. I was so publicly disdainful of the nun who was our homeroom teacher, I was finally punished by being removed from my office as class president.

Then, when I was sixteen, I traveled forty miles from home, to Trinity College in Washington, D.C. Soon my sense of myself began to unravel. College, with rules and regulations that seem laughable today, offered so much more freedom than I was used to that I was terrified. Before long I was smoking a pack a day, stumbling blindly through my textbooks, trying to figure out why other girls were getting good marks and I wasn't. I couldn't concentrate, couldn't focus, was obsessed with self-consciousness. I almost flunked out that first year. I had little sense, anymore, of who I was.

The feeling of devaluation I'd had in high school continued. I don't know if my classmates thought of me as coming from a family without money, but I did. I entered college with a scholarship arranged by my father through a priest he knew on the faculty. I worked in the kitchen to pay part of my expenses but never actually saw the money, as it was handled as a deduction from my tuition bill. For spending, I got an allowance of five dollars a week. I could count on a check being in my mailbox every Monday. In four years my father never missed. I asked him once if instead of the weekly checks he could send me a month's money at a time, but he said that it wasn't possible. If I ran out before the month was up, he wouldn't be able to give me more.

In the face of this adult logic I succumbed. If I couldn't make five dollars last a week, why should I imagine I might make twenty dollars last a month? I'd get behind. I'd get seriously behind. I was already living on the edge, feeling the perilous imminence of poverty.

Father is the beginning of a girl's romance with romance, her first prince, the potent embodiment of patriarchal reality. He believes in the myth himself and, knightlike, lance in hand, shield held high against the enemy, does what he can to ward off danger. The danger, in this instance, was my own as-yet-unproven inability to deal with money. My father cut off at the pass any possibility that I might screw up my finances and cause trouble for him. He promised protection, I would acknowledge over and over, years later, lying rigid with fury on my analyst's couch, but what he delivered was control. The lesson I was learning, so young, was of my own incompetence.

SHUTTING DOWN AND SHUTTING UP:
PREPARATION FOR ROMANCE

What happens to females earlier in life that makes them so wary of expressing their true thoughts and feelings that it not only ruins the possibility of genuine relationship, but also cripples their ability to become joyfully independent, emotionally and financially?

Those who studied only *young* girls would not find the answer to this question, for before puberty most girls are feisty and outspoken. It's when they arrive at the crossroads between childhood and adolescence that a shift takes place. When she interviewed girls on the edge of adolescence, says Carol Gilligan, she sometimes felt she was entering a feminine underground, "led in by girls to caverns of knowledge which then suddenly were covered over, as if nothing was known and nothing was happening."[3]

What she was being shown was how girls learn to *not* know what they know — essentially, how they come to repress what causes them too much conflict. At the end of childhood the phrase "I don't know" begins slipping into girls' language. Gilligan heard so many "I don't knows" in girls of twelve that she began to understand that the phrase was more than just a tic. It represented true loss and feelings of powerlessness. They *had* lost something. They'd lost the memory of who they were in childhood. *I don't know,* said Gilligan, marked a gateway to the underground city of female adolescence.

The dissociative forgetting was a protective defense that allowed their entrance into the false, cultural version of "femininity" to be less painful.

Adults — including, and especially, women, Gilligan found — offer girls little support for standing up and fighting for themselves. Rather, they track girls into "goodness," obedience, and perfection. It's because women have covered over, or denied, their own painful pasts that they are disturbed by listening to girls who are struggling against society's assault on them.

It wasn't for another few years, when the American Association of University Women published its report *Shortchanging Girls, Shortchanging America* that the trauma of adolescence for females was clearly documented for the first time. Eighty-five percent of girls reported being sexually harassed at school — over half of these in the classroom. The harassment was sufficiently troublesome that a third of these girls didn't want to go to school because of it. Fifty-five percent of middle and junior high girls were having sex — and many were regretting it. Most, as well, were hating their bodies.[4]

"The challenges facing adolescent girls have never been larger than they are today," wrote Jane Brody, in the *New York Times*, in an article called "Girls and Puberty: the Crisis Years." Brody reported on a large survey, conducted in 1997 by the Commonwealth Fund, which found that " 'more often than not, young girls entering puberty experience a crisis in confidence that renders them vulnerable to risk health behaviors that they may not have the strength or will to resist.' "[5]

By high school age, only 39 percent of girls were highly self-confident and older girls had less self-esteem than younger ones. " 'In contrast,' " the fund reported, " 'older boys were more likely to be highly self-confident than younger boys, with more than half of all boys in high school indicating high self-confidence.' "

Not surprisingly, depression comes hand in hand with loss of self-esteem. " 'An alarming 29 percent of girls reported suicidal thoughts, 27 percent said they were sad "many times" or "all the time," and one-third of older girls said they felt like crying "many days" or "every day." ' "

Eating disorders among girls are rampant in the late 1990s. Up to 25 percent of adolescents — 90 percent of them girls — regularly purge themselves to control their weight, the Fund survey found.

Girls report " 'a disturbingly high incidence of violence, with 18 percent of girls in grades 5 through 12 reporting some form of physical or sexual abuse,' " more than half of which was perpetrated by a family member.

Is anybody listening?

At the beginning of their work at Emma Willard, Gilligan's researchers found that even *they* were unable to hear the girls' troublesome messages. Unresponded to, the girls began shutting down left and right. At that point, the researchers recognized they were going to have to restructure the whole project if they wanted to create an environment in which the girls felt free to actually *talk.*

When they did, out came the truth, at last, about the tremendous losses girls experience as adolescence looms. Talking to girls at one-year intervals, as they moved from childhood to the edge of adolescence, the Gilligan team witnessed a "shift from engagement in a rich social world of childhood, in which thoughts and feelings — both good and bad — are spoken about directly and publicly, to a struggle at the edge of adolescence to hold on to what they think and feel and therefore know, to authorize their experiences. . . ."[6]

To learn how growing girls slowly shift their method of dealing with others, Carol Gilligan and Lyn Brown asked them to interpret one of Aesop's fables.[7] The fable of the moles and the porcupine contains some of the relationship issues girls and women seem to find so difficult.

What was novel about this study was that it asked girls to talk about the fable each year, thus allowing researchers to trace changes, as the girls grew older, in their unconscious attitudes about self and others.

Here's the fable the girls were presented with.

It was growing cold, and a porcupine was looking for a home. He found a most desirable cave, but saw it was occupied by a family of moles. "Would you mind if I shared your home for the winter?" the porcupine asked the moles. The generous moles consented, and the porcupine moved in. But the cave was small, and every time the moles moved around they were scratched by the porcupine's sharp quills. The moles endured this discomfort as long as they could. Then at last they gathered courage to approach their visitor. "Pray leave," they said, "and let us have our cave to ourselves once again." "Oh no!" said the porcupine. "This place suits me very well."

When Jesse was eight, her take on this situation was that moles and porcupines make a bad combination and ideally shouldn't be together. The solution, she thought, was to make the cave bigger.

A year later, her response to the fable had become more equivocal. Maybe the moles should take a stand, should say, " 'I'm sorry, but please get out. This is my house. I'm not going to let you in anymore, so leave.' " But Jesse couldn't tolerate the possible consequences of so firm a stance, worrying about what would happen to the porcupine. " 'It's like having a baby in your house,' " she said.

The researchers note that the voices of parents and teachers have been inculcated in Jesse's speech. " 'You should be nice to your friends and communicate with them and not . . . do what you want,' " Jesse finally summarizes. Her wish for the porcupine and the moles is that they " 'are happy and they don't have to fight anymore. They could just be friends and they could stay like that forever.' "

Harmony would reduce conflict — at least Jesse's conflict.

By the next time she's interviewed, at eleven, Jesse has begun to view authentic encounters with others as potentially dangerous. Now she's willing to be nice to get her friends to play with her, rather than because she feels like being nice. And her response to the story of the moles' predicament has undergone a major change. While the moles *could* say, Get out, I don't want you here anymore, " 'that would not be a nice way to do it,' " says Jesse, " 'because the porcupine would feel left out.' " The solution, now, is to make the hole bigger, " 'because it would be nice to have a neighbor in the house.' "

Jesse's slide, definitely, is toward compliance. Though speaking up about her feelings was no problem at eight, by nine she had begun to equivocate, and by eleven she completed covering up her personal truth if she sensed the potential for conflict. If a girl doesn't like another girl, it's better to pretend she does.

Jesse, at eleven, may be more sophisticated in her under-standing of herself and the world, but she is also "more likely to stay in relationships in which she is hurt, more willing to silence herself rather than to risk loss of relationships by public disagreement."

A perfect girl in the making.

It is, of course, a universal question, how not to fail oneself while relating honestly to others. But what the research shows is that girls tend to reframe the problem as one of either having to respond to others and abandon themselves, or respond to them-selves and abandon others. "The hopelessness of this question," according to Gilligan, marks "an impasse in female psychological development."[8]

What I found stunning about Lyn Brown and Carol Gilligan's study of girls like Jesse was their documenting of childhood confusion that has changed little, so far as I can see, since I was a little girl. The book they wrote about this study, *Meeting at the Cross-roads,* brought me up against memories I had put aside because they were too painful. Brown and Gilligan's research on girls would allow me to see how I had begun, as a child, to choke back my own voice.

"PRUNELLA": A GIRL'S ALTER EGO PROTECTS HER

Last winter I met a young woman who belongs to the second generation of researchers in the new area of the psychology of girls.
Having just received her master's degree from the Harvard School
of Education, Elizabeth McLeod was taking what she had learned
out into the field. She and a colleague were starting a center in San
Francisco that would intervene in the lives of twelve- and thirteen-
year-old girls, to prevent them from having to give up so much on
their way to becoming women. It was a project whose roots were
planted in the soil of Elizabeth's own girlhood.

While taking a course with Carol Gilligan called "A Radical
Geography of the Psyche," Elizabeth, at thirty-three, had recalled
for the first time in years the extraordinary lengths to which she
and three friends had gone as young girls trying to become what
society expected of them without losing their aggressive and creative childhood selves. Sitting in my living room in front of the fire,
one snowy winter morning, she shared her story with me. Tall,
blond, slender, in her straight-legged black jeans and black boots,
she seemed the apotheosis of cool.

But a desire to be cool, I would learn, was something Elizabeth
was still vehemently trying to get past.

The struggle had begun in 1974. Elizabeth recalls the period of
her life between eleven and fourteen as being mostly dominated by
desire to be accepted by the popular kids. "I remember the 'war on
Caroline' when for months everyone ganged up on her. Every day,
the power shifted." Elizabeth was always on the periphery, with
one foot in the "in" group and one foot in the "out."

But it was in the out group, she knew intuitively, that the real
Elizabeth — the creative girl, the feisty girl, the girl who may have
looked nerdy but who really didn't give a damn because she had
more interesting things to think about — would be allowed to stay
alive.

Known then as Betsy, Elizabeth and her friend Gigi were writing notes back and forth to one another one day in Mr. Thompson's fifth-grade reading class when they came up with imaginary characters they named Priscilla and Prunella. Unwittingly, the two girls were beginning an extraordinary adventure in creativity and self-preservation that would last, growing more and more elaborate, for two important years.

Unlike the "cool" girls, Gigi and Betsy, who were trying to figure out what being popular was all about, Priscilla and Prunella were oblivious to the styles and fads of the seventies. "My new imaginary twin, Prunella, was both childish and grown-up; she still loved to play the games which I'd outgrown, but unlike me, she had already entered into the world of boys and dating."[9]

Elizabeth can vividly recall that time, when she and her friends felt excruciatingly self-conscious, preoccupied with the pressure to be smart and nice and friendly and feminine and mature and, most of all, "popular." Prunella, by comparison, embodied all the traits and characteristics that seemed increasingly unacceptable for an eleven-year-old girl. She was free to be outspoken and silly.

But she was free within the support of a group of like-minded alter egos: Prunella and her friend Priscilla joined up with two other girls who had taken the names Prunisia and Preteesia. The four alter egos still played the way they had in third and fourth grade but also ventured into territory as yet unexplored by the cool "real" girls: the world of boys.

"Not only did Prunella have a boyfriend," Elizabeth told me, "she was exploring her sexual feelings in a way which *we* wouldn't have dared."

The four girls formed a club whose acronym, P.R.A. (which stood for Popular Recreation Association), was taken from the fact that all their names began with PR and ended with A. The girls in P.R.A. "vacillated between being little girls and young women, with their hair in ponytails and still wearing black patent leather shoes;

they also had boyfriends, and they wore bras and makeup before we dared."

Studies have found that gifted girls are more likely than gifted boys to be shunned by their peers.[10] Undoubtedly, the members of the P.R.A. were gifted, the very sort who get shunned for being different from their less-talented classmates. The P.R.A. had its own art club, called the M.M.S., the Masterpiece Maker's Society, and the girls filled up notebook after notebook with drawings of themselves and their boyfriends. Drawings of Prunella showed her as a baby, a child, a young adolescent. (The adolescent pictures seemed to illustrate a fascinating hybrid of little girl and sexual girl: breasts and hairbows, overalls and chic eyeglasses.)

They wrote novels with love scenes in which the characters "made out" with their boyfriends. "While we were often embarrassed by the P.R.A. girls' fascination with their growing bodies and their bold expressions of their feelings and urges," Elizabeth recalls, "our 'twins' were a constant source of entertainment for us."

By the end of sixth grade, all the members of the P.R.A. were writing and producing plays, painting, creating alternative yearbooks, and completing their novels. "Since Prunella and I shared the same body, and Prunella had so many projects and creative endeavors going on, there was less and less time for me. It got to the point that even when I wanted to 'come out,' Prunella would push me out of the way. I'd be trying to talk normal, but suddenly I'd be snorting and bucking my teeth; Prunella had clearly taken over."

Psychiatrists might call this "multiple personality syndrome." But clearly these girls were preserving something deep and real in themselves.

One summer night late in August, on the very eve of seventh grade, Betsy was sitting on her front porch when her friend Stacey dropped by. "Stacey understood the importance of imagination, and she respected Prunella and P.R.A. However, Stacey said that she feared that I was losing my connection to reality. What got my attention was her claim that the summer before I had known all the words to the top ten radio songs, and that this year I couldn't even identify their titles."

That hot August night, after Stacey's visit, was the beginning of Prunella's death. By the time seventh grade began, only a few weeks later, the P.R.A. clubhouse was unoccupied, and the drawing and creative writing stopped. "My friendship with the other girls in the group started to deteriorate, and we were never as close again."

"I had two conflicting needs," Elizabeth explains. "I wanted to develop a self that was unique and creative, and also a self that was socially acceptable and fit into my peer group." The peer group wanted to be pretty and stylish and up on the latest music. "It was also important to be smart, nice, neat, and modest. People with these qualities were the ones boys noticed and girls wanted for their friends."

Carol Gilligan describes this pressure as the "tyranny of the perfect girl." "In white middle-class America she is the girl who has no bad thoughts or feelings, the kind of person everyone wants to be with, the girl who, in her perfection, is worthy of praise and attention, worthy of inclusion and love."[11]

Elizabeth resumed her struggle to be accepted into the popular group, and for the next several years maneuvering the social scene became her hobby. She never returned to drawing and painting, playwriting and acting, but she did continue to write throughout her adolescent years. "But I stopped writing stories and poems," she recalls. "Instead I filled up journals and diaries with thoughts, fears, hopes about friendships and romance."

Prunella had been Betsy's link to the creative, carefree world of her childhood. "When she was extinguished," writes the thirty-three-year-old Elizabeth, "my imagination, too, suffered a kind of death."

The question is how to retain self when we are constantly encouraged to accept the convention of feminine selflessness. Gilligan thinks coming of age in a patriarchal, or "male-voiced" society, is inherently traumatic for girls. Dissociation, for them, becomes a "brilliant psychological mechanism" because when they can't find resonance outside themselves, they create a protective resonating chamber. "My friends and I came up with a unique alternative," says Elizabeth. "We created imaginary twins to embody our silenced voices, and P.R.A. was our resonating chamber."

Teresa Bernardez, a psychoanalyst and training supervisor on the faculty of the Michigan Psychoanalytic Counsel, sees a direct developmental link between the perfect, self-denying girl and the psychologically distressed woman. In learning to be "cool," girls find that expressing anger is not an option. The lesson stays with them for years. "I have found the damaging psychological effects of this cultural prohibition against the expression of anger on their own behalf again and again in adult women," says Bernardez.[12]

She believes therapists must acknowledge out loud what girls and women cannot identify for themselves: the oppression they experience in their families and by the culture. Their symptoms come from an effort to *deny* this oppression, Bernardez believes. They show a woman's attempt to connect to a thwarted desire to be a more authentic person. Therapists who recognize this have a chance of helping "the young, sagacious and brave girl of earlier years to emerge." *All* women, Bernardez believes, carry inside of them "this girl who has been abandoned and betrayed."

The adult women who conducted Gilligan's studies of girls at various schools (studies which came to be known as the Harvard

Project on Women's Psychology and Girls' Development) began to recall how their own childhoods had betrayed them in ways similar to what the girls with whom they were interacting had experienced — how, even worse, they had betrayed themselves!

When I interviewed Elizabeth McLeod, she told me that so far in her life she has never been able to get a handle on finances. She could do brilliant work at school and commit herself devotedly to developing programs for girls, but she could not get on top of her own bills and debt. "It's my next project," she said, "I've *got* to do it."

But there flashed onto her face the same questioning look of despair I've seen so often when the subject of money comes up with women. *Will I do it? Can I do it? I'm not sure. I'm afraid not.*

The period of dissociation so many girls go through in late childhood and early adolescence, in which they feel they cannot be themselves and survive, contributes to the lack of reality they later experience when it comes to taking care of themselves financially. Financial independence is fraught with conflict for women. But girls have learned very well the lesson of splitting off, or denying, conflict. They are not taught to negotiate conflict, and as a result are left with a gap in their emotional intelligence. Psychologically they remain dependent.

WITHOUT A BRIDGE

The disconnection between girlhood and adulthood perpetuates itself, since adult women often are not in a position to help girls bridge the terrifying adolescent impasse. Without that bridge, girls split, disconnecting from the past in a way that leaves them without a solid emotional foundation that would give them a road into the future.

This split was the source of the feeling I'd had as a girl that there was no bridge — and thus, no future. One day I was a child, the next, I was out there in high heels and keyhole necklines, trying to imagine that I was a woman. My mother had not been there to help me through the adolescent passage. The teachers had not been there. No one had been there.

What develops, as a result of such abandonment, is a kind of false maturity, one that glosses over the inner girl and her still rampant dependency. Once I was on my own, in New York, I began having, over and over again, a dream that, had I known how to read it, could have revealed my own lingering dependency. The dream dismissed the external reality of my academic history, which eventually became one of graduating from college with honors. This dream, like all dreams, was about *internal* reality.

At the end of my senior year I discover that if I am to graduate, there are certain things I have to do, tests to take, credits to make up. Somehow, there isn't enough time. Through some small but fatal error I won't graduate. This is clear early in the dream. The balance of the dream is taken up with worrying about what I will do with my life now that I have fallen off track.

The one thing I can think of is going home to my parents and taking courses at the local university, but this never becomes a real plan. For one thing, it isn't clear to me exactly what I would have to do to graduate from another college. Would I have to start over again from square one? Or was it even possible to start over? Had I ruined my only chance to get out of my parents' house and have a life?

The dream is about feeling unready to move into adult life. In it I actually kept myself from graduating so I could stay in school — or, actually, so that I could go home to my parents. The most nightmarish aspect of the dream was its feeling of stuckness. *I felt: the glue that surrounds me is of my own making.*

This powerlessness, I think, is deeply related to the self-betrayal girls learn in childhood. Women do not really *believe* in their ability to make it. They can't rely on themselves; the social environment, in not having supported their truth, has taken away their power.

Parents are ambivalent about their daughters' futures. They know that they risk crippling their daughters, but it's as if they can't help themselves. What if they push the poor girl out the door and she can't make it? So they hedge their bets, offering the wrong kind of "help" — paying their daughters' bills, for example, instead of helping them learn to figure it out.

As parents we need to resolve our ambivalence. When we over-protect girls we're succumbing to our own fears and encouraging theirs. The overprotection of girls tells them, essentially, *I don't think you can make it out there in the world without me carrying you.*

My daughters received financial assistance from me throughout their twenties. My son didn't. He expected, and I expected, that the first order of business when he got out of grad school would be to get a job and pay his bills. He got a job selling shoes at five dollars an hour. He paid his bills.

For my daughters, the way I looked at it, the first order of business was "finding" themselves. They had identities to develop. They were bright, talented, and trying to figure out what was involved in creating a life. I was tremendously identified with them. *At the time, I had no idea that inner security had anything at all to do with financial security.*

My feeling, upon graduating from college, of being trapped in the past was the result of my having disconnected from want-ing — from any personal sense of desire. Desire is the bridge to the future, and, simply, I had none.

The new female psychology centers on a serious question: What can be done to prevent girls from succumbing to their fears of being alone?

Women, Carol Gilligan believes, are concerned with survival. At bottom, they are afraid of ending up alone on a cold planet. And so they sacrifice themselves, hoping that if they devote themselves to others, they'll be taken care of in return.

It isn't lost on Gilligan that women's inclination to care for others comes in part from their own concerns about security. But depending on relationship in this way boomerangs. It also undermines personal development.

Women today are caught in the gears of a social revolution. The majority of women are supporting themselves. They are also supporting others. Even those living with husbands, as we saw in the previous chapter, are contributing half or more of the money to their households. Yet the dream of security supposedly offered by men and marriage continues to seduce them. The wish for security, as we shall see in the chapter to come, results in the diminishment of aggression and self-confidence in young women. They are still being taught to give up their dreams and settle for the romantic ideal.

In the late 1970s and early 1980s, I made gains in my struggle to become independent. In beginning to face my own dependency, I began relying less on my man for support — both financial and emotional — and became more reliant on myself. My long-sought assertiveness allowed my relationship with my partner to expand, making room for autonomy and mutual respect.

When The Cinderella Complex was published, my life changed in many ways. I was asked to do things of which I would never have thought myself capable. In Tokyo I gave a university lecture attended by so many people they had to put TV monitors in the hall outside the auditorium to accommodate the overflow. In Italy I participated in a public debate about women's fear of independence with some of Italy's feistiest feminists, including no less an idol than filmmaker Lina Wertmuller. I had dinner, afterward, sitting next to — talking with! — the mayor of Rome. This was a world I had never imagined, but I was relatively comfortable with it because I knew I had accomplished something. In identifying *The Cinderella Complex* I had given women a tool with which they could begin to change their lives.

In the years after the book was published, my partner and I grew apart. I was becoming a stronger person, and my sense of what I wanted was changing. I had begun to feel that I needed to be on my own. In a relationship, when you give up the "I" to become "we," you can lose sight of what you feel and think as an individual. Things can become hopelessly entangled. Instead of two people relating to one another, the arrangement can end up a hodgepodge of mutual dependency.

Yet it was tempting to play it safe and just hang out. My partner and I had been together fifteen years at that point, and I knew that statistically the odds of my entering another long-term relationship were pretty low. The specter of a lonely old age — the stereotypical nightmare of the single woman — rose up to intimidate me. Yet I felt both his discontent and my own. Perhaps neither of us was comfortable with the changes that had taken place in the other over the years. L. had become a successful businessman. The things that interested him no longer captured my attention. And although he would have said otherwise, I'm not sure he liked my being as independent or as successful as I had become. It seemed to him that I needed him less, and I *did* need him less, at least in the old way. Ten years my junior, he was in the process of resolving certain major life issues. We were not at all in the same place. Although L. had never said so, he may have wanted at least the opportunity to have children. With me, that would have been impossible.

For a while I waited for something to "happen," nursing the dependent delusion that people make the decision to split up together. Then I realized that if I wanted this move, I would have to be the one to initiate it. What happened then was interesting. L. said that if I hadn't brought it up, he might have taken the path of least resistance and stayed on in the relationship indefinitely, even though he, too, wanted to separate. "It's ironic," he said, "but of the two of us, it turns out that I'm the more dependent one."

You can't have an authentic relationship if you relinquish who you are; that was one of the chief conclusions of Gilligan's work with girls. Women sometimes spend years wriggling around trying to accommodate that contradiction. Primarily, we're protecting our wish to be loved and our conditioned belief that we can't have love without putting the needs of others ahead of our own. Resisting the pull of the Romance Myth requires a different way of evaluating what we need and a new concept of goodness, one that respects and honors the self.

Chapter 6

THE ROMANCE MYTH: HOW FEMALES GET SIDETRACKED FROM THE GOAL OF SELF-SUPPORT

In my first analysis, which began in the seventies, I spent years trying to understand why, at twenty-four, I had been so infantile, so dependent, so hopelessly childish as to have married the wrong man and caused sorrows for myself and my children for years to come. It was a typical way to frame the problem, coming straight from the mouths of the analytic fathers.

In my second analysis, in the nineties, with a woman, a feminist, I began to see things I hadn't recognized before. For years I'd been telling myself the story of my marriage in the same way, the fifties way. I had tried to take full responsibility for the failures in my life, even though, as a girl, a part of me had been crushed. But now I began seeing it differently. My relationship with "the man" — my father, the Church, the Pope, the catechism, the very structure of institutionalized patriarchy — had affected me profoundly. I'd developed ways of looking at myself in relation to men, and to the world, that were ultimately destructive. Money, financial planning, a commitment to supporting myself throughout my life, remained hazy ideas to which I paid lip service. But psychologically, I would came to understand, I was inhibited *against* supporting myself. Most women are. Unconsciously they feel that becoming financially independent is like shooting themselves in the foot.

CAPITULATING TO DADDY

When I'd been living in New York for four years — same job, same friends, few dates (talking to a man, whenever I actually met one, made me nervous) — I was introduced to a man who took a great liking to me and began pursuing me. I was taken with his unguarded interest in me, his verbosity and intelligence, and his odd, downtown life, which seemed mostly to involve going to bohemian bars in the Village. The people in these places never wore suits or dresses, or even had jobs, so far as I could see, but they all talked as if their lives were taking place in their brains. Even the women — painters, writers — were outspoken, brash, holding their own in the booze department. I felt like an ingenue but they fascinated me. After a few India Pale Ales, or maybe some cognac, Ed would begin to recite Yeats in a bellowing brogue. He'd grown up in Sheepshead Bay, but his syntax was Shakespearean.

After about a month of seeing this man, he screamed at me drunkenly in a cab one night because I wouldn't go to bed with him — and the next night I slept with him. That I felt desperate is obvious, at least in hindsight. I was afraid he would walk. He was thirty years old and had actually lived in Paris. What did he want with a half-baked half-virgin who was still afraid of life?

I wasn't sure I wanted him, wasn't sure at all, but I wanted the chance to further assess matters. His life seemed exotic in some ways but was also disturbing. He was out of work, having lost a job as a magazine reporter for getting drunk at a press party. He told this story as if the episode were an aberration. I knew in my heart it wasn't. The people he talked with in the bars below Fourteenth Street were more acquaintances than friends. But they all seemed joined in rebellion against the establishment, the bourgeoisie, as they called it.

And they certainly were joined in drink. But then, so was everyone, in those days.

I deeply suspected that I belonged in the bourgeoisie. But maybe not, entirely. I had never met any people like these and I felt my world opening up a crack for the first time. This was new. This was not anything I'd been told about. No one could stand in the wings and warn me because no one I knew knew about this either. Not that it would have made much difference if they had. When I stepped off into the downtown world with this off-center man (when he drank he got really off center), I didn't look back.

I knew I was leaving my uptown world almost from the beginning. Soon I was feeling contemptuous of those who worked nine to five and actually thought their jobs were relevant. Looking back, it was a perfect setup for me, a new way to feel superior, a way to acquire value by joining an elite. My parents belonged to the bourgeoisie, and now I could feel superior to them, too.

All of this was happening very rapidly. I would meet Ed every night after work. I wasn't seeing my roommates. He and I were sleeping in an apartment on Carmine Street that belonged to his brother. I actually don't remember my sexual experiences of that time. I think we were mostly drunk when we did it. I was falling down a well, a tunnel; I had stepped off into the downtown world.

When I'd gone two months without a period, a friend, not one of the Catholic girls, made an appointment for me with her gynecologist and went with me. I couldn't believe what was happening. A cab to the doctor's office, an examination of a sort I'd never had before, a quick talk with the doctor, and suddenly my life was not my own anymore.

Pregnant. The news was stunning. I had been in complete denial. I called Ed and told him on the phone. He was thrilled and insisted I come immediately and meet him at a bar. I went downtown in the same sleeveless linen sheath I'd worn to the doctor, and sat down in the dark bar and told him I wasn't getting married. I was going to have the baby and give it up for adoption. My religion didn't permit abortion, and I couldn't have imagined such a course. I had something living inside of me. Much as, before, I had denied the possibility of pregnancy, now, with the doctor's pronouncement, it was as if the Pope himself had made me with child. The word of the male doctor, not my own body, was what made it real.

But I couldn't keep the child as my own, I felt sure, because nothing about this situation was right. I'd only been seeing Ed for a matter of weeks. He begged me that afternoon, in the dark, empty bar, to marry him, and I felt touched that he wanted to but unmoved in my determination to go on with my life as a single person. Of this much I was sure: it wasn't his decision, it wasn't our decision, it was my decision.

But I didn't tell my parents for another three weeks. I was terrified of their reaction and had to force myself to leave my office desk and go down to the pay phone in the lobby and call them. I always thought it had been their moral judgment I was afraid of, and I'm sure that was part of it. But I think, now, that I was also afraid of acknowledging the separation that had occurred. That they'd lost touch with my life I hadn't been able to admit to myself. Now, to make that call was to say, "You don't know me anymore."

And they didn't. An unspoken parting of the ways had occurred after I left home and came to New York. I felt they disapproved of New York. To give them this news would be like bringing them their worst fear on a silver platter. Daughter leaves home for Sodom and Gomorrah and brings back a pregnancy.

But also, I think I knew they wouldn't support me in my decision, wouldn't offer help. And they didn't. My father went into the bedroom and closed his door for three days, my mother told me later. When he came out, he had decided what I had to do. I had to get married.

"I don't want to get married," I told him.

And then, with hardly a beat, I got swept into his view of it. Unable to hold on to my own sense of what I wanted, I aligned myself with my moral, upright, all-knowing father. My responsibility was not to myself, he pronounced, but to the child.

Of course. How could I have been so demented?

Mine was destined to be a life of selflessness, a concept, certainly, that Catholic school had pummeled into my head since the day I entered first grade. My father was just reminding me of obligations from which, momentarily, I had lapsed.

"Love, according to [male Christian] theologians, is completely self-giving, taking no thought for its own interest but seeking only the good of the other," writes theologian Valerie Saiving. Woman tucks herself neatly into such a cultural framework, believing that "having chosen marriage and children and thus being face to face with the needs of her family for love, refreshment, and forgiveness, she has no right to ask anything for herself but must submit without qualification."[1]

But is it possible something solacing lies in being submissive?

Ed, delighted by my turnaround, went with me to see my parents. My father feared the Church might slow down the proceedings because Ed hadn't been to Mass in years. In my father's black-and-white way of thinking, a nonpracticing Catholic was virtually the same as someone who'd never been baptized. Hence, he believed the Church would view ours as a "mixed marriage" and require endless weeks of counseling to get Ed ready for his promise to raise the baby Catholic. Ed had no trouble making such a promise since he was already a Catholic. But my father had constructed this problem in his mind and now needed to do battle with it. He called his old friend Father Hagmaier, in New York, and asked what he could do "to expedite things." I felt like part of a corporation.

My father hadn't seen Father Hagmaier in years, hadn't kept up with his career. It turned out he was now getting a doctorate in, of all things, psychology. He was preparing for a career in marital counseling! When Hagmaier heard my story, and met Ed and heard his story, he counseled me not to get married. I can only use the words of the current generation to describe my father's reaction when he heard this. He went ballistic. "God damn it," he shouted into the telephone.

I was in the phone booth in the lobby at work again. I'd had my two sessions with Father Hagmaier and felt both vindicated and supported in my original decision. There were many "red flags" in Ed's history, the priest told me. He cited Ed's being thirty and having already lost a job because of his drinking. He cited the fact that Ed's father was alcoholic and had been institutionalized for years, nobody quite knew for what. Father Hagmaier suggested I place the baby in foster care so as to give myself the time I needed to decide whether I wanted to marry and keep the baby or give it up for adoption. "Take your time," he'd said. "Get to know this man to see if you really want this relationship."

I passed these notions along to my father, but they cut no ice. He gathered unto himself the full force of his moral authority: "You made this decision in the act of conception!" he boomed into the telephone. "You are responsible for this child!"

In the act of conception. What a concept. It had such a Latinate ring. It took me right back to Catholic school, the nuns, the priests, the *Baltimore Catechism*, the rules I'd been reciting, the sins I'd been enumerating in dark confessionals all my twenty-four years. With those words my father got me, once and for all. There would be no more talk of going ahead with my own life. I was going to be married. Suddenly, it seemed like the right thing to do.

Girls have a tendency to think of males as being honest, courageous, and strong. Their role models for viewing men as paragons of virtue are their mothers. In the face of my impending doom, my mother was silent. This was serious business, too serious for her to express herself — too serious, certainly, for her to disagree with my father and hold out help.

But didn't she identify with me? How could she not have, regardless of whether she had ever been in such a situation herself as a young woman? Was there no connection, any longer, between the two of us?

I don't remember any discussions with my mother, except for her explaining to me that I could not tell my nineteen-year-old brother what had happened to me because my father feared he would become "demoralized." She and my father would tell friends and family that I had been married secretly, five months earlier, and I would be expected to go along.

Perhaps my mother was cut off from her own past.

Or perhaps she was traumatized by fear of my father. I could only guess. At this crucial juncture in my life, my mother did what she had always done when she didn't know how to talk to me: she sewed. This time it was a maternity dress made of brown serge. So serious. So dowdy. Like being turned into some kind of nun-mother overnight as payment for my sins. I felt thankful to my friend Nancy, a theatrical costume designer, who took the bull by the horns and said, "Raspberry," when I asked her what I should wear down the aisle.

Nancy dug out an elegant pattern from *Vogue* and made me a suit of raspberry-colored mohair with a big inverted pleat in front. By the time I actually got down the aisle (the interventions of Father Hagmaier notwithstanding), I was five months pregnant. The suit, and a gold lace mantilla from one of my roommates, helped me hold my head — and my stomach — high.

For a long time I would experience the difficulty of my new life as punishment for having gotten pregnant, for having "had" to get married, as we used to say. But that interpretation, in the light of what I have since learned about girls and women, no longer seems adequate. The feeling that something was wrong with *me* preceded any "sin" I might have committed. That I had always felt diminished revealed itself in the fact that I never had any hopes or dreams for myself. I couldn't imagine a home, a family, a car in the driveway, a kiddie pool in the backyard. Nor could I picture an office, a laboratory, a university classroom of the sort in which my father taught. Any notion I may have held of the world ahead was dismayingly dim.

Why this blank screen rising up before me, permitting no glimpse of a future? That void, when I think back on it, was terrifying. Most girls growing up in the fifties envisioned two little overdressed figures atop a tiered wedding cake, at least. I saw nothing.

LOSING HEART

When interviewers asked girls at a prominent Ivy League college why they were applying for Rhodes scholarships — what, that is, they planned to *do* after completing their studies — these bright, achieving students could think of nothing to say.[2] Academic awards were as far as their imaginations took them. Successful on the outside, they were disconnected from desire, "from the yes! within," and were unable to project themselves into a future.

That yes! is essential if we're to become comfortable with the idea of supporting ourselves — of not only believing we can take care of ourselves, but of *wanting* to. Unfortunately, for many girls the yes! becomes hedged. True desire — "wanting, lusting, craving, longing, needing in all and every way" — becomes subverted in females, write Elizabeth Debold and her coauthors, Marie Wilson and Idelisse Malavé, in *Mother Daughter Revolution*.[3]

And yet desire is at the very root of self-efficacy. It's what pumps us up, enlivens us, gives force to what we do. When desire is forbidden or compromised, we become separated from that force. A split occurs and we no longer experience the deep source of our wanting. This wreaks havoc with our sense of personal power. For the female students applying for Rhodes scholarships, as for so many girls, there had been no propelling sense of a life to be developed, no way even to imagine continuing out into the world. It was as if the adventure was over before it began.

As we shall see, girls are systematically robbed of the ability to take charge of their lives. They learn submission and deference. In school, they are bullied in the classroom and harassed in the halls. Even teachers who *want* to provide an atmosphere of equity fail. Girls are left weakened and defeated. In a very real sense, they give up on themselves.

Into this void, as inevitably as night follows day, comes the great romantic deterrent. As girls enter adolescence, the culture begins telling them "true love" is no longer the love of their mothers, siblings, and girlfriends, it is the love of a man — and only a man. This man-love, packaged as "romance," is supposed to make up for the childhood integrity they're losing. "Perfect desire, perfect love, and perfect happiness are held out as women's reward for giving up the power of psychological integrity, passionate child love, the child world of girls and women," Elizabeth Debold and her coauthors report.

Today, in spite of the women's movement and the massive education and professionalization of females in our society, the Romance Myth persists, catching both men and women in its web. Men are still cast as heroes — the mentors, the protectors. And women still seek, and feel frightened and vulnerable without, protection.

What girls give up for the love of a hero is nothing less than their potential for becoming a force in their own lives. Yet no one talks about what this barnacled position does to women's efforts to support themselves — to take full charge of their lives.

In interviewing women for this book, I found that self-created financial stability — without which inner security and a sense of freedom are virtually impossible — is something that is known to, planned for, even wanted, by very few. Because of the way women have been socialized, they don't know *how* to want it.

A woman today earns her own money, sometimes piles of it. But, as Annette Lieberman and Vicki Lindner note, in *Unbalanced Accounts,* "*Nothing in her psychological or cultural history has equipped her to imagine taking care of herself for the rest of her life.* Neither rescued nor freed from her rescue fantasy, she can become financially paralyzed."[4] (Emphasis added.)

Financial independence has nothing to do with how diligently one works. Most women plow through double-shift days and still dream at night of becoming bag ladies. They are earnest, committed: they *care*. But not about themselves.

It is remarkable how thoroughly young females in our society continue to be taught dependency. When I began to see what is happening in schools and in families, as the first studies of girls appeared, in the late eighties and nineties, I began to better understand my own story of financial downfall — and the stories of other women.

Females are actually taught that they are unable to rely on themselves for answers.

They are taught that males have the skills to survive, and they don't.

They are taught today — as clearly as they were taught yesterday — that they must depend on someone else.

PUT-DOWN IN THE CLASSROOM

In 1990, alarmed by early findings of the Harvard Project that the beginning of adolescence initiates a crisis in girls' lives, the American Association of University Women conducted a nationwide survey on self-esteem in adolescents. Disturbingly, it found that while 60 percent of girls and 67 percent of boys felt happy with themselves in elementary school, by high school only 29 percent of girls still liked themselves, as compared to nearly half the boys.[5]

Twice as many boys as girls consider their unique talents to be what they like best about themselves, the AAUW reported. What girls like about themselves (when they like anything at all) is their appearance. Poignantly, adolescent boys dream bigger dreams than girls do, "and they are more likely to believe that their dreams can become reality."[6]

When the AAUW came out with its troubling news, in a report called *Shortchanging Girls, Shortchanging America,* journalist Peggy Orenstein found herself deeply concerned. This was the most extensive national survey on gender and self-esteem that had ever been conducted, and it produced a picture of girls' lives that was shocking. In spite of the changes in women's roles in society, the report noted, many of today's girls fall into traditional patterns of low self-image, self-doubt, and self-censorship of their creative and intellectual potential. During adolescence their self-regard drops way below boys' *and never catches up.* Girls come out of their teenage years with reduced expectations and less confidence in themselves and their abilities than boys do. They are more vulnerable to feelings of depression and hopelessness and are four times more likely to attempt suicide.[7]

Orenstein wanted to see for herself what was happening in girls' lives to produce these dramatic losses. She spent a year with eighth-grade girls at two California schools, reporting meticulously on their appearance, their attitudes, their dreams and fears and behaviors. She interviewed their parents and teachers as well. It would turn out that watching those girls took the reporter back to her own adolescence, twenty years earlier — and to the depressing recognition that remarkably little has changed. When she was thirteen herself, Orenstein writes, she lowered her hand in math class, "never to raise it again, out of a sudden fear that I might answer incorrectly and be humiliated."[8]

At sixteen she lost forty pounds, "refusing food and binging on laxatives, eventually losing the ability to eat at all."

At twenty-one she became "paralyzed during the writing of my senior thesis, convinced that my fraudulence was about to be unmasked."

In *SchoolGirls,* her book on the eighth-graders, Orenstein writes that adolescent girls "learned to see boys as freer, with fewer concerns, ultimately more powerful. Girls' diminished sense of self means that, often unconsciously, they take on a second-class, accommodating status."

Even though some teachers were consciously attempting to run gender-unbiased classrooms, a "hidden curriculum" was being perpetrated. While few of the girls Orenstein spoke to had ever been told directly that they couldn't do what boys could do, they were learning this lesson anyway, and paying an enormous price. Without a strong sense of self, she noted, girls enter adulthood "less able to fulfill their potential, less willing to take on challenges, less willing to defy tradition in their career choices," and as a result, their financial security would be jeopardized.

There would be other factors affecting their ability to support themselves. All in all, Orenstein's prediction for their futures was apocalyptic. "Their successes will not satisfy and their failures will be more catastrophic, confirming their own self-doubt. They will be less prepared to weather the storms of adult life, more likely to become depressed, hopeless, and self-destructive."

As I followed Orenstein's report on the classroom, visualizing what she had seen, hearing what she had heard, it became all too apparent that her conclusions (and the AAUW's) were in no way overstated. Girls' treatment in the schoolroom, in the mid-1990s, is little short of crushing. How could anyone, growing up in this way, retain the belief in her ability to care for herself without someone stronger, more powerful, more skilled to lean on?

But, of course, it was the same way I had grown up!

Bold, brassy, and strong-willed on the outside of the classroom, thirteen-year-old Amy retreats to a different position within. As she takes her seat, arms folded across her chest, hunched forward toward her desk, she seems to be making herself smaller. Gone is the brazen playground persona. In class she hardly says a word.

Orenstein notes that the boys sprawl. Nate leans his chair back on two legs and begins a conversation with a friend. The teacher, Mrs. Richter, has given them colored squares to code into prime numbers. When she asks them to call out the prime numbers they've found, Nate booms out, " 'Eleven!' " As they continue into the twenties and thirties, the boys scream louder and louder, competing to see who can get the numbers out first. The teacher lets their intimidating behavior slide. One girl, Allison, who'd been raising her hand to get the teacher's attention, gives up.

After the boys have reached a hundred, Mrs. Richter asks whether 103 is prime or composite.

Kyle shouts out, " 'Prime!' " but Mrs. Richter tries to give someone else a turn. Kyle doesn't go along with this. "He begins to bounce in his chair, chanting, '*Prime! Prime! Prime!*' "

Orenstein notices that when the girls do speak, they obediently follow the rules. Allison raises her hand and waits her turn; this time, she manages to get a response. When Amy volunteers, she, too, raises her hand, but alas, her answer to an easy multiplication problem is wrong. She "turns crimson, and flips her head forward so her hair falls over her face."

Occasionally girls do shout out answers, but usually in response to the easiest questions, Orenstein reports. "When the girls venture responses to more complex questions the boys quickly become territorial, shouting them down with their answers."

While the teacher doesn't say anything to condone the boys' behavior, she permits it. The hidden curriculum holds sway.

Beginning a new lesson on exponents, Mrs. Richter asks, " 'What does three to the third power mean?' "

" 'I *know!*' " shouts Kyle.

Instead of calling on Kyle, the teacher turns to Dawn.

" 'Do you know, Dawn?' "

Dawn hesitates, and begins, " 'Well, you count the number of threes and . . .' "

" '*But I know!*' " interrupts Kyle. " 'I *know!*' "

Dawn is overridden and shuts up.

" 'I *know!* ME!' " Kyle shouts. " '*It's three times three times three!*' "

" 'Yes,' " says Mrs. Richter. " 'Does everyone get it?' "

" 'YES!' " shouts Kyle.

Later the girls explain to the journalist that they hate answering questions for fear of being wrong and for fear of being corrected by the teacher. " 'Boys never care if they're wrong,' " Amy says. " 'They can say totally off-the-wall things, things that have nothing to do with class sometimes.' "

Speaking out in class, and being acknowledged for it, Orenstein points out, is important because it's reinforcing. The kids who *don't* speak out in class have no opportunity to enhance self-esteem through exposure to praise. Nor do they get to learn from their mistakes.

* * *

In every classroom Orenstein visited there was at least one boy like Kyle or Nate who demanded "constant and inappropriate" attention and to whom the teacher deferred. In the reporter's own count of who speaks up in classrooms — who yells out answers, who is called on by the teacher, who commands the most interaction — the ratio hovered at about five boys to one girl.

"Ignored by their teachers and belittled by their male peers, girls lose heart," Orenstein reports. "They may become reluctant to participate at all in class, unable to withstand the small failures necessary for long-term academic success."

Even though she seemed overpowered herself by the boys in her classroom, Mrs. Richter retained a clear sense of the damage being done girls, and how their lowered confidence inhibits them against taking risks. By high school, boys take more risks and do better on tests. Girls give up, even though they have the skills, because they are so afraid of being shown to be wrong. Boys are different, the way Mrs. Richter sees it. " 'They can get all the homework wrong, but they don't care as long as they tried. And then they figure out *why* it's wrong instead of being embarrassed about it. That makes them more confident.' "

What she doesn't say is that boys can afford to be wrong because no one publicly humiliates them for it.

What happens in math and science classrooms can have life-altering effects on women's ability to create financial security for themselves. No matter what field they enter, *women who take more than two college math courses are the only ones who subsequently achieve pay equity.*[9]

Both girls and boys who pursue math and science end up with higher levels of self-esteem than other children. Studies show that girls who like math and science are more likely to aspire to careers as professionals.

Karen Karp, an assistant professor of mathematics education at the University of Louisville, has developed a program called Feisty Females. Its goal is "to train elementary and middle school mathematics teachers in how to give female students the power to attack math problems with the success more often associated with boys," the *New York Times* reported.[10] Karp devised storybooks with strong female characters like Cinder Edna, who doesn't hang around waiting for someone else to solve her problems. Nor does she max out her credit cards. "She buys a dress on layaway, puts on her sensible loafers and takes the bus to the ball, where she meets the prince's cousin."

Studies indicate that girls actually have better math skills than boys in early childhood. But they lose the edge as they grow older, when, as approval becomes important to them, they become too tied to rules. " 'In math, you really need to take risks,' " says Ms. Karp, whose program is funded by the National Science Foundation.

My father, a mathematician, thought I should be able to learn math. But when he tried to help me, he became so exasperated and short-tempered that the experience, for me, was humiliating and I gave up.

Years later, when my daughter Gabrielle demonstrated brilliance in her high school math classes, I marveled. Where did she get this talent? Wherever she got it, it seemed to irritate her male teachers (she sometimes corrected them), as did her gradual withdrawal of interest during an unchallenging senior year. One teacher, appearing more annoyed than concerned, threatened her with failing the regents exam in trigonometry. Instead, she came out in the ninety-ninth percentile. She also was awarded a full scholarship to Harvard and invited to enter with sophomore standing. At high school graduation, every Four-H Club honor any graduate in that rural area might have gleaned was duly mentioned at the ceremony — but not Gabrielle's scholarship to Harvard. She had not played by the rules. She had not kept her mouth shut. And the system duly punished her.

SLUTS R US: THE TRAUMA OF SEXUAL MATURITY

Girls are not only squelched intellectually, they are put down for their sexual development. Simultaneously they become objects of both desire and ridicule. The message confuses and frightens them, causing them to retreat further from their strengths and seek shelter in the Romance Myth.

Even before their teens most girls find themselves being thrust into the precarious world of adult female sexuality. By age twelve more than two-thirds have begun to menstruate. Their breasts have budded, their bodies' contours changed. This visible newness, and the way the culture responds to it, Elizabeth Debold and her colleagues believe, thrusts girls out of the world of childhood in a way that is harsh and abrupt. They feel flung out of safety, dangerously unmoored. While boys are generally enthusiastic about the adolescent changes in their bodies, equating them with greater control and power in the world, most girls equate their physical changes with a loss of control.[11] Almost overnight their girlish expressions of curiosity, outspokenness, and pleasure are taken as sexual.[12] Suddenly they are being identified with the commercialized images of women, women as objects of desire.

And they are both desired and denigrated for being desirable. This confusing paradox gets taken into the psyche and — for many women — never resolved. A group of women I know, divorced in their forties and free to date again, refer to themselves as "Sluts R Us." It is meant to be a joke about their enjoyment and pursuit of sex, but it connotes shame.

Today, the power dynamics of sluts and studs being acted out in the schoolrooms of America would be laughable were it not so insidiously destructive.

The scene in one California classroom is vividly described in *School-Girls*.[13] The subject in Mrs. Webster's class is how diseases get transmitted sexually.

She starts by drawing the Greek symbol for woman on the blackboard. " 'Let's say she is infected, but she hasn't really noticed yet, so she has sex with three men.' "

Onto the blackboard go three symbols for man. A heavyset boy stage-whispers, " 'What a slut.' " The class giggles.

The teacher, who apparently hasn't heard the comment, continues diagramming how an epidemic works. The first man has three sexual encounters, she explains, drawing three more female signs. " 'The second guy was very active; he had intercourse with five women.' " As she draws with her back to the class, two boys stand and take bows.

The third guy was " 'smart,' " she continues; he didn't sleep with a woman. This didn't impress the boys a whit. " 'You! You!' " they began pointing at one another, mocking the very idea of the nonsexual male.

Typically, in high schools, boys are considered sexual players, girls who have sex are considered sluts. Sexual activity is terrible for girls' reputations, but great for boys'.

I've heard women in their twenties refer to certain young men as sluts, but of course they're using a female slur. Mostly the concept is limited to females, and it's meant to shame. "What would happen if we whispered the truth to girls," Orenstein asks, in *SchoolGirls*, "if we admitted that their desire could be as powerful as boys'?"

What would happen, indeed?

Desire in girls is discussed only in terms of whether they should say yes or no — and to boys, not even to themselves. Educator Michelle Fine says that sexuality, as taught in high schools, supports the idea of "the male in search of desire and the female in search of protection." The subject of girls' pleasure is evaded; their sexuality is discussed in terms of reproduction — menstruation, the ovaries, the uterus.

By not discussing women's sexuality, the culture supports its repression and the idea that sexual pleasure for females is shameful. Shame is inculcated in girls when they're very young — while at the same time sex is *available* to them when they're very young. Some studies have found that over half of middle and junior high school kids have had intercourse at least once.[14] From the first, a girl's consideration of her emerging sex drive is tinged with guilt.

As a girl comes into sexuality, she begins to experience her own feelings of lust and yearning, and she feels safer thinking they are inspired — even caused — by a particular boy. He could be a boy with food stuck in his braces, a less-than-gallant way of behaving toward girls, a stale odor emanating from his infrequently washed body: it makes little difference *who* he is. Onto this paragon of ordinariness she will fasten everything — her happiness on Wednesday in having a date for Saturday, her feelings of worth and attractiveness, those deep yearnings from inside her body which, she believes, only nearness to *him* can produce. She thinks he actually *makes* those feelings inside her.

As she hands over her connection to her body, she splits off from her desires and yearnings, puts them, in effect, in his hands; *gives* them to him. And in absolving herself of responsibility for her yearnings, she loses touch with the power they confer. Because she wants those feelings she believes *he* creates, she puts herself in thrall to him. She begins to think that she wants *him,* when in fact what she may really want more than anything is her lost sense of self and her dream of being an adventurer in the world.

Losing that sense of herself has ramifications that long outlast girlhood. Striking out in her twenties to pursue a career and taking responsibility for her economic well-being are crucial to a woman's breaking out of financial dependence and dysfunction. But the ability to take charge gets seriously undermined in girls, not the least — and this has *never* been adequately acknowledged — because their bodies are not respected. The important contribution Elizabeth Debold and her colleagues made in *Mother Daughter Revolution* was in showing that as a girl sends her connection to her body underground, so does she send her desires, her dreams, her hopes for the future.

" 'I feel scummy,' " Evie tells Peggy Orenstein in *SchoolGirls*. " 'Even though I didn't actually do it, I feel like a total slut inside.' "[15]

Evie had been badgered for sex for two years — in sixth and seventh grades — by a boy she'd been " 'in love with.' " Orenstein found her story — a story, as she puts it, of male aggression and female defense — to be typical.

To protect themselves, girls deny their natural instincts and try to become "good." This is not so much a question of morality, says Orenstein, as of survival. Girls have to monitor their budding sexual desire. "They must keep vigilant watch, over each other and over themselves."

The price of all this vigilance is enormous. "When being desirable supplants desiring, sexual activity takes on a frightening dimension: it becomes an attempt to confirm one's self-worth, one's lovability, through someone else," Orenstein concludes.

Parents and teachers think they're protecting girls by focusing on the dangers of behaving sexually, of victimization, of pregnancy, of disease. While there are real reasons for those fears, there is also the reality of female desire, and girls aren't taught about that. As a culture we give girls no clue as to how they might navigate between danger and desire toward a healthy eroticism. "Sexual entitlement — a sense of autonomy over one's body and desires — is an essential component of a healthy adult self," writes Peggy Orenstein. Yet we deliberately infuse girls with shame.

Sex is frightening for a female adolescent. It's *made* frightening by abuse and belittlement. In a recent study the great majority (eight out of ten) of those girls who experienced sexual harassment at school reported having been touched, pinched, or grabbed. Well over a third reported being harassed every single day in school.[16]

Coming of age sexually poses a disturbing dilemma for most girls. They feel they must retreat from the dangers that would result from an open expression of sexuality. Girls need a safe environment in which to work through the challenging transition into adult sexuality. Instead, most experience this time as dangerous and as unpredictable as a minefield.

"Many girls, particularly middle-class girls, 'disembody' by distancing from the sexual knowledge and feelings in their bodies so that they feel safer and less vulnerable," write the authors of *Mother Daughter Revolution*. But of course the tactic backfires. "By not being able to 'own' their sexuality and integrate it within their ideas about who they are, girls find themselves taken by surprise by the urgency of their feelings, and they become confused into 'love.'"[17]

Being reared in an atmosphere of physical fear and humiliation is tantamount to brainwashing: *Girls are still being bombarded with the message that they're inferior.* They're not capable of taking care of themselves. They will not be expected to take care of themselves! By the end of high school, if not before, they will have learned that the real out for them is the romance story — and all the solacing protection it implies but does not deliver.

THE FALLACY OF ROMANTIC PROTECTION

"I don't remember how the impression was made that I wasn't going to have to support myself," says a woman in my journal-writing group. "It was implied, in a sense, that the ship will come in, the knight will arrive, the dream lover will appear — the 'one,' the perfect one, the only one."

Whether these words are told us or not, women are fed the Romance Myth as their hidden curriculum. If we behave properly, if we give up desire, if we put others' needs before our own — we will be protected. This notion — protection in exchange for compliance with traditional female roles — is at the very heart of the Romance Myth. And the story continues to be believed in, even though most women are shocked to discover (usually earlier rather than later) that the promise of romantic protection is little more than a cruel hoax.

It was frightening when I began to recognize, at the age of twenty-five, how unstable life was going to be *because* I'd gotten married. I had been programmed to expect something different. What I ended up with didn't seem normal. In the beginning, at least, it seemed almost perverse.

And then, of course, I became accustomed to it, feeling that *this* was reality, and that the other story — the rose-covered-cottage story — was what they told little girls. Eventually, like the Santa Claus story, you came to understand that it wasn't true. At that point, and only at that point, could you be said to have begun growing up.

There was no cottage awaiting me after I complied with my father's directive to get married. The apartment Ed found us had a long, dark hallway off which were two small bedrooms and a chipped and fractured bath. At the end of the hall a tiny kitchen opened onto two small rooms with an archway between them. The floors were of soft, splintery wood. The walls had cracked and been painted over many times. Light came from ceiling fixtures, harshly illuminating everything. There seemed to be nowhere to lie down and feel protected.

146 • MAXING OUT

The place hadn't been cleaned in a long time. The moldings were grime-encrusted, the kitchen and bath ancient and mildewed. God only knows who'd lived there before and under what circumstances. I thought: This is where our little family is going to make its nest? Each day I woke up, looked grimly at the wan light seeping through the filthy windows and felt utterly defeated.

But Ed was proud. He said he loved coming home from his new job as a bartender and having to halloo down the hall to me, sitting waiting for him in the room at the far end. The night of our wedding we slept in that room on a mattress on the floor.

This apartment had none of the pretensions of the bourgeoisie, unlike the place where I'd lived with my roommates. *It* had been sterile to the point of meaninglessness, I told myself. But I kept thinking of its two bathrooms, its air conditioners, and its new refrigerator. It had been in a high-rise building near the East River. There was even a doorman, that token of security for nice young women. The elevator had Muzak. *What was I to make, now, of this line-up of dark, dirty rooms? What did it mean about my future? What did it mean about me?*

As I thought about the new studies of girls and recalled my own childhood, I began to see how being tracked into the Romance Myth undermines a girl's ability to learn to take care of herself. It encourages her to think that this is someone else's job. Instead of being aware of my own deepest yearnings, I had looked outside for guidance as to what I *should* want, and so I ended up losing myself to the illusion of romantic protection. That I should *want* such protection, should feel I required it, had been tied by conditioning to my sense of being female.

Now my research was beginning to coalesce. A picture was coming together, based on the reports of women I'd interviewed, the studies I'd read, and experts I'd talked to about women's difficulties in embracing financial independence. *Everything* is related to females' attitudes toward men, and our internalized attitudes about ourselves in relation to men. Given the setup, it could not be otherwise.

The setup, as we have seen, includes girls "losing voice" as they approach puberty, unaided by adult women in their lives, who themselves have forgotten how traumatized they were at the same age.

It includes girls watching in horror as their bodies develop, because their female parts are being sneered at by boys.

It includes girls being afraid to participate in the classroom because boys overpower and humiliate them, calling them stupid. And because female teachers, implicitly siding with the boys, do nothing to correct the situation.

At the very same time society begins criticizing girls, it starts pressuring them to enter the Romance Myth — to begin believing in boys as their salvation. It's a one-two punch: the attack on girls' competency, followed by the promise of protection, are what give the myth its devastating potency.

And young females succumb, as recent surveys of girls' romantic attitudes about their futures attest. *Fully 81 percent of teenage girls in a recent California study do not expect to work outside the home when they have children!*[18]

In Denver, in 1992, a study of schoolgirls found that *most* did not expect to have to work full-time as adult women. They planned to get married and raise children. (It's noteworthy that many of these girls were living with divorced mothers who were actively discouraging their daughters from pursuing work and were telling them, instead, to find a man.)[19]

Seeing how difficult their mothers' lives were as they juggled jobs with work at home, girls often fantasized romance as the way to financial liberation, Linda Christian-Smith writes in *Becoming a Woman Through Romance*,[20] a study of how girls are affected by romance novels. To girls from poor and working-class backgrounds, the false hope these stories offer can be particularly cruel.

Mothers often support daughters buying into the Romance Myth. By the time she reached seventh grade, Victoria, a girl interviewed by the Harvard Project, was reading romance books side by side with Mom. Because Victoria's father had died when she was young, leaving her mother with "a rough life," as Victoria put it, she herself was hoping to marry the man of her dreams and have a happy life.

The Harvard researchers to whom Victoria told this story noted that neither Victoria nor her mother was able to conceive of her life solution as coming from herself. Victoria dreams of marrying "the perfect prince," a man who "is going to be at least six foot and have a beard and mustache and he's going to be really nice and gentle. . . . He is going to be rich, too."[21]

Sharon Thompson, a researcher in adolescent sexuality, tells how fifteen- and sixteen-year-old girls "rush into full-blown narratives about sexual and romantic life" that sound as if they've come straight from a paperback.[22] Girls get so seduced by these stories that they actually think they can organize their lives like a plot.

Compare the virtues of Victoria's phantom lover to the guidelines Silhouette Romances give would-be writers of its novels. The hero is expected to be eight to twelve years older than the heroine. "He is self-assured, masterful, hot-tempered, capable of violence, passion and tenderness. He is often mysteriously moody," Christian-Smith writes.[23]

The heroine, by contrast, is a plain little thing, an ingenue who manages to transform herself, stunningly, when she dresses up. In her life she's "in transition, unhappy with her job, or just starting out," the publisher suggests. And "she is usually without parents or a 'protective relationship.'"

Alone in the world, that is. Abandoned to her own puny resources. The struggle for the heroine of a romance novel, according to Elizabeth Debold and her colleagues, is "to turn her relative powerlessness into power by holding the hero prisoner of his own emotions until he simply must marry her (and, thus, share his economic power and privilege) or lose his mind."24

STELLA TAKES CARE OF HERSELF, AT LEAST FOR NOW

Her parents grew up in the sixties, members of the human potential movement who taught themselves how to conduct the fast, jivey group therapy of the seventies. Rocking emotions, dramatic change. It was a time of permissiveness, of reaction against the conservatism of the Eisenhower years and rearing from parents who'd grown up in the frightening time of the Great Depression.

Both Lewis and Monica had IQs that might have produced Ph.D.'s, surgeons, heads of corporations. But something got off track somewhere. People were "dropping out," doing their own thing. Pot became a regular ritual in the lives of a lot of adults, smoothing the edges of disappointment. The pleasure principle took the ascendancy.

Not that Lewis and Monica didn't provide well for Stella and her brother. First, they lived in a brownstone in the museum area of Philadelphia and had the nanny. Every afternoon they left to go downtown, where they would spend the evenings running their groups for successful but unhappy professionals who came as soon as their workdays were over, two, sometimes three, evenings a week. Primal Strategies was at the cutting edge, in Philly, in the nineteen seventies, an avant-garde combination of primal scream therapy, addiction-breaking encounter groups, and love, love, love.

The Andersons' groups became the talk of the town. Lewis and Monica made good money. Sometimes Stella and her younger brother accompanied mom in their carriage, when the sitter didn't come through. There was always someone on hand to take care of them when mom went into the big room and led her group members through the rituals of "getting angry," "feeling the fear," and even puking into a bucket when the anxiety surrounding such feelings became too intense. People would relive their traumas from early childhood and feel better. They would learn to trust others enough to let themselves be seen in the throes of confusion and come away feeling less isolated.

But eventually the founders of Primal Strategies became disenchanted with city living. Was this where the Sixties Generation really wanted to raise its families? Hardly. Too much crime. Too many drugs. Too much filth on the streets. The Andersons picked up and moved to New Hope, bought a huge, ego-gratifying house, and continued their therapy work, only on a less grand scale. Both mom and dad saw clients and tried to help them with their problems. But as the economy began to shift in the eighties, people became more interested in material goods and less fascinated with human potential. They were on the trail of adventure, thrills of every sort, and spent their money on kayaks, sound systems, high-end entertaining, and the cocaine that often went with it.

Not that Lewis and Monica didn't continue to make a living; it was just harder. Work was more sporadic. Clients came in because they wanted to get hypnotized to quit smoking; they didn't come in because they wanted to *change*. Therapy became short term — shorter and shorter term as, in the nineties, managed care took over and insurance covered less. Money, or the lack of it, became more palpable as an issue, and Stella's mom and dad didn't look at it in the same way. "My mother used to tell me, 'Pay your bills first, and then get what you want,' " Stella, twenty-five, recalls. "My father, it was, 'take what you want, and then pay your bills with anything that's left.' " She laughs when she says this, but knows it has influenced her own relationship to money. Her principle? *Don't overspend, don't amass debt, and save if you can.* Otherwise you end up on the subtle yo-yo of insecurity. Borrowing is tantamount to relying on someone else, and Stella doesn't do that. She relies on herself and only on herself — at least at this point in her life.

When she was twenty-three, she bought a new car with cash she had saved from her first job. When her cost of living skyrocketed after she left Boston for New York, she took an extra job showing commercial real estate in the evenings to supplement her regular salary.

All seemed well enough. Stella was notably more responsible than many of the young women I'd interviewed, who feel obliged to spend money maintaining their images, keeping their social lives revved, and making up for deprivations they'd felt since childhood. It isn't until we start talking about her future that the classic female ambivalence about self-support emerges. Stella told me that in a few years she wanted to get married and have children. Would she expect to be supported by her husband, once she got married? I asked.

"Well, I think we would all like that," she said, referring to her generation, "but I don't think we *expect* it."

Yet people are telling her to expect it: her father, for one, although he says it "kiddingly." Also, an older man at work who tells her, when she says that she doesn't like throwing money away on rent and would like to own her own apartment, "Well, it doesn't make any difference because eventually you'll get married and your husband will take care of you."

"If you don't expect to be taken care of, how will you take care of yourself when you marry?" I ask.

"I'll only take off for six months or a year after a baby is born," she replies. "And I'll maintain my relationship with a company and return to it."

So far, so good, although one wonders how many young women *think* that that's what they'll do, until the deliciousness of being home with a baby and being taken care of by a loving, money-making husband lures them from their more practical sensibilities.

There remains, for many young women, a distinction between what's appropriate when you're single and what's permissible when you're married.

Also they distinguish between what's "mature" for a female and what's "mature" for a male. Stella told me of her roommate, a divorced, childless woman a few years older than she who can't live

152 • MAXING OUT

152 • MAXING OUT

on what she earns and is helped out financially by both her parents and her boyfriend. "Sometimes I look at Alice and feel contempt. Other times, I think it's nice that she's looser than I am about money. She says she's more interested in having fun than in worrying about money, and I like that lightness about her. It's charming."

"Would you think it was charming if a man her age were being given financial help by his parents and girlfriend?"

"Absolutely not."

"What do you think the difference is?"

"I guess I would expect a man to be able to support a family."

"So your expectations for men and women are different."

"I guess they are."

"But developmentally, Alice is being kept a child."

"That's true."

"And you wouldn't find her behavior acceptable in a twenty-nine-year-old man."

"No."

When Stella was fourteen her parents ended their marriage but remained close friends. It was never quite clear to Stella who was paying for what, even though her parents lived separately. But as she approached college, she remembers, it was her father who helped her buy her first old car, and who offered to help her with her college loans (he never made good on this promise). Her father also bought some of her clothes.

"Did you think of your mother as having had a tough time, financially, after she was on her own?" I asked.

Stella says quickly that she didn't. She thought that any financial difficulties her mother had were "her fault." "She could have worked more. My father says now that there were some years when she didn't work."

It seems a classic case of the divorced father's financial contributions to his children being in the form of easily recognizable specifics, like car insurance or clothes, while the mother's day-to-day care and financial nurturance is not recognized as such. Mothers are often blamed for the divorce in the first place (and indeed are more likely than their husbands to instigate the breakup). Thus, they "deserve" what they get.

Stella's ambivalence about what's appropriate for women — her thinking of her roommate's helplessness as "light" and charming reveals how divided she is about her own strict financial autonomy — takes a different form from that of the girls of divorced mothers who confessed to wanting romance and a man to take care of them. She wants to be on her own but is not quite sure how this will compute, once a seemingly reliable man appears on the scene. This has not happened, so far, in Stella's life, so for the moment, at least, she is independent.

But her entire generation is in conflict with this independence, just as their mothers are. "For me and many of my friends, our parents' divorce marked the first time we began to sense both the transience of money and its enormous power to shape our emotional lives," writes Rebecca Johnson, in a *Vogue* article titled "For Love or Money." "Money, we learned in those formative years, when suddenly there wasn't as much of it anymore, is not just the ability to buy stuff. It is freedom. Freedom to walk away from a bad job, a bad town, a bad man."[25]

Johnson's article is about the split between what her generation of women want and what they think they should want, vis-à-vis financial independence. "I was born too late for mad money," she says. "By the time I was old enough to date, the idea that a woman would leave her house with just enough cash to get herself home was so anachronistic, it verged on ludicrous. We pay for ourselves. Or, rather, we pretend we want to pay for ourselves. You know, that vague, girlish move toward the purse while the man says, 'I've got it.' "

Unless he says something more along the lines of, " 'Your share comes to thirty-nine dollars with tax and tip.' In which case, we pony up. And then secretly resent him," admits Johnson. "This is one of the creepy effects of feminism that nobody likes to talk about. *Even as we espouse parity, we never quite manage to fall in love with the man who makes us buy our dinner."* (Emphasis added.)

I fell in love with such a man but then spent the next fifteen years wondering if he really loved me. Women who marry the man who pays their way may momentarily feel loved, but invariably, the arrangement collapses. In *The Gift of Fear*, Gavin de Becker writes about how women know, intuitively, when they are in physically endangering situations, but that something in them wants to deny this, wants to remain the trusting young girl, and too often they ignore their intuitions, risking rape and worse. I believe women have the same intuition about financial support. They know, when they give up their jobs and allow husbands to support them, that they're playing Russian roulette with their financial security. There's at least a moment, a brief window on reality, when they can *see* the danger. But then the window shuts.

Like Stella, many of the women in Johnson's generation are at least struggling with the issue of self-support. Johnson tells about an old lover who was more conservative in his spending than she. He also liked the idea of fifty-fifty dating. "The end came one cold New Year's Eve when he insisted we take the subway to a black-tie party. As I waited for the train, shivering in my stiletto heels and spangly earrings, something in me died toward him."

This may not have been the man for Johnson, but looking back, she admits she learned something from him. "We have worked so hard to make our own money, and we still make so much less than men, that it is hard to let go of it, so we, or at least I, have hoarded it, still waiting, however unconsciously, for a man to come along and pay the bill."

If nothing else, playing this game can put you in demeaning situations. "What I should have done that cold New Year's Eve," she says, on hindsight, "is pay for the cab myself."

The new female psychology suggests to me *that it is the dampening of our desires and the denigration of our skills when we are very young that lead girls to become fearful about survival.* The story men are given for organizing their lives is the hero legend. The story women are given is the Romance Myth. It slams into full force at adolescence, when a boy, a man, marriage, becomes, for the girl, nothing less than salvation.

CAUGHT IN THE ROMANCE MYTH: EVELYN'S STORY

"I know how to work hard," Evelyn says. "At the same time, I've learned, 'Well, if things don't work out, they still work out.' Instead of, 'If things don't work out, you have to *make* them work out.' "

With her charmingly decorated but poorly heated cottage, her patched-together Volvo, her famous perennial gardens and feeling for clothes, Evelyn has always radiated a certain style. But she is never free of wondering where the money will come from for next month's bills.

Soulful in demeanor, beautiful, Evelyn is trying to make sense of what happened to her since the breakup of her marriage. When she comes to be interviewed by me, in my hotel on the outskirts of Chicago, there is no question that she is in crisis, emotional crisis, financial crisis. I learn that she gets by, barely, on jobs that do not build to anything. She has made a virtue of making do. She has made a virtue of waiting. Now, with her fortieth birthday having rolled by, she is looking back, trying to understand what has led her to the precarious state in which she finds herself.

In Evelyn's family, growing up, it was always "the man" who was going to pull things through. Theirs had been the usual fall from grace ever since her father had left, when she was two and a half. Daddy continued building his life and career, while mother, at wit's end, with neither skills nor wherewithal, tried to rear two little girls alone. Like *her* mother before her, she believed that the only way she could take care of herself and kids was if she had a man to support them.

Within a year, Evelyn's mother was having an affair. Alvin became the center of her life at that point, and two young girls' childhoods came to an end. "Her whole world was about *him*, not us," Evelyn recalled. "She'd say, 'Don't drink the milk, save it for Alvin.' She'd do his laundry and not ours. She would iron his clothes, go out drinking with him all night, and then when it was time for her to do the car pool, she'd be so hung over she'd tell me to call a cab. It was so humiliating, having to pick the other kids up in a cab."

When they give up on themselves, diving headfirst into the romantic illusion, mothers violate their daughters' trust in them. Evelyn was soon thrust into a classic role, handling notes for the milkman, gathering up the clothes for the dry cleaner, compensating for her mother's incapacities. She was also learning the message of passivity. "My mother didn't make things happen for herself, ever. She always ended up in a crisis. Somehow my father would come through for her with a car or some old furniture from the model units in apartments he'd built."

Says Evelyn, "Now I'm looking at how I've gotten myself into those same kinds of situations." She has begun to face the difficult history that eroded her confidence, making her so available to the seduction of the Romance Myth. "It's in my psychological makeup, I think, because it's what happened to my mother. My mother was totally devoted to my dad. He comes home one day and says he doesn't want to be married anymore. She finds out that he's been having an affair with her best friend. Leaves her, marries her best friend, and she's destitute, so to speak, with two young girls. I was only two and a half, and I must have gotten her pain *cellularly*. I mean, we're talking on the unconscious, preverbal level. Aside from the obvious, which was growing up having to hear that complaint, that whining, self-pitying complaint."

Evelyn tries to give her mother any credit that's due. "My mom's a fighter, too. She's got a resigned side to her, but she's also a survivor."

Her way of surviving was to give over her power to men, pitiably eking out a living for herself and her two young daughters with whatever crumbs were thrown her. "So that's the challenge," Evelyn concludes, "going beyond this image of my mother I've been looking at. Now the question is: Can I believe in myself and my capabilities, beyond what she believed in?"

Elizabeth Debold and her colleagues observed the same cycle of submission and self-doubt getting passed from one generation to the next. They saw adult women being emotionally unavailable to younger women because their own adolescent traumas had been covered over and denied, leaving them unable to be open to and supportive of what girls were going through. It was too threatening to them.

Just when girls most need a guide through the whitewater rapids of adolescence, they look about them and see their mothers and their mothers' friends hiding what's going on in their own lives. They watch them bolstering men with fragile egos but never speaking openly about male vulnerability. They see women and girls being sexually harassed — or are so, themselves — and no one talking about it.

The authors of *Mother Daughter Revolution* observe that mothers who are cut off from difficult girlhood memories experience "a complicated mixture of anger, anxiety, and jealousy when their daughters begin to mature." The feelings, which mothers often can't acknowledge, prevent them from connecting authentically and guide them "to act in ways that will feel competitive and hateful to a daughter."[26]

From the time her mother and father split up, Evelyn had felt her mother's confusion acutely. As an adult, she was living her life in response to her mother's desperation and to the missing father who had always objectified her. Who, when she was six and seven, would talk to whoever would listen about what great legs she had. "It was never about my schoolwork or my dancing. The only praise I got was for how I looked."

As Evelyn approached puberty, her father began making money. At the same time, things at home had gotten worse. Her mother, by then, was suffering from the breakup of a seven-year affair with the milk-loving Alvin. Evelyn wanted out and convinced her father to send her away to school.

"It was Quaker-run, a farm school, coeducational, very liberal. It was the best thing I ever did."

Things began to look up. The following year, for off-term, she went to a performing arts school in Paris. It was the summer of 1973. She was seventeen. "I had intended to dance, primarily, and to learn French. But I took a theater course that ended up, to my surprise, being my real strength. The director went nuts for me. It was thrilling to be able to do something that was such a natural and that I loved so much."

But is it possible that the real thrill had come from the director's going "nuts" for her?

By summer's end Evelyn was invited to join the repertory theater associated with the school. "I went back to Vermont, intent on finishing up and returning to Paris. I thought, 'Wow, my future's cut out for me.' "

Back at school, her grades suddenly soared. "My self-esteem had gotten a big boost. Suddenly — honors! — across the board."

But just when it seemed she had really gotten herself on a positive path — had created, through grit and determination, her own bridge to the future — romance appeared. "I fell madly, head-over-heels in love. I'm sure I was in a lot of terror about leaving school and entering my life, but I truly fell in love with this boy. I clung to him and gave my life over to him. All of a sudden it didn't matter whether I had a life of my own. He became everything."

CREATING THE HERO — THEN COUNTING ON HIM

The flight into romance has long been considered normal for women — the appropriate adult outcome of their entire psychological development. "The stage of life crucial for the emergence of an integrated female identity is the step from youth to maturity, the stage when the young woman, whatever her career, relinquishes the care received from the parental family in order to commit herself to the love of a stranger and to the care to be given to her offspring," wrote the influential psychoanalyst Erik Erikson in 1968.[27]

Wittingly or not, Erikson was offering women the romantic promise *par excellence*. And a generation of therapists, unfortunately, followed suit.

But the safety promised by the Romance Myth is a delusion. Financially, women who marry end up with less stability than women who don't. They experience the shock of this reality either during the marriage or — and especially — after the ball is over.

By the time Evelyn entered her thirties, she had developed a thriving massage therapy practice and was spending a lot of time at an ashram in Boulder, where she was trying to learn more about her spiritual self. The experience was strengthening for her but she was making just enough money to stay abreast of her bills. When she incurred an injury, a herniated disk, she had no savings and no disability insurance. Suddenly, she went from economic stability (or so she'd thought) to financial jeopardy. The experience frightened her, bringing to the surface, again, all the vulnerabilities she had felt since childhood.

"I remember that at the time I didn't think I was looking for anyone. I had my own business, I was very involved in the ashram, I was living there three days a week, and I was, I thought, happily *not* in a relationship. I thought that one day I would meet someone, and that the man would share my spiritual values. I imagined us meditating together in the morning."

But then, out of the blue, it happened, that great chemical urge that seems to have so little to do with intelligence or psyche or planning. Once again, she was totally, blindly, in love. "I never expected the kinds of regression that occurred as a result of being attached to this man."

"This man" was one of those guru psychiatrists, a maverick who had long since veered from the constraints of his profession, bent on more freedom, greater glory, and more access to women than living by any code of traditional ethics would allow. He was an innovator, a charmer, a runner of workshops in which he was the star.

Evelyn met Lyle at one such, and there was a powerful attraction from the first. Almost immediately they began living together, he still married, but not admitting it at the time. Eventually, they got married.

The fact that Lyle was older only added to his charm. "There was a lot of passion between us, and we shared a lot of dreams," says Evelyn. "But for me, there was the pitfall of believing, here is someone who will take care of me."

Like Cinderella, she would do her part. More than her part. "I figured I'd take care of him as well, so it wasn't as if I was getting a free ride. We would take care of each other, only differently."

But "taking care of" someone is almost invariably a trap. It feels good, it feels tender, it feels womanly — because women have been conditioned to experience caretaking in this way. We've been trained to do chores men feel are beneath them and to get from doing them the warmest of glows.

"What, actually, did you do to take care of him?" I asked Evelyn, wanting to better comprehend the daily quality of life with this prince.

"It was fifties kinds of stuff that I did," she said, recalling her perfect domestic efficiency. "I kept a clean, beautiful home. There were always groceries, there was always clean laundry, he always had clothes, things were always picked up from the dry cleaner. I kept his life in perfect order because he was in total chaos. I thought, 'Well, that's my job,' and if one was paid to do those things, mine would have been considered a full-time job."

Besides housekeeping, she also helped him with his business. "I must have edited three or four chapters of his book, and I was good at it. I was constantly doing paperwork for him and mailings. I would assist him in his workshops, do a lot of planning, put all the materials in order. I did a lot, and basically I think that what *he* did was fund me. And that was the exchange."

It was one aspect of the exchange, for beneath the surface a kind of ego-merge was going on wherein Evelyn participated in her husband's ideas, gathered fire from his grandiosity, was inspired by his creativity. In all, she bought into his own notion of himself, and then some. Not large enough in his own eyes, he became larger in hers, and he fed off the inflated image.

But so did she: she turned him into a prince, allowed him to exploit her, and ultimately resented the hell out of him for it. Evelyn recognizes now that she has hooked up with men for financial support and for bigger dreams than she has been able to generate on her own. "But each time I did this, the resentment grew larger. I wasn't living my own life, after all, I was living theirs. I think it catches up with a woman when she's not living up to her potential."

It also catches up financially. Writes Elizabeth Debold, *"The flight into romantic, obsessive love — and often away from any sort of serious life planning or desire to live fully in the larger world — may be women's largest and most debilitating survival strategy."* [28] (Emphasis added.)

One day it dawned on Evelyn that all of her efforts had gone into priming *his* ability to make money, while she, in truth, had been reduced to practicing the same limited skills. "When Lyle and I split,

I didn't have the funds to return to school, and basically was plunged back to where I started, with few skills and no money. And I thought, 'I've given six years to this!' "

How often we feel embittered as an ill-conceived marriage comes limping to an end. But all along there has been a modus operandi, a psychological agenda of which the woman herself may not be aware. In such marriages, suggests the brilliant psychoanalyst Louise Kaplan, the woman's scheme is "to appease in order to maintain a life-giving, vital relationship with the almighty other."[29]

It's not that we *want* to suffer, or like it, or derive pleasure from it, Kaplan writes, distinguishing her insight from Freud's notion of "female masochism." It's that we're willing to endure suffering for the sense of having a *life!* By devoting herself to Lyle's career and giving up her own, Evelyn had put herself in an extremely precarious position. Yet she didn't get the full picture of what was happening until Lyle met another woman (one whose glorification of him was still undimmed by reality) and brought the marriage crashing down.

Now, at last, the truth of Evelyn's situation pressed home. Plunging into romance had provided her with no safety at all. She was back to square one. "I feel as if I'm starting from where I was when I left college without a degree, with no career I was committed to. I have life experience, but I feel very much at the beginning, as unsure as I ever did at sixteen, eighteen, twenty-five, or thirty."

That, then, has been Evelyn's problem, her lack of connection to her own power. It reveals itself in endless questions that never get answered, steps that never get taken. It reveals itself in deadly passivity.

"I've always felt, 'Too late, too late.' By the time I get this done, I'll be too old. I don't really know if this is exactly what I want; what if it's the wrong thing?

"Or 'By the time I get this done, who knows where I'll be?' Or

'I don't have money. I have to work in order to have the money. I guess I have to work first to get the money to go to school.' So then, while I'm doing the work to get the money, I forget the goal. At some point I become petulant, or indulgent, and feel, 'This is too hard, I have to treat myself to something.' So let's say I *save* three hundred dollars, or a thousand, or whatever — that could get drained on a vacation or a course. And before you know it, I'm in the same position as ever."

From such a position, the fear of destitution is understandable. Bag lady dreams underlie dreams of romance. And dreams of romance supplant dreams of flying — dreams not only of success, but of the ability to self-regulate, to provide for ourselves over the life course in a sustained, reliable way.

If you don't *have* yourself, why would you feel responsible for yourself? Just as *he* is made responsible for our sexual pleasure, our Saturday nights, just as *he* is made into our liaison, or bridge, to adulthood, so, ultimately, does *he* become responsible for us, not only for our livelihood and our safety, but also for our very excitement about life.

Of course, the Prince is all the more powerful for his traits being primally familiar. The men in Evelyn's life were always profligate spenders, poor money managers, drinkers, men who had other women in the wings and fell for one of them whenever they felt the need to make the flight on which men are more likely to embark — the flight from commitment. They were men who moved in, then flew. Men who were "brilliant," in chaos. Men who were just like daddy.

Evelyn's story illustrates how culture and family join in making girls feel powerless. That passivity often continues into adulthood, affecting their ability — even their desire — to become financially responsible. It is as if, in youth, girls' spines get broken. By the time they are adults, they have become acclimated to the injury, and they continue life unaware that they have been left with a structural deformity. They think that fear, anxiety, and the need for someone else to lean on is normal.

THE END OF THE ROMANCE

It's interesting to me to look back and see how in many ways the major task throughout my life has been to convince myself that I am capable of taking care of myself. My father's message was so powerful, reiterated daily in the smallest interactions, or lack thereof. We didn't really negotiate anything in our family. I was given rules to follow, curfews. I was told no or yes. Thus, I had little experience of affecting my own fate. Daddy did my fate. I obeyed. Even when it came to marrying, Daddy told me what I must do.

My father wanted me to take responsibility for myself, but he didn't help me build a bridge into the adult world. He kept me dependent, a child — then grew furious when, at the age of twenty-four, I continued behaving like one.

Soon after my second child was born, I started writing; immediately — and this still seems like luck — I began earning money from it. After several years I was offered a monthly column of tongue-in-cheek housekeeping tips by *Cosmopolitan* magazine. I thought the regular money might allow us to move to a larger apartment.

The first ad I saw was thrilling — a six-room apartment on West End Avenue for a ridiculously low rent. To impress my potential landlady, I wore a new coat with a red fox collar. I hoped the fur collar would create an impression of financial solidity. I brushed my long blond hair and put on heels: the perfect image of a young matron with children and a work-a-daddy husband taking care of everything. She bought it.

It was only several years after we moved into the big, solid apartment building that Ed "dropped out" of a job for which he'd lined up no replacement. In the seventies, some of us construed the corporate world as dehumanizing and "dropping out" to be a sally in the direction of a better life. Ed hoped leaving a demanding job would help resolve his conflicts about writing. Better to take a construction job, he reasoned, one whose concerns he didn't have to bring home with him, and be clear-headed enough to write at night.

Ed left his job as communications director for the Corporation for Public Broadcasting and started slamming up Sheetrock in brownstone renovations. He got trim and muscular but nothing much changed save my dawning realization that nothing *would* change. Though less stressed, he found writing no easier. At night he began working on the same sort of project he was paid for during the day, stripping layer upon layer of paint off the paneled wainscoting in our dining room.

The fact that this was a rented apartment didn't dim his enthusiasm. Chip by chip the paint came off, slowly revealing the oak solidity of an earlier time on the Upper West Side, before it had turned slightly down-at-heel, becoming a low-rent, large-apartment neighborhood that attracted artists, musicians, and writers. Most of us, though we were striving for a new kind of consciousness, as well as freedom from the straits of industry and government, still yearned for the protective predictability of our middle-class childhoods: those high-ceilinged, oak-paneled dining rooms stood for that.

Looking back, I see how being married, or even living with a man, as I would do later, was a recapitulation of my parents' life. So long as I was married, I was judicious with money — proud of being the one to manage the household affairs, budget for clothes, determine the wherewithal for an occasional small vacation. Oddly, I never imagined that *lack* of money was the main reason I continued on in a marriage that was becoming increasingly desperate. When my first book was published, conferring professionalism on me at last, the thought hit for the first time that maybe I could make it on my own.

166 • MAXING OUT

Ed never managed to get all the paint off the dining room paneling before I decided the marriage had to end. Once the decision was made, things happened very quickly. Yet I kept the scarred dining rooms walls for almost a year, still attached, in my mind, to the notion of myself as married, still unable to think of the apartment as my own.

Then one night, after the kids were in bed, I put down the first coat of primer. Within minutes, the revealed oak was covered. Within a week I had my dining room back in all its pristine white-painted glory. I had a dinner party, the first of many, celebrating my state as a single woman with a whole new life ahead. There would be legs of lamb; there would be wine. I aspired to a kind of elegant bohemianism. I wanted ideas spoken of at my dinners. I wanted moderate outrage. One night, when a man rose from the end of my long table to empty a glass of wine onto the head of another man he felt wasn't taking him seriously, I felt I had arrived. Here was conviction, emotion. Here was a kind of soft-bellied intellectualism holding sway at my dinner table, and I didn't even need a husband to produce it.

But I did, apparently, need a husband to keep me on track with money.

On my own, I became unsure. Freedom seemed to unleash the frailties of adolescence. I bounced high, I bounced low. There were episodes during which I worried obsessively about how the children and I would survive. There were mildly manic times during which I felt supremely confident and threw money away on clothes and dinner parties. I think I was trying to make up for the fun I didn't have when I was younger.

I will say this: I have no shame about that young woman trying to find herself and create a life and develop a career while she cared, alone, for three small children. I only wish, for her sake, that she had known then what I know now: *Coming to grips with money is of the essence for anyone who wants both freedom and the experience of inner security.*

MISTRESS OF YOUR OWN FATE

When I was in my forties, I sent my mother a photograph of a beautiful, historic house I'd purchased with the man I'd been living with for a number of years. Apparently, the house made my mother anxious, even envious. She wrote back, "I couldn't help but imagine the house after you'd died, with a sign out in front saying 'Colette Dowling lived here.' "

My mother was quite old before she was able to view me without envy. By then, living alone, she was able to discover a modicum of freedom for the first time since she was young. With that, I think, she was finally able to feel connected to me. I learned that she had never felt confident in her ability to help me make a way for myself in the world. She didn't understand my needs, and she felt too cut off from me. But she had not been oblivious of the conflict that had lain so long between us.

Nor, by the end of her life, was she oblivious of the fact that she had abandoned me to a man — her husband, my father — and that he, too, had abandoned me. We were able to talk about this when, after my father died, my mother emerged from beneath the mantle of her own oppression with the energy to look at her life straight. By then she was in her eighties, but I was grateful for her acknowledgment of me, and us. At that point, I came to understand what had happened to my mother, and while what she had done for me hadn't been enough, she had not been able to do more.

A child tries to find herself in the midst of her parents' agendas. A child may be smart, but smart isn't enough. She must be strong, even aggressive, to create an agenda of her own, get in touch with the excitement of her own life. She must constantly be staking claim to her own thoughts, her own feelings. I see, now, the price that was paid for my heavily conditioned passivity.

What is it about aggression that's so threatening? I asked my therapist once. "It means being captain of your own ship," she said. "Mistress of your own fate."

I had never *wanted* that responsibility. I shrank from it, but then I wondered why I was always anxious. I had every reason to be anxious. Deep down I knew the possible endpoint of my passivity: I could *be* that bag lady. Through doing nothing, I could actually *make* that homeless future for myself.

Chapter 7

WAKING FROM THE DREAM OF RESCUE

The night after my nine-year-old Saab was finally done in by a minor accident and I'd had the far worse experience of discovering that I'd let my insurance lapse, my unconscious state — rocky, to say the least — revealed itself in a dream.

> *I was planning to renew my sexual connection with L., from whom, in reality, I'd been separated for six years. The fact that he had a girlfriend in no way dissuaded me. I thought I'd just ask both of them to get AIDS tests, and then I'd move in. I had no doubt that this was possible. If I wanted to go back, I could go back. All that needed to be worked out was the logistics.*

The loss of my car — and not knowing if the bank would finance another one, as I'd been consistently late in repaying a loan — took me to a financial and psychological bottom. It was almost as if I'd *created* the bottom. Who would help me? Who *could* help me? This is it, the end, I've nowhere to go. *It was as if I'd brought about the thing I feared most.*

169

But in the dream I ran for shelter — the shelter of my most recent relationship. Though in reality I had no desire to return to it, I did, unconsciously, seek rescue. The dream flagged that, ever so clearly. (Flagging, in fact, may be the main *point* of dreams.) I even constructed a mother image for myself — the girlfriend. I would be accepted not only by L., but by *her*. The three of us would be friendly. It would be kind of like mommy, daddy, and baby Colette — only sex was involved. Or maybe sex is always involved, at least for a woman who believes herself, at bottom, unable to survive on her own.

I think the dream represented a very particular type of shelter: protection from my own destructive impulses. Clearly, I was out of control. But during the years of living with L., I had functioned with temperance, able to plan, able to defer gratification, able to build a terrific credit picture. In those days, if I needed a loan I could barely get the application filled out before someone was handing me a check. The green lights were all there: impeccable payback record; pristine timeliness; no wild expenditures.

This shipshapeness, I would eventually come to recognize, was not due to my own discipline, but to his.

It was all so . . . logical. We had separate accounts for our personal money and a joint account to cover living and housing expenses, which we split. We both put our deposits into the pot each month and I was religious about it, never again wanting to experience the humiliation of being called on my dependency problems, as I had been, years earlier, in a disturbing confluence of events that led to my writing *The Cinderella Complex.*

Soon after beginning to live with L., I'd collapsed into a state of blissful housewifery, letting him pay all the bills while I baked cakes. But that had never been our deal. When, after a year, he confronted me, saying I was taking advantage of him, I was mortified.

It was definitely a moment in the life of a young feminist, brought about by a man who'd been to school with a lot of other young feminists (L. was in the first class at Sarah Lawrence College to have males as well as females.) He knew I was getting away with something. I was ten years older and had more professional credentials than he. I'd simply given up all ambition and allowed him to start supporting us.

It was a great struggle for me to face what I was doing and change, but I did. I began contacting editors for writing assignments and making a living again. We put ourselves on a monthly budget and soon I was experiencing financial security for the first time since leaving my parents. It was pure joy to buy our first house and be able to make, with ease, the monthly mortgage payments because L. had figured out what we could actually afford. When repairs had to be made, we discussed them and put extra money into the account. It was all so calm and systematic.

And it was all so male-initiated. I had no idea of the degree to which I was relying on L. to keep my compulsivity in check. For fifteen years I lived that way, and then, boom! As soon as I was out of the relationship, I knew no restraint. What I paid for a house, when I bought one on my own, was determined not by planning, but by what I could get the bank to give me for a mortgage. They were generous with me, in part because of eighties economics and in part because of the credit rating I'd built up while functioning as the extension of someone who was rational with money.

On my own was I was not rational. I took tremendous pleasure and feelings of power from spending. My goal was not to save. My goal was simply to have enough money to cover my monthly spending. Succeeding at that felt grand.

Grand is the telltale word, here. I'd bought out L'.s share of our five-bedroom house, telling myself it was only temporary, until I got used to the major change of living alone. But in the early poor years, I'd never expected to live in a big, beautiful old house and now, having achieved it, didn't want to give it up. It would have felt to me like going down in life, or going backward. So I hung on.

Not only hung on, but expanded. With a child still in college, my necessary expenses were high, but that didn't stop me from installing perennials and fruit trees and bluestone walls — from building, as my father lay dying, a huge new studio. I wanted to live in that house like a proper matriarch, someone who'd been widowed, let's say; *not* someone who'd had to earn it all herself — and had to keep on earning it!

I think I felt there was something slightly déclassé about my situation, though I doubt I could have admitted it at the time. I was still in too much conflict. I had cast my fate in the feminist camp, but to do that, I had had to deny the teachings I'd grown up with.

Eventually I was forced to take out a second mortgage. I didn't see that as a bad thing, of course; I saw it as further indication of my fabulous financial credibility. If the bank thought I was worth a second mortgage, it must mean that I could *afford* a second mortgage!

I should have sold then and moved to something I could manage, but of course I wasn't acknowledging that I wasn't managing. I was late with tax payments and beginning, occasionally, to be late with monthly bills. I'd stopped making annual contributions to my retirement account. It was costing me too much not only to keep the house I was living in, but to maintain the smaller house across the street.

Initially I'd bought the small house with the idea of having a place to live when I was old and gray and, in the interim, using it as "income" property.

It was never income, it was always outgo. And *I* managed not to become old and gray by virtue of coloring my hair.

Coloring my hair and rose-tinting my glasses. Eventually I came to what I thought was a clever financial decision. I would renovate the small house and sell the big one. I would save money *and* get to exercise one of my lifelong ambitions — to "re-do" a moldering old cottage and turn it into something charming. To pick the colors and decide on the floors.

But you know the rest.

For a while I chose to think it was a run of bad real estate luck that had put me in the hole. I'd had to buy out my partner at a time when the market value of the house was high. I'd run into unexpected costs in renovating the old cottage. Then, when the government demanded I pay my taxes, I'd had to sell both properties even though the bottom had fallen out of the market.

It took quite some time before I was able to see how my whole life had led inexorably to this point. I had been trained not to regulate myself, but to rely on controls provided by someone else. That particular training is a devastating aspect of the Romance Myth, but it isn't talked about. *Women are simply thought childish with money. The complex web of restraints that prevents them from developing financial independence has never been examined.*

I have come to think that women unconsciously sabotage themselves financially as a way of perpetuating the Romance Myth. We seem caught between two models of economic survival: the traditional, in which women were taught to depend on men, and the modern, in which we are expected to be Brave New Feminists who depend on ourselves. We're not confident in our ability to do the latter, so we veer ambivalently toward the former. Financially ungrounded, we are confused and often self-deluding in the stories we tell ourselves about both our men and our money. We *want* to be independent, but we don't know if we can trust ourselves.

And we certainly don't know if we can trust *them*.

The dilemma creates emotionally and financially entangled scenarios of nightmare proportions.

HERO WORSHIP

Thirteen years and four children later, she sits in an almost empty
house, children gone, unable to contemplate the fact that she will
soon be having to get out. It's hard to believe. It's . . . bizarre.
Her ex, a week earlier, had come to cut phone lines and strip the
burners from the stove so she couldn't cook dinner for their children. She subsequently got a temporary restraining order to prevent him from entering the house again — but so what? It was so
empty it was unlivable. And he took the children.[1]

At thirty-five, Bette, thin and blond, had recently turned to running and lifting weights as a way of keeping herself sane. A serious-
looking woman with high cheekbones and curly hair swept up and
back, Bette is reminiscent of Dorie Previn after Andre left her. Both
women looked as if they had lived more than they would have liked.

Thirteen years earlier Bette had been a lovely, hopeful woman,
though her young life was spinning out of control. Too many
parties; too many weekend binges. At nineteen, she was feeling
terrified by her own impulses.

Then into her life came "the man" — huge, six feet seven, a
295-pound athlete who knew what he wanted in life and was
determined to get it. Brian Holloway, Stanford graduate, son of a
retired air force colonel, grandson of the first executive director of
the United Negro College Fund, was twenty-two and on his way to
becoming an All-Pro offensive tackle for the Patriots and Raiders.

Bette McKenzie, a physical education major at Bridgewater
State College, was searching for a savior.

It's understandable that she would see one in Brian. Her daddy,
after all, had been a hockey pro — "Pie" McKenzie, right wing for
the Boston Bruins. Now, she says, she should have known better
than to become so identified with her father's and her husband's
celebrity. And her mama had warned her not to marry an athlete.
" 'She said they have affairs and they leave you.' "

Daddy had suffered from alcoholism, and was known to have had affairs.

Bette ignored her mother's warning, she told a friend, who later wrote her story in the *New York Times*. She and Brian married during a National Football League players' strike, in 1982. He made all the arrangements for the wedding. And the night before, he whipped out a prenuptial agreement that said she wouldn't share in anything he purchased or that was in his name. Bette was upset, but God, the families were already gathered! She signed.

For three years, she told her writer friend, she was happy; then life turned hellish. " 'Brian never wanted me around other athletes' wives.' " He preserved his control by keeping her isolated. " 'He said, "I want you in the country, barefoot and pregnant." I didn't realize he was serious.' "

In 1988, he put her in a pumpkin shell — an old farmhouse on two hundred acres of land, an hour from the nearest city in upstate New York. But, his N.F.L. career over, Brian was often away on the lecture circuit. And she was stuck on the farm. In winter, it reminded her of Stephen King's *The Shining*. It wasn't long before she was deep in a depression.

But during the eighties, Bette had not only had four children, she'd managed to finish up her bachelor's degree at Wellesley. Still, Brian kept her under glass, and her isolation was making her increasingly dispirited. Whenever they were with others, he did the talking for both of them. Holloway was control personified. "The sense of 'being taken care of' that had drawn Bette to Brian became dependence," the *Times* reported. They didn't even have a joint checking account. As Brian parceled out the money for everything, including groceries, Bette beecame increasingly self-doubting. It was a classic situation, involving the kind of brainwashing that occurs when one person in a couple has a great deal more power than the other — and intends to keep it that way.

Eventually a woman friend suggested to Bette that they go into business together. As the venture progressed, Bette began feeling strong enough to want to leave the prison of her marriage. As so often happens when a wife decides she's had enough of a controlling partner, the "nightmare," as Bette called it, began fast forwarding. There were "raids" during which Holloway came and took bed sheets, clothing, furniture, kitchenware. "The house is a shambles," wrote the *New York Times*. "It appears to be vandalized and abandoned."

The house, in any event, was his.

Eventually, at least nine domestic disputes made it to the police blotter, and by 1997, according to court papers, Holloway owed more than eleven thousand dollars in child support.[2]

Today, as much as she exercises in an effort to build herself back up psychologically as well as physically, there remains "a haunted quality in her blue eyes." When she leaves the house, she unplugs the phone and puts it in the trunk of her car, where she also carries a hair dryer, her court documents, and some clothes. She sleeps with the phone at her pillow and her car keys in her hand. Though Holloway has never threatened her physically, she says, she feels intimidated by his size, and by the memory of his violent profession.

The story of Bette and Brian began with two bright, articulate, college-educated people deciding to make a life together. It ended with one having all the power and money and the other without a home. It was, pronounced the *Times*, "the story of a sense of male entitlement, and of a woman who was subconsciously drawn to it."

It was also the story of a woman who was born and bred to get caught in the Romance Myth, and who today is having a painful awakening. What advice would she give to those about to embark on the same path? Says Bette, " 'I'd tell young women, especially those involved with athletes, to be independent, to be able to support yourself financially. Don't have a baby unless you can bring it up yourself.' "

That last caveat is one I've never heard stated quite so bluntly, although it certainly reflects women's reality: *Count on someone else for money and protection and you lose.* Yet — and remarkably — in spite of her enlightenment, Bette still rationalizes her former husband's behavior. " 'As long as he had football, as long as he had the outlet of being a warrior at war, it wasn't so bad,' " she told the *Times*. " 'But all that energy, all that intelligence needs a channel. Once he figures it out, there is no limit to his potential.' "

Therapist Martha Kirkpatrick says that in her experience, divorcing women are stunning in their insistence on believing they'll be taken care of by the man they are leaving or being left by. "Regularly in my practice, no matter what the marriage experience has been, no matter how fearful the expectations of punishment, no matter who initiates the divorce or why, the woman begins by announcing she is lucky that her husband is an honest and responsible provider and will not cheat his family of adequate support."[3]

Many women draw their feeling of being valuable from their relationship to a man. They may not have an inkling of this; they may even, on their own, appear boldly "independent" in demeanor. Then they enter a relationship. The more involved they become, the higher the emotional stakes grow. Ineluctably, the woman's sense of herself begins to be shaped by how she's being perceived — or thinks she is — by her Prince. Her achievements are no longer valuable unless *he* values them. And she can't be certain that he does value them unless he constantly reassures her.

As such a relationship describes its inevitable arc, a shift takes place: our lovely, hopeful young woman begins to lose whatever shred of self-esteem she had to begin with. Slowly but surely she stops valuing her own integrity, stops feeling she has any importance of her own. Jean Baker Miller, a psychiatrist and scholar-in-residence for Development Studies at Wellesley College's Stone Center, says of a woman named Paula: "Though she took care of a huge household, the things she did with great ease and efficiency counted only as they produced an inner sense that Bill would be attached to her intensely and permanently, and that this, in turn, would make her worthwhile."[4]

If Bill didn't express enough interest in or concern for Paula's activities, she would drop into a downward spiral and her life would begin to feel empty. What she did no longer mattered. Yet, while Paula was convinced her husband "didn't care enough," she had little evidence of this. Objectively, he seemed like a perfectly good husband and father. If she were being rational (she felt) she would *know* he cared. Why didn't she *feel* he cared?

At that point, Paula would start to conclude there was something wrong with her.

Hero making, like compulsive eating or drinking or talking, is something we do to allay anxiety. The most highly accomplished women are capable of overvaluing men in their intimate relationships and suffering an escalating diminishment of self-esteem.

Jean Miller Baker tells of Barbara, "a rigorous thinker with a big position at a university," who struggled with the feeling that nothing she did was worthwhile — *unless* she had a "significant other" in the wings affirming and applauding her.

She also writes of a shrewd and highly successful saleswoman who didn't feel her financial acumen amounted to a hill of beans unless there was a man who "cared" about her. With a man in her life, Beatrice felt stimulating and energetic. But when no man was on the scene, she collapsed. It was strange, on thinking about it, she told Miller. She could be doing the very same things she had been doing in her life *before,* but without the man, she couldn't "feel" her feelings. Any event she attended lacked pleasure and significance. Her nerve endings might have stopped functioning for all the pleasure she was able to experience when she was on her own.

It isn't so much that women like Beatrice feel like "half a

person." It's "like being not a person at all, at least no person that matters," says Dr. Miller.

Her need for a more powerful "other" from whom she could draw value affected Beatrice at work, as well as in love. At the office she could accomplish prodigious amounts so long as she had at least one person in a position of power over her. Knowing this (although not conscious of it), she made sure never to let herself have the top job.

If we feel safer in a one-up / one-down relationship, we will try to maneuver people into positions that create the desired imbalance. Both in her personal life and at work, Beatrice always managed to get some man into a position of being higher up on the totem pole. One down, and looking adoringly up, was where she felt comfortable.

The psychoanalyst Karen Horney described this very phenomenon. Writing about a woman she called "Clare," Horney showed how remaining dependent fends off anxiety — a concept anyone caught in the one-up/one-down cycle needs to grasp if she wants to extricate herself.[5])

Clare had been madly infatuated with "Peter," a young man who — though still professing his love — was in fact withdrawing from their relationship and driving her to despair. Nothing seemed to have any meaning for her, except when she was in the presence of her love.

She was so entrenched in the relationship that her entire mood depended on what Peter was doing. She had noticed how her mood had swung up sharply one evening when he gave her an unexpected gift of a scarf. It was ridiculous how terrific that scarf had made her feel. But later that evening, when he was listless about making summer plans with her, Clare became depressed and couldn't enjoy sex.

That night she had a dream in which she saw a large, beautiful bird flying away from her until she couldn't see it anymore. When she woke up, she was anxious and had a sense of falling. Then a phrase occurred to her: " 'the bird has flown.' " The dream, she realized, expressed her fear of losing Peter.

Until the dream, Clare hadn't seen how anxious her relationship with Peter was making her. Her extreme joy over the scarf came from the momentary relief from fear that being given a gift provided.

But why so much fear?

It had to do, she eventually came to understand, with her belief that she couldn't exist without someone buffering her against life and its dangers. That — not true love — was why Peter was so important to her.

WHAT'S LOVE GOT TO DO WITH IT?

Clare was still far from understanding the full extent of her anxiety about being deserted — her fear, had such a social phenomenon been as evident then as it is today, of ending up on the streets. Bag lady fears are about being out of control, of feeling weak, of being convinced we can't survive on our own. Those fears, psychologists believe, are influenced by gender expectations. "Even when weakness is real, women can go on to strength and ability once they can convince themselves it is really all right to let go of their belief in the *rightness* of weakness," wrote Jean Baker Miller, thirty-four years after Horney wrote about Clare.[6]

Miller says it is especially difficult for men, "with *their fears* of weakness, to see why women cling to it."

Today, it is difficult for *women* to see why they cling to weakness. Horney was masterful at getting at the whys. To do that, one has to take the plunge and dive beneath the surface.

Clare had reached the point where it was harder and harder to continue believing in her romance. A tremendous discrepancy existed between her "passion" for Peter and his withdrawal from

her — and his often having no excuse. Now she was really struggling. She told herself that all she wanted was Peter's love and
affection and support. Was that too much to ask?

Oversimplification is a trick of the needy, allowing them to perceive their demands as being so pure, so "normal," that only the
ineffectualness of the partner could account for their needs not
being met. Clare would come to discover that what she demanded
in a relationship was not so pure and normal after all.

One night she noticed an odd reaction to a movie. Usually she
didn't cry during films, "but on this particular evening tears sprang
to her eyes when a girl in wretched condition met with unexpected
help and friendliness." It was peculiar, she thought, the next day;
"the crying had occurred not when the girl in the movie was badly
off, but rather when her situation took an unexpected turn for the
better."

Such scenarios, Clare realized then, had *always* made her cry.
As a child, she had cried when the fairy godmother heaped unexpected presents on Cinderella. What was the connection, she
wondered, between this type of crying and her joy over being given
the scarf? Suddenly, Clare went back to a frequent daydream she'd
had in college: she used to think of it as the daydream of "the great
man." In it, a man of superior intelligence, wisdom, and wealth
made sexual advances because he sensed her potential. He knew
that if he gave her a break she could be beautiful and achieve
greatness. Pygmalion-like, he devoted all his time and energy to
her development. "She had to work hard under his guidance, not
only at becoming a great writer but also at cultivating mind and
body," Horney wrote. "Thus he made a beautiful swan out of an
ugly duckling."

So even in college Clare had dreamed that her success would
occur through her connection to a man more evolved than she.
She'd have to work hard, but in return, he would shower her with
presents. Best of all, she'd never have to ask for anything!

Suddenly recognizing the similarity between her college

daydream and her relationship to Peter, Clare felt stunned. She had mistaken for love something that largely consisted of expectations that she be presented with gifts — not only material gifts, but gifts of her own growth and development. This revelation shocked her. "Her love was at bottom no more than a sponging on somebody else!"

Because Clare had always repressed her own wishes, like the young women Gilligan and Debold studied, she needed somebody who could do the wishing *for* her — someone who would *guess* at her desires and fulfill them without her having to do anything. By now it was unavoidable: Clare had to acknowledge her fundamentally exploitative attitude toward Peter.

At the same time, she saw *him* more clearly. There was something fraudulent in this man. He promised love but kept himself distant. Essentially, he was wrapped up in himself.

It was as if "a spell had been broken," Horney writes. Clare's dream of the beautiful bird had been about her glorification of Peter. She could now look back and see a lifelong pattern of hero-worshipping. "Always, because of her expectations, she had hitched her wagon to a star. And all the stars had proved to be candles."[7]

Clare was close to bedrock. She had been pitifully dependent. She had lost her dignity clinging to a man who didn't really want her, and whose value she doubted anyhow, although she'd never allowed herself to see it. How *could* she see it as long as his personal qualities were masked by her glorification of him?

Clare realized that *she* was the one who'd been devaluing everything she did on her own, or with anybody but the " 'beloved.' " This made her partner — *whoever he might be* — all the more important, and further alienated her from herself and others.

It became clear that Clare's "weakness," her feelings of " 'I can't,' " had in fact been resistance: " 'I won't.' " Could it be that she had "actively refused to turn to anything else in life, like a child who refuses to eat anything if he does not get apple pie?" This question battered away at the bulwark of her notions of romance, for beneath it lay the pay dirt implication that she used "love" to perpetuate her own refusal to grow up.

Karen Horney's brilliant insight that dependency can be the hidden kernel at the center of "love" raised, for me, the question of whether women's feelings of victimization aren't *always* about a girlish refusal to take responsibility.

THE DREAM OF RESCUE

Melissa and Harold are in business together as management consultants to large firms like Xerox and Federal Express. Each also does individual consulting on the side. It's a first marriage for her, a second for him. Leftover baggage from his earlier marriage has colored theirs.

"Before we married, we made a verbal agreement that if he died before I did, I was not going to force the application of New York state laws on what I was due, financially, as his wife," Melissa told me. She thought, at the time, that it was a reasonable request on his part. But as the years passed, and she started feeling more confident about her own position in Harold's life, his when-I-die-you-get-zero policy became less acceptable. After fifteen years, Melissa finally confronted him: she wanted him to make out a will, and she wanted to be in it — *substantially* in it. "Originally he had a hard time accepting that I should actually have some of the money. I don't think he feels that way anymore. I *hope* he doesn't feel the same way anymore."

The amount he first suggested leaving her wouldn't be enough for her to live on in her old age, Melissa told him. "He got annoyed. 'You don't trust that I would leave you enough,' he said. I said, 'Well so far you haven't suggested you were planning on doing that.' "

Harold was viewed as the money-savvy one in the relationship. Yet both had doctorates. Melissa had been working in the business for fifteen years. Harold had made quite a bit of money investing. He also charges more for his work. "We have contracts from corporations, plus the private consulting we do. He charges two hundred dollars an hour for consulting, but I'm comfortable asking one twenty-five. I think sometimes these consultants ask for too much."

Interesting point of view. "Suppose you were on your own," I say, "would you try to earn more?"

At this, she veers from the subject of earning to talking about a cushion. "Realistically, if I combine what I'm getting when my parents die with what he's leaving me, I'll probably be okay."

"You said you stand to get interest on half a million from Harold. Plus an outright amount of . . . how much?"

"I can't remember. Somewhere around two hundred thousand."

For someone who's so concerned about what she's getting — and who, essentially, feels financially insecure — how come she doesn't *know* what her husband's decided to leave her?

"You're not real clear on the numbers," I suggest.

She laughs. "I don't do well with this. He's giving me his insurance stuff. It's over two hundred thousand. I think."

"Plus, you've said, a minimum of a quarter of a million from your mother. Plus your investments. Plus your income. All in all, it sounds like you are in pretty good shape.

"Maybe it's because I don't sit down and do a budget, so it all remains vague."

"Have you figured out what you need to invest in order to have enough to live on when you stop working?"

"No."

"Wouldn't you feel saner if you did?"

"What I want is to be able to say: 'Charlie, invest enough money for me that I don't have to worry.' "

Charlie is a former lover who's been handling her limited investments so far. "So you'd hand the inheritance over to him to take care of?"

"Absolutely."

"What do you gain by not controlling it?"

"I think that *is* controlling it. 'Charlie, *you* do this. I do what I do, you get paid to do this. I don't want to have to bother with it. I just want to know that you're going to competently take care of it.' "

"So, finding someone you can trust to handle it is taking control of it?"

"Yes."

"What happens if you've picked the wrong person?"

"I know I haven't. I've known Charlie for twenty years. He's pretty conservative. He cares for me as a friend as well as a business thing. I'm not worried about that."

Some women like having men in control because it creates a brake on their own impulsiveness. Having to account to someone for their spending helps keep the lid on Pandora's box.

For Melissa, as for Bette, a man holding the purse strings had had the same underlying attraction: *Here, I'll be safe. Here, I'll be protected against my own worst instincts.*

It was the same destructive lesson I'd learned from my father: "I'm in charge here, and lucky for you, since you're unable to manage on your own."

Melissa's father, she told me, had given her the same message. In our mates we were able to recreate the illusion of safety.

ONE LAST FLING WITH THE HERO

He was thirty-five, she was forty-five. Of the two, she was the known figure in the university town, a vocal and highly respected journalist, single mother of two. He was a scientist whose research in quantum mechanics actually made money for him because of its ready application to industry. When they met, Michael was in the process of getting a divorce. Sylvia, twice divorced and long since accustomed to the single life, imagined she would never again be interested in marrying. "He was getting a divorce and I thought

I could be a friend to him while he was going through it," Sylvia recalls. "We had lunch together once a week and practiced our Italian."

But sex was there from the beginning, and soon they were off and running. Michael courted her with trips to Europe, rare wines from his collection, and an unusual empathy for the tribulations of women. They fell madly in love, and they were happy, at least for a while.

Then Sylvia began to struggle with the question of what to do with her life. She had never made a lot of money and she was rearing two kids, the elder of whom was now fifteen. It had been a long haul of being "the responsible one." With this stable man having entered her life, the lure of the romantic fallacy began pulling at her. She had always thought she wanted to be a poet. Could she just slip into Michael's orbit — into his lovely cultured lifestyle — and begin writing poetry full-time?

This was a struggle. She was fifty-three — a "public intellectual," as she told me — and once again was feeling swept away. She resisted. Something about this wasn't right. "Michael was going to be traveling for several weeks. I decided to take a sabbatical at a Trappist monastery."

Where did her contemplation lead her but back to the safety all Catholic girls are promised in return for playing it the way they're taught. In the monastery, Sylvia returned to the dusky, incense-flooded atmosphere of her girlhood: the nuns, with their pale subservience, had been her mentors, the female saints her idols. The priests alone, in God's image, were the mysterious "other." At the monastery, all the romance of Sylvia's youth assailed her senses. "By the time I came home I was ready to really throw myself into the relationship with Michael."

Yet the picture she had painted for herself of what it would all be like was based on her own private fantasies. "I decided I was going to take one of the upstairs rooms in Michael's house for my studio. Before he came back I started moving my things in. To me, this was very symbolic, because I was placing myself — my *work* self — in the center of his space. I thought that when he came home he would be happy about what I was doing, and I would move in. But he wasn't happy."

That Michael might have a different view of things came as a surprise; the hero fantasy is so all-consuming it doesn't actually include the other person. Michael, in his travels, had come to the conclusion that the relationship was going pretty well and now he could recommit himself to work. "We'd been having a honeymoon," says Sylvia. "We were both thrilled to death with the relationship, exuberant, very much in love and very comfortable with the amount of time and energy we were putting into the relationship. Then he started withholding some of his time to do his work. I felt very threatened, very hurt and rejected."

Sylvia had felt secure in the womblike merger of the honeymoon period; now the demands of two separate, individual personalities were making themselves known. "All along we'd done a lot of cuddling at night, a lot of pillow talk. But before we got together, Michael used to use that time at night to read. He felt he had to reclaim that in his life, because his work is quite competitive and he was losing ground."

When Michael explained his need to recoup some time for his own pursuits, Sylvia felt hurt all over again, and she upped the ante. "I started putting a sexual spin on things. Suddenly, I started feeling we weren't spending enough time making love, and I became accusing."

Finally he started becoming annoyed with her. "I was brought up short, realizing I had become demanding."

"When you're not in good connection with the more heroic form of the lover within *yourself* — when you're in some kind of struggle with that inner hero," a Jungian psychotherapist, Barbara Koltuv, told me, "you can't get on with anything that you want to do in your own life."

The woman, in such a scenario, hasn't included in her image of herself the idea of being her own adventurer. The adventure is still experienced as happening outside — something accessible only through her relationship with a vibrant, active, heroic "other."

Sylvia was feeling unable to free herself to do the things she wanted to do but was also dimly aware that it wasn't really Michael who was standing in the way. When the two of them went off on a vacation to the south of France, the time away from her regular schedule helped Sylvia to become aware of some of her own issues. "One night we had a few glasses of wine. Then I started to cry. I told Michael I was jealous — jealous of his professional life, jealous of the passion he had for his work."

Sylvia was both attracted to his passion and envious because it was making her recognize what was cut off in *her*. "I was afraid I'd lost it for my own work. But I also realized how *much* I had let this man subsume me. It was embarrassing to recognize this. He's not a big guy. He's not domineering. He's not overbearing. He's kind and loving and liberating."

"So you, then, mentally made him into something you needed him to be."

"Yes," said Sylvia, "just because he's a man."

"But also because of how you've been affected by your own development — by your own ability, or lack thereof, to pursue the things that *you* really are passionate about."

For the woman, the man becomes a kind of coatrack onto which she hangs all her needs and unlived adventures. She wants to be swept up into *his* adventure. "Usually the feeling is that 'he' could take you away from all this," says Dr. Koltuv. " 'He' could take you to places you couldn't go by yourself. That's the scenario of the hero and the lover."

What a burden this becomes for the hero. And what a disappointment, inevitably, for the lover.

Many women have a tendency to make men extremely fascinating and powerful. They feel they're going to get to access that power indirectly, even though they actually create the power in their own minds. It's a purely mental operation, one women take part in unconsciously.

After their talk in France, Sylvia had a painful insight. "First, I got into this incredible funk, feeling, 'Everything I've ever done is absurd and ephemeral. I've spent my life doing journalism when I was supposed to be one of the great poets of my generation.' I mean, I know that I've ended up being damaged, in the past, by choosing men who were babies because they couldn't dominate me. And here was this man who was good with money, who was taking me on all these exotic trips where I didn't have to pay a dime, who wined and dined me, who knows all about the very finest things, who has exquisite taste, who is very high-minded, and in my own quiet way I just attached myself to this old script, thinking, 'Okay, Sylvia, you've done a really good job. You've achieved much more than anyone ever expected, and now you're going to be let down from this cross you've nailed yourself to. He's going to put you up in a little garret, and you're going to be able to write your poetry after all.' "

When she asked him if he'd ever consider remarriage, Michael told her, "I'm very committed to you but I can't honestly say, at this point, whether I'm ever going to want to marry again. We're just going to have to see how things unfold." This was *not* what she wanted to hear. In her increasingly desperate quest for support, Sylvia began expressing the part of herself that felt weakened and demoralized. "I would say things like, 'I'm really tired.' Or, 'I don't have enough money.' I kept throwing these things at him, and he refused to pick them up."

"Were you hoping he'd say, 'Don't worry about money, I have enough for both of us'?" I asked.

"I know that seems pathetic. I think it goes back to the way I was treated by my father. He always used to say, 'Don't worry, Syl.' He made it plain he never expected I would have to take care of myself. He used to say, 'I have three children. One's on cloud nine, one's on cloud seven. . . .' I was the one on cloud nine. But there was a payoff for me. I was the one my father loved the most, and I always thought it was *because* I was on cloud nine. *Because* I didn't know how to take care of myself. *Because* I couldn't deal with the real world."

Barbara Koltuv says that many women experience dealing with money as being "what men do. They don't have to think about it, themselves. They expect to be taken care of with money but they don't expect to have to *make* the money."

Sylvia admits, "It's always been a struggle for me. I make enough, but barely enough. At this rate, I'll have to work indefinitely to support myself. And that's a *horrifying* thought. So along comes Prince Charming, and I think, '*Ah! Here it is. Finally.*'

The initial relief, simply, at being with a man who could take her on vacations she couldn't have afforded herself soon led to making Michael responsible for her entire well-being. Sylvia would give up her small ranch house and move into his gracious Victorian. She would be able to resume the creative life she had long ago given up. She would reap the delights of his exquisite wine collection, his taste in art and antiques — *and* she would become a full-time poet.

On the contrary, as Koltuv and other Jungian therapists point out, the giving up of independence wreaks havoc with creativity. If Sylvia were to follow her romantic fantasy, she would soon enough lose touch with her innermost self. That "garret room" in Michael's house would produce not the visions and dreams that lead to poetry, but would haunt her, as envy of her lover, coupled with her dependency on him, grew.

Sylvia was fortunate, at that point, to have a flagging dream.

I dreamt that I was moving into a new house. It was a wonderful house, the kind of house that I would love to be moving into. The kitchen looked out onto a beautiful garden with open double French doors, and the sun was shining. It was extremely colorful. All the colors of the flowers were repeated in the chintz upholstery on the chairs. Very comfortable chairs. And Michael was helping me move in. He was behind me and he was carrying potted plants. And in the kitchen there were plants growing right up through the kitchen countertops. There was this wonderful sense of the exuberance of nature, that wouldn't be contained out of doors, that was bursting right into the house.

Seated at the table was this gorgeous hunk of a guy. I think he was wearing a blue shirt, a blue denim shirt. And medium build. And he is looking at me very deliberately and saying, "Now I want you to tell me exactly when you're going to marry me." And I felt confused, and I started saying, "I'm very flattered by your offer, and I would love to marry you, but you see I have this other boyfriend." I was making these excuses but really wanting to say yes.

In thinking about the dream, Sylvia concluded she was *really* wanting to say yes to her own life. The vivid male figure, the "gorgeous hunk," was a clue.

"I always take a male figure in a dream to be part of one's own animus," says Barbara Koltuv, of the dream work she does with her women patients. "If you can wholly understand what that male figure is like, if you get comfortable with it, it doesn't trip you; if you don't, it takes you over."

The gorgeous hunk was Sylvia's "animus," the unlived part of her life, and she was getting ready to have a go at it. "I knew this guy was the real Prince Charming."

To push further with her insight, she decided to write a letter to herself from Prince Charming's point of view. "You have the right to claim anything and everything in your dreams, so I decided that I *was* Prince Charming. I wrote the letter to myself *from* Prince Charming, and it was a real love letter. His words to me were so loving, so appreciative, and so cherishing of me in ways that I really am. He told me that he loved me for my honesty, my integrity, my intelligence — and not just my intelligence but the *quality* of the intelligence I have, and that he was going to fulfill all my biggest dreams, but that in order to do that we were going to have to make a pact, and I was going to have to fulfill my end of the bargain."

The basis of Jungian theory is that what you construct, in the dream, is all parts of yourself. The strength comes from integrating them. When Sylvia was in her envious mode, before the night of the Big Insight, in France, she was projecting her inner wish for productivity and adventure onto her lover — and then being disappointed in him because he wasn't "giving" her what she wanted. The Prince Charming dream told her she'd finally gotten things into perspective.

"As long as you think it's 'out there' somewhere, you have to wait until 'he' comes along and does it for you," says Dr. Koltuv. "If you've been working with that energy in yourself, doing the kind of work Sylvia did on her dream, you'll eventually come to realize *you* have it. It isn't 'out there.' "

"The role that Michael played in the dream was the very role that he wants to play, and *is* playing, in my life," Sylvia said. "That is, he's helping me move into that house, which is the place where I *really* want to live. And he is in a completely supportive role, and he is also helping me to draw out my best sense of self. And yet I still have Prince Charming."

Writing the letter had been a powerful exercise. "Right away I started putting things into place. I enrolled in a seminar Merrill

Lynch was offering on women and money. I placed a phone call to establish a Schwab account. I'm finding that I'm much more efficient in my day-to-day life. And that I have the time — time that was there all along — to do my writing! I'm working very actively on three major writing projects."

Jung recognized that when a woman has integrated the animus into her consciousness, she can begin to live out her full potential. That animus acts as a "soul figure" for her, it "helps her become a whole person by turning the energy that was formerly repressed into active and creative endeavors,"[8] writes June Singer, in *Boundaries of the Soul,* a book on Jungian psychology.

Once she'd gained insight into the connection between wanting a marriage commitment from Michael and "getting tired" of worrying about money, of having always to "make it happen" for herself, Sylvia recognized the flaw in her thinking. She *felt* the destructiveness of it in the fiber of her being, and energy was released — energy she found transforming. "I realized I had unfinished business," Sylvia said, after working on her Prince Charming dream. "And that I loved my life, and it wasn't over at all. And this was a critical opportunity."

RESCUE IN REVERSE

What of women whose fathers were not in control — who were gamblers, let's say, or profligate spenders, or dreamy artists who just couldn't/wouldn't deal with the financial chores — and whose mothers had to pick up the slack?

Here the terrain gets trickier, the psychological maneuvering less obvious. Here, men need to be taken care of, protected against *their* worst instincts. Here, the *women* need to be in control, although they cannot let it appear that way. And being in control, as we shall see, doesn't necessarily mean providing for their own

financial security. It means navigating the ship in such a way as
to preserve the illusion of equality in a relationship that otherwise
would provide no sense of emotional security.

Sometimes, as we shall see, this can only be done at the risk of
financial security.

He was the kind of father endowed with almost magical qualities
by the children who love him, a gambling man who threw it around
when he had it (to this day his daughter describes him as generous),
and who grew depressed and indifferent when he didn't. The family
lived in a neighborhood beyond their means while he raked it in
on real estate and film deals — until the time the sheriff came to
the door looking for daddy. From then on things grew increasingly
grim, with the family moving from house to house and neighborhood to neighborhood as father tried to keep one step ahead of
his addiction to gambling. "But no one, at Christmas, would have
guessed we were poor," says Eileen.

Christmas, as gamblers are so often able to manage, almost
made up for it all; Christmas, with its bounty of gifts under the tree,
made them seem almost normal. Even today, Eileen sees those
Christmases as almost an heroic accomplishment on the part of her
father, given the vagaries of their lives the other 364 days a year.

Eileen was almost twenty when her mother and father finally
split, at which time she and her sisters took over their mother's support, which they continued until the day she died. "Did you resent
having to do that?" I asked her. "No," she said. "I did it because I
felt she'd missed out on things, and she needed it."

As a child, Eileen had felt sorry for her mother, not because
of anything her mother said, she insists, but because for ten years
they lived in a rich neighborhood and in their house there were no
servants. Her mother did the cooking and cleaning and the child
care and went to the PTA meetings. Her father was out in pursuit
of "deals."

The sense one gets, listening to Eileen, is of someone who has clung fervently to the same family story. Most people revise their histories as life goes on. Those from what have come to be called dysfunctional families may hew forever to the same story line. "There were so many secrets," Eileen says, "and I was their keeper."

No wonder, in conversation with her, there are so many lapses, so many details Eileen can't recall, even the seemingly innocuous ones, like whom she went to for help in investing her divorce settlement. Eileen actually can't remember the answer to this although she's sure "someone" must have.

The worst secret of all is the truth. It is the secret that plays itself out in one's life year after year, regardless of what one thinks one believes. First, in Eileen's life, came the husband who "took care of everything," like Good Daddy. Daddy who could make Christmas appear out of thin air. "We lived in Europe. Robert's family was interested in art. My needs were taken care of. My husband wanted me to look nice and bought me beautiful clothes. And he accompanied me on those shopping trips. That's the way it was done. I never spent money while I was by myself, except when I did the marketing."

Eileen split up with the benevolent husband when she was still young. Boredom, she says now. Robert hadn't "grown," as she had. Eileen returned to the States, got a job in an art gallery, and from that point on earned her own living.

But then an interesting switch occurred. Eileen's next relationship was with a man who'd never grown up — the ne'er-do-well side of her father, the man who took money from his children when his "deals" fell through. Marcus was Bad Daddy — charming, lovable, but essentially exploitative. He moved in with Eileen, along with his young son, and for the first five years he didn't contribute to the rent. Basically, she supported them.

"I didn't even realize it was happening," she says. "First they were on the West Coast in their own house, then they came east and moved in with me, and I just kept on paying all the bills I'd always been paying. In some ways it was like me being able to take money from my husband when I was married. It didn't seem unusual, it just seemed like it was family money, there for everyone."

Families that treat the needs of everyone, parents and children, as the same, produce adults unable to experience appropriate boundaries between themselves and others. What's yours is mine, what's mine is yours, we'll all go down together. Thus, Eileen didn't really mind that *she* was the one earning all the money; she still experienced her security as coming from her connection with the other. For fifteen years, Marcus would get jobs and lose them, blaming his job losses on the market, even saying that women were getting all the jobs. "It was a long time before I began thinking there must be some reason why he was always the one getting the boot. For years I just felt we were making a life together and if he needed my money, he could have it. I never felt he was selfish. But by the end I felt he was selfish. Very, very selfish."

By the end, Marcus had gone through all her savings, including the money from her divorce settlement. After they separated, she was so broke she asked him to help her out for a while. Within six months, he was telling her he could no longer help; he had his own bills to pay.

"Then," she says, "I found the two custom-made suits on my Am-Ex bill."

While she has no bitterness toward her husband and their life together, she *is* bitter about Marcus. "I didn't learn anything from that relationship, except never to get in one like it again." She recognizes that she was taken advantage of, but she makes no connection between the life she lived with Marcus and her childhood with her parents.

It hadn't only been daddy who was sly and secretive about money. Eileen's mother, she and her sisters would learn much later, had actually been investing in the stock market while allowing her children to pay her bills. "I think at one point she got some kind of inheritance. Isn't it ironic that she was investing while I was working so hard to support her?"

Her father, too, would take money from his daughters. But once, when he wanted to come to see Eileen, he actually borrowed money from someone else — and she remembers that occasion fondly. Her mother never came unless Eileen sent her the money to do it. Her father's borrowing the money to see her meant he really wanted to see her. He did it the time when, at twenty-seven, she left for Europe with a ticket her boyfriend had sent her. Daddy came to the airport and drank wine and threw confetti, he was so happy for her. Eileen's sister has told her Eileen was daddy's favorite. She says they used to have a "date" every evening when he came home from work. She would go into the den and sit on his lap.

After Eileen returned from Europe and was living in New York, daddy would sometimes travel to see her unannounced. "I'd come home from work and he'd just be sitting there on the step. He never told me he was coming. He wouldn't even know what was going on at the time. That's the way he was. He just popped in and out of life."

Before he died, he told Eileen he felt he had not been a success in life. When she tells this, tears come. It was the saddest she had ever been, the day her father told her of his sense of failure.

Now she lives alone and says she wouldn't even let anyone inside the house who wasn't willing to pay his way. "I can't say that if I fell in love I wouldn't let myself be taken advantage of again, but never to this degree."

SELF-DEBTING: A WOMAN WHO CARES FOR OTHERS AT THE EXPENSE OF HER OWN SECURITY

Tara is a pretty woman with a dark, boyish haircut and a beautifully modulated voice. She came up to me in Seattle after a lecture I gave for a local women's organization and said she had a money story to tell me. She was on the fence with it, and maybe, she said, I'd have some ideas.

Tara had worked at many things: among them, as a magazine illustrator and as a buyer for stores specializing in women's clothing. Now in her forties, she is in her third marriage. Recently her uncle died and she inherited money. Altogether, she has close to a million dollars. But she's having a very hard time hanging on to it — and not because of her own spending, but because of her proclivity to be a caretaker, what Debtors Anonymous calls being a "self-debtor."

During her three marriages, Tara has never been supported by a man. But in this third marriage, things are different. "Richard's been in this precarious financial situation basically since I've met him, although I didn't know it for a long time. He really covered it up. Not through any attempt to deceive, but just because . . ."

She lets the "because" drift off.

"By an absence of the information he gave out to you?"

"An absence of information. Also, he has this coin collection, so he was slowly selling off coins. His money waxes and wanes, but now we're in this extended period where his business is making nothing and it's scaring the shit out of me. I'm afraid to sit down and total it up, because if I do I'm going to get really upset. I think that in the last year and a half he's gone through, for *work*, somewhere between thirty and forty thousand dollars of my money. He has a phone bill that's well over a thousand a month. So, you know, I don't think he's taking the money and going out and buying expensive cigars. I'm sure it's going . . . to work."

What kind of financial agreement did she and Richard have? I asked.

"It's very difficult for me to *get* one," she replied. "I sat him down when I inherited the money and I said, 'Look, I want you to participate in this, but I have to tell you the truth. I can't put half of it in your name because it makes me too nervous. But I really want you to be a part of it; I mean, our life is together. Tell me what *you* think.

"I mean, he's certainly far more knowledgeable than I am about investing and matters like that. He's also much more risk oriented. And so I keep on saying to him, in one way or another" (and here her voice grows abruptly softer), " 'Honey, we need to hang on to this money for when we're older because it's sort of like everything we spend now not only makes it smaller, but takes away from the interest it can accrue over the years. So I'd rather spend less now and know that when I'm seventy, which I no longer feel is so far in the future, we can have flexibility *then*.'

"And he says things like 'Don't worry, honey. I'll make money; we'll have money; we won't run out of money; I'll inherit some money from my mother.' "

"It's pie in the sky."

"It's pie in the sky. I mean, he's *not* saying, 'I'll make a million dollars,' but on the other hand he's not going to inherit that much, either. He gets half the value of his mother's house, and I don't think it's worth a hundred thousand dollars."

Basically Tara was treating her inheritance as his money, regardless of whether any of it was in his name, wasn't she? I asked.

Tara disagreed, although what she said next indicated that she *had* in fact given him carte blanche to spend. "I didn't want him having to come to me and ask me every time he wanted something, so I said, 'Let's open a joint checking account and I'll put a chunk of money in and when you get some money you can put some money in, you know, we'll both . . . but right now I have it and you don't.' What I'm trying to *do* is basically get him to some kind of time limit on this stuff. It's a very complicated thing, because at what point do you say, 'You know it'd be cheaper for you to sit home and watch television and do *nothing*?' "

Tara is clearly annoyed, but she avoids putting into a simple declarative sentence what *she* would like.

"I know one thing. I'm *not* going to feel comfortable if he blows a big, big chunk of money."

"Isn't that pretty vague? You're not establishing any limits or boundaries with this situation."

"Yeah, but that's very *hard* for me. I mean [sighs], one of the things I like so much about Richard is that he's nondirective. He doesn't make demands. Not that he doesn't express preferences, or concerns about things, but basically he loves me, he's happy to be with me, and he's not trying to change me. It's a very nice feeling."

The unstated arrangement between them, she says, makes it difficult for her to say to him (here she makes her voice bold and bossy), " 'Okay, when you hit the fifty thousand dollar mark.' Or, 'Okay, December one.' Or, 'This has to stop.' I mean, I don't know how to *do* it. It's driving me nuts."

Jean Baker Miller says that women often feel people are demanding too much of them and they resent it, but they can't allow themselves to admit that they resent it. It's gender training, again. "They have come to believe that they should *want* to respond at all times and in all ways. Consequently, they cannot let themselves openly call a halt to the demands or even take small steps to limit them."[9]

When I suggest to Tara that she seems to be confused about what her rights are, she disagrees. It's not about rights, she says. It's about protection. "He's so fragile, in some ways, that I really don't want to make him feel bad. He feels like shit already. He's not making money and he's spending my money. He's not being 'manly.' " She laughs nervously at her ironic reading of "manly." Surely they're beyond such plebeian gender stereotypes; but what *is* manly? What is grown-up and responsible? Something's happening here that's affecting Tara profoundly, but she isn't sure what it is.

Richard isn't out to suck up all her money. He's disorganized in his own life, and he looks at Tara's windfall very differently than she does. Probably he looks at many things differently than she does, but their differences that might be perceived as "demands" are unlikely to get addressed. Tara permits the situation to remain amorphous, essentially to allow Richard to determine how things are going to go. It's a situation that could easily blow up, the question being when. After all the money is shot?

"Part of what gives me pleasure about this money is thinking that when I'm older, I'll be protected from the shopping bags on the street." Her fear of ending up with shopping bags is countered by an equally strong fear: "I don't want to threaten him and make him feel uncomfortable."

I try to open up the window a little on the dilemma. "What if the shoe were on the other foot?"

"If the shoe were on the other foot, I would not be able to take the same percentage of money from him. I mean, *yes*, if he had five million, I'd be able to blow a million."

Worrisome, also, to Tara is that she doesn't understand what his business is about. But she does know "it's speculative; it's all about the *possibility* of a big payoff."

When she was sitting down with her financial planner, Richard came into the living room, sat down with them, and said, "I'm Tara's highly speculative position."

"It's accurate," she says. "The possibility of a big payoff is there. I'm just not someone who *wants* a highly speculative position. I would, maybe, with a small sum of money, but basically, I'm not a gambler."

"But you don't say that to him. You don't say, 'I need to have more control over my money. I need to bring this thing to a head because of my own psychological needs.' "

"I know, I know. I just have this feeling I don't want to *unman* him. I just don't want to *do* it."

Tara's mother was well supported by her father, a renowned filmmaker, until he blew everything through misguided investments and overspending. He was an artist, after all; he didn't have to worry about money. To the end, his way was spendthrift and grandiose. "When the electricity was turned off because the bill hadn't been paid, he'd bring home a fresh goose liver for dinner and roast it over the fire," Tara recalls.

Finally provoked to leave her husband, Tara's mother was left with his tax debt. The divorce occurred when Tara was eight. She and her mother went to live in a one-room apartment, where they stayed until the tax debt was paid off. At that point, Tara was sixteen years old. You could say that Tara, too, had helped pay off her father's debt.

"Psychological and social difficulties have come from the distortions taught to women," Jean Baker Miller points out. "Indeed, women have been led to believe that if they act and think effectively they will jeopardize their chances for satisfying emotional experiences."[10]

Tara expresses that kind of constriction. "We're born into this society. When Richard and I first started seeing each other, before I even *knew* what his financial position was, when we went out to dinner Richard almost always would pay the bill. He still does. I do the cooking. I pay for the groceries. It's classic men's work, women's work. But that strikes me as cute. It seems very harmless. And every time he takes me out and pays for a meal, I always thank him. Every time I pay for a meal, he always thanks me."

Today's women who have money of their own play out the traditional male-female "romance" in an attempt to override the vast economic difference in their situations, and the *anxiety producing* power imbalance their money implies. Many women are afraid that if they become competent with money, they'll jeopardize their relationships with men. Tara has her own view of it. Richard is a nice person, she says. He accepts her pretty much as she is. She wants to be able to do the same for him. Whatever this boat is, she's afraid to rock it. But she's watching her money dwindle not so slowly away. Tara experiences herself as having her hands tied. If she does nothing, her nest egg will evaporate. If she takes charge and puts limits on Richard, she'll lose the comfortable, laissez-faire relationship she has now. She could even lose the relationship. She sees it as a no-win. Act, and she loses; remain passive, and she loses. When I ask Tara what her worst fear is concerning money, her answer comes without a beat: "I'm afraid of growing old and having no money."

When I tell her it's every woman's fear, the bag lady syndrome, she says, "I'm not afraid of ending up a bag lady, because I'd kill myself first."

Tara has always taken care of herself, in the sense of earning her own money. What she doesn't do is take care of herself for the long run. The romance story is too important to her. A significant part of her particular romance story is the similarity between her husband's qualities and her father's. Richard is clever, charming, earnest in his wish to please, but unable to get it together.

Her story also reflects similarities between her mother's conflicts and her own. Tara learned from her mother to keep a firm grip on the purse strings and spend responsibly.

But she also learned her mother's battle between dependence and independence. Tara recalls that her mother was terrified of having her independence limited. (During a third marriage, in her sixties, she would become irate if her husband so much as asked her where she was going.) Tara may be keeping the upper hand on her fear of dependence by being with a man she can't rely on financially.

The Romance Myth entraps women in a compulsive acting out of their childhood histories. The trauma from childhood is repressed — forgotten; but the adult repeats the scenario over and over again in her unconscious attempts to master it.

PROJECTIONS

When I came across Jungian writer June Singer's story of Diane and Ian, in *Boundaries of the Soul,* it was the first time I understood what had really happened between L. and me — why I had been so willing to rely on him financially, and why, initially, he had seen me as someone in need of his protection.[11]

When Ian met and fell deeply in love with Diane, he saw her as much younger, someone he wanted to protect. (In fact, she was about the same age as he.)

Diane was widowed young and had been rearing her children alone — a task that required her to become hard-working and efficient. But she acquired those traits in extremis, Singer points out — "not because it was natural to her, but because it was an absolute necessity" if she and her children were to survive. When Ian came into her life, she saw someone strong, reliable, and both willing and able to take care of her and the children. Things went well for a while, but then, inevitably, the projections that each placed on the other began to disintegrate.

Relying on her newfound sense of security, Diane began to be less interested in the home and things became disordered. She lost her job and made no attempt to find a new one. She said she'd have more time for Ian — which he liked — but at the same time, since she was bringing in no money, her financial demands for herself and her children increased — which he *didn't* like. Her children, now, needed college; she needed a new car, the house needed repairs. Ian kept paying because he was afraid that if he placed financial demands on her, he'd lose her. "Eventually they found themselves deeply in debt. Each blamed the other. They also blamed each other for the other ways in which each had failed to measure up to the other's expectations."

Finally, Ian and Diane went into couples therapy. For each, the major task was confronting the reality of who the other person actually was. "Each one had to withdraw the projections and recognize that they would only retrieve the marriage if each would take responsibility for the parts of themselves that they had expected the other to provide for them," Singer wrote.

Each had to come to know the opposite within, and to let that part develop and grow. This was the only way each could become more whole, could function more independently; could respect the other for who that person was, and not for how that person could serve them.

"The thing that is hardest to get at in our own psyche is what takes on the image of the opposite sex," June Singer explains.

For the woman, this is the animus; for the man, the anima. "The animus of the woman is . . . the repressed Other, the unconscious Other that she has been prevented from living out."

One of the tasks, for someone in Jungian therapy, is bringing that repressed animus out into daylight. So long as the animus remains an unconscious part of us, "we can find ourselves powerfully attracted to another person, usually of the opposite sex, who bears some resemblance to the inner figure. We unconsciously project the inner image onto the other person, who immediately assumes the form of someone infinitely desirable, the person we had always hoped to meet, the 'soul mate.' " Whatever we believe we are lacking in ourselves appears, then, in the form of the beloved. "He or she is everything we need to feel complete, and we expect this person to fulfill the empty spaces in our heart and home."

Of course when we meet such a paragon of perfection, "we take the surface appearance to be deeper than it really is," Singer observes. Essentially, what we do is create our own add-ons — and we imagine them belonging to the other when they don't. Then we become furious and disappointed when that person turns out not to be who we imagined.

DECONSTRUCTING THE PRINCE

One doesn't have to be married, or even in so-called "love" to relate to men by turning them into heroes and then suffering the humiliating devaluation that goes hand in hand with idealization. I discovered myself regressing to my old standby of hero making when I was in my fifties. It wasn't a husband or a lover or some dashing older male relative; it was my Pilates trainer.

Not long after beginning the study of Pilates, a rigorous form of mind-body work, I became attached to a completely faultless vision I constructed of my teacher. But this time I learned something about hero making, or the process of idealization. I discovered I'd been using it defensively all my life in my relations with men. The perfect, princely image of them I created in my mind made authentic relationship impossible. At the same time, that hero making turned *me* into ashes, for there is no way to glorify the other without diminishing oneself.

A choreographer and former principal with a major dance company in New York, David was a natural target for my fantasies. Tremendously energetic, he was continually engaged — the dance company, a new work he was choreographing, a new piece of equipment he was building for the studio, a deck he was constructing on his barn. He seemed to be able to exist without sleep, flying to Texas for a five-hour rehearsal, driving up to Woodstock from the city at four A.M. and beginning to teach at eight because he was out late celebrating his wife's birthday. It was David's *energy* that appealed to me, his life force. He was interested in everything, each student held an appeal for him, and he *worked* it, worked his life with a sense of ownership and power that filled me with awe.

The women teachers at the studio were good at what they did, but for me, the charge was missing. I went to David for two private sessions a week, as much for the charge as for his teaching.

The charge in part came from how he made me extend my-self — psychologically, as well as physically. He'd reach out and grab a leg and put it through its full range of motion in a way that I never would have done on my own. I would never have *imagined* my own full range of motion. David taught it to me, hands on, like Geppetto the toymaker willing life energy into his puppet.

Not that David thought of me as a toy. I would have balked at that. He treated me as if he thought I was without limits. "Try this, try that. Turn it out. Turn it out further." I liked the challenge. But I also liked the powerful sense of being directed, made to push the limits. I liked someone telling me, essentially, that I could do it, but even more, someone seeming to breathe his own energy for life into my clay.

But then, at last, I began to see that something was happening that I didn't want happening. In exchange for a vague if compelling vision of perfection I had imposed on this man, I was giving up the chance to know someone with whom I could have a real sense of communion. Intelligent, compassionate, committed to many of the ideas and beliefs that inform my own life, David could be a true friend if only I would let him down off the pedestal on which I'd placed him.

And I? I could feel more powerful, more engaged in my own life if I did not insist upon giving that power over to someone else.

Why had I become this sort of person? What confluence of culture and childhood would bring me to this — an accomplished and ma-ture woman who continued to feel that the life blood beat in others' veins, but not her own?

The answer to this question has nothing to do with competence. It has nothing to do with intelligence. Nor does it have very much to do with accomplishment. The weight of my whole psychologi-cal history lay beneath my conflict: to the degree that I wanted Geppetto's life for my own, I was consigned to devalue what *I* had, in an ongoing cycle of envy and self-debasement. And I wanted that life because, long ago, I had foresworn my own inner prince.

"There is a mystery about the unknown," writes June Singer, in *Boundaries of the Soul*, "and the unknown is often the unconscious Other within. When we see another person carrying the qualities and potentialities that we do not see in ourselves, we envy the Other within."[12]

This notion is at the base of the modern psychological understanding of penis envy. Metaphorically, says Singer, "penis and womb represent that mysterious Other which seems most desirable and yet most unattainable."

Since adolescence I have liked hanging out with the boys: the boys *have* it. As my husband, and later the man I lived with for many years, spoke passionately about some subject, my inner sparks would fly. I interacted with these men. I got charged. No matter that it was the image of *their* life that was supplying me with energy. I was borrowing passion, attaching myself to someone else's desire.

What has always attracted me to particular men is the idea that they possess a certain energy, a life force. I had a powerful model for this in childhood, where I became attached to a father who dominated the dinner table each night with his fiery displays of anger, his struggles, and his passion. This man — the original Prince in my psychological makeup — had *ideas*; he wanted the rest of us in the family, me especially, I thought, to *get* them. He was fevered with his own self. At some point I began to resist his powerful energy, sensing that if I didn't, I'd be swamped by it. And so, at the age of twelve or so, I began arguing with him. I fought for my own psychological existence. I grew disdainful.

But inside, I continued in those early years to be attracted to males with energy, frissons, the life force. It wasn't just their large ideas about life I found compelling, it was their day-to-day living as if everything they thought and said and felt *mattered*. They — their stories — affected my engine like sparks arcing between two wires.

I *needed* them. I reacted to and was inspired by them. I argued and disagreed with them but I *wanted* what they had. *They owned their experience.*

So it wasn't just protection that was the Prince's lure. It was his *life* I hoped to breathe in, like a contact high. Boys talked about tennis and car engines. They made endless jokes, most of them irreverent if not dirty. They fought with the adult world, did parodies of their teachers, teased and provoked one another, had girlfriends who somehow were less important than all of this put together, or who, at least, were just one part of the whole. The whole was the force — their pure animal energy being stimulated by the world around them. They were open to the world, brash, unfearful. *They were not afraid of experience.*

To have access to their vitality, which I very much wanted for myself, I hung out with the boys. I had girlfriends, too, but our experience together was more limited, directed mostly by the search for boys. Boys, ah, theirs was the life. They actually bought their own cars. And they knew how to fix them. They stayed out as late as they wanted without their parents restricting them. They gestured, strutted, *moved,* as if the world existed for their adventure.

Not so, girls. Girls struggled for acceptance, a feeling of connection with others, the wish, above all, for a boy to complete them. *Only let me be with you and I will have a life.*

Women are brought up to develop the "pervasive sense" that a man has an entirely mysterious strength — some very important ability that enables him to manage in the real world, says Jean Baker Miller. "This element becomes increasingly foreign for the woman; it takes on the quality of an almost magical ability that men have and women do not."[13]

Men are strong, bold, aggressive, daring, energetic — they *make* their lives exciting. Women are nurturing, gentle, quiet; they are willing to put their own ambitions on the back burner, anxious about taking risks, keepers and holders of the family secrets.

Because society assigns certain human traits to each gender,

210 • MAXING OUT

those same traits, when they appear in the opposite gender, are considered downright unnatural. This polarization is so extreme that the woman who embraces her boldness, aggression, and curiosity does so, she fears, at the risk of losing something. Not only might she end up alone, she could lose her very feelings of centeredness as a woman.

On the other hand, the woman who submerges her masculine side, though she may not end up alone, will be unable to enjoy the thrill of mastery. This woman will intervene against the expression of her own energy, cutting it off rather than risk being dominant, self-sufficient, and (she fears) isolated.

The unconscious solution of the adult woman, thus, is an extension of the very same defense she began to adopt at twelve and thirteen: if she doesn't want to be alone, she must find as painless a way as possible of being half a person. Those, she believes in her soul, are her options.

BECOMING A PLAYER

One can do many things in life and still not feel like a player. I had done much in my life but I discovered, through analyzing my interaction with David, that I still did not experience myself as a player. When David talked about raising sixteen-foot beams to support the deck he was building on his barn, I would think, "*That* is being a player." He did it with help, of course. (Not even David can lift a sixteen-foot beam by himself.) But he couldn't wait to get home, after a long workday in the studio, to put in more hours on the deck before dark. "I'm beating up my body, the pickax is ripping up my hands," he would tell me the next day, with obvious delight, "but I'm mastering this deck!"

David, for me, was the adventurer. He entered life in an active, undaunted way. He *engaged* with many people and got gratification from it. He pushed himself to his physical and emotional limits (sometimes too much so, but I didn't focus on that). He put in a long, full day, with many activities. He didn't oversleep. When he worked at something — the teaching, the deck, making a new ballet — he was *focused* on it.

I had always lived in a dreamier state — a bit self-protected, a bit disengaged, controlling time and energy as if they were in dangerously limited supply. As a result, I felt as if I didn't accomplish enough. I was understimulated; huge parts of life's adventure were passing me by.

Diving into a project *because* it gives a sense of mastery, enjoying the mastery, and knowing that one enjoys it — this, to me, is being a player.

As individuals, men, certainly, can be as dysfunctional as women in their handling of money. The difference lies in the cultural expectations placed on each and the degree to which these contribute to, or detract from, an individual's ability to develop financial independence.

Men are taught that there's no back door. Ultimately, they're going to be responsible for earning a living and supporting a family. Forget that, these days, women do as much to support a family as men; this is cultural myth we're talking about. The willingness — and ability — to take it all on are considered the very essence of masculinity. This is why boys are permitted to shout out their answers in a classroom and girls are taught to admire that aggressiveness and back off in the face of it. Boys are going to go out into the world and make things happen with their male hands. Girls are going to defer and admire. That is part and parcel of femininity. They are going to blush and hang their heads when they get an answer wrong, while the boys will toss off mistakes as insignificant and simply shout out another answer.

Because our ideas about gender identity are rooted in the issue of survival — women are faced with an impossible mandate: to accept responsibility for their own survival means they have to give up their sense of being *women.*

By the same token, men who slack off financial responsibility are seen as less than masculine. They are basically viewed as boys and lose — in the eyes of both men and women — their gender potency. Thus, in a powerful and primitive way, we are all encouraged to associate manliness with money: money making, money managing, money investing.

Men learn not only to survive with money, but to control with it. Controlling is considered *part* of surviving, so it, too, is accepted as appropriate masculine behavior. Note the language Brian Holloway used, in a fax sent by his lawyer's office to the *New York Times* stating that he had been "unjustly charged" with dastardly behavior by his former wife, after cleaning out their house of anything that would make it livable for her: "Athletes, Celebrities and Business Leaders are required to be ever vigilant . . . it would be negligent not to have a prepared strategy in place."

The prenuptial agreement in which Bette agreed to get nothing if they divorced was apparently part of the "strategy." Ditto the removal from the house of the children, the stripping of the burners from the stove. We're not talking, here, about a drug-addled maniac. Drugs were not part of Brian Holloway's picture. We are talking about a man's ordinary sense of entitlement, blown to heroic proportions in an athlete encouraged by the culture he lives in to think of himself as godlike.

What women do, or don't do, with money is ever influenced by the overarching question of how they are going to survive. And they are not at all sure — nor should they be, given the inequities that continue to exist in wages, taxation, and Social Security — that their best chances don't lie in the Romance Myth.

As the twentieth century draws to a close, women are being pulled between two poles — the presumed protection of traditional romanticism and the vibrant self-sufficiency of the Brave New Feminist. There is visible tension in the lives of women today as they try to extricate themselves from the web of the Romance Myth — the false promise of protection and control — and attempt to enter life fully on their own. It takes every shred of analytic intelligence and emotional courage they can muster, for the odds, as we have seen, are still piled against them. Society doesn't *want* women experiencing the power of financial self-sufficiency. For them to do so would be to tumble the tower of gender inequity once and for all.

But women are afraid that if that tower tumbles, they will be left with no help at all — not even the modicum they get now from a system that still places its bets on men.

Chapter 8

ATTITUDES OF THE AMBIVALENT

One day in the winter of 1995, I wrote down in my journal three episodes that let me know my financial recovery was far from complete. A few days before Christmas, I had driven to New York with new friends to see a performance of Handel's *Messiah* and have dinner at a nice restaurant. Shortly after we drove off in their car, I realized I'd left my wallet behind. I had to borrow two hundred dollars from people I'd only begun to get to know. How humiliating.

Barely a week later, visiting my mother in South Carolina, I saw a good lease deal on a car. Pleased that I actually had enough cash to pay for two years of the lease in advance, I went ahead, high on the image of my new car with its shimmering, British-racing-car-green finish. But in my euphoria I neglected to check out New York State's registration requirements. I could easily have gotten the necessary form signed in Charleston and been done with it, but no. I spent several weeks driving around unsure of what, precisely, my legal situation was.

Driving the car north, at around midnight, I was stopped in Roanoke by the Virginia state police. Something about how I only had one plate displayed and I was supposed to have two. I sat there watching the twirling lights in my rearview while they made their call. Apparently someone determined that I wasn't a criminal, because the cops let me proceed on my way with a warning. But how unnecessary!

A week later I was driving to New York City from my home in Woodstock and again made the "mistake" of leaving my house with no cash. I arrived at the George Washington Bridge at nine-thirty on a Saturday night with no money to pay the toll, only hoping they'd let me cross the bridge. I was asked to pull over and explain myself, because I still had the lousy one plate on the car. I had to show my leasing papers *and* explain why I had no money. The toll officer checked my birthdate and must have been moved to pity because he decided to "believe" my story — due primarily, he said, to the fact that I was a Pisces. "I'm a Sagittarius myself, so I don't know why I'm doing this. I can be a real bastard."

The whole thing felt surreal. Yet getting to cross the bridge made me feel both relieved and thrilled.

It gets worse. I had thought that when I arrived at my hotel I would be able to cash a check. However, the hotel's check-approving company apparently had some damning information, and the hotel wouldn't take my check. I knew I had money in my account so could only assume my recent history of check bouncing had caught up with me. My son had to pay for my dinner that night *and* put my room charge on his credit card.

I could no longer deny that I was caught up in some kind of sickness. It was as if I were putting myself in these vulnerable positions deliberately. What, possibly, could I be gaining from the experience of feeling put down and humiliated?

This hellish period occurred a year before my mother died, during a time when she was very ill. I think the fear of being unable to take care of myself was geysering right to the surface and causing panic. Ordinarily I wasn't someone who left the house without money, and I'd done it twice within several weeks. And there was that thrill when the toll officer let me onto the bridge — the giddy little rush because I'd "made" someone (even a Sagittarius!) take up my defense. It meant I had the ability to manipulate others into helping me.

In our mothers' generation there were women who never wrote a check until their husbands died. Today's women reveal their ambivalence about independence in their lack of planning for the future. Many have no savings, no investments, no tax-deferred retirement plans. Women I've interviewed tell me they plan to work "forever." They actually use that word. Partly it's because they enjoy work, but just as likely they haven't acknowledged the necessity of financial planning for the future. Like the adolescent who thinks she'll live forever, the new, liberated woman can contemplate no end point. That expectation that she can work until the day she dies signals a new kind of defense for the woman who still has trouble with dependency. Rather than acknowledge that no one will be there to take care of her, and taking action *now* to create security, she just keeps on "doing what I'm doing" and hoping to hell it'll all work out.

What will become of these women, one wonders, when they are in their eighties and nineties? Many imagine hovering together in their old age. Said a woman in an investment club I visited, "My oldest friend is forty-nine, a freelancer who has debt but no savings. When I asked what she was planning for her old age, she said, 'I'm going to kill myself or I'm going to move in with you.'"

Another woman, contemplating the isolation of an older friend who'd been put into a nursing home to live out her last years, had formulated a plan for how to wind down her own life when the time came: "I'm going to join the Peace Corps and go to Zaire and get shot."

It's more than possible for a woman to appear ambitious and independent and still not be aware that rescue is the end point of her long-term financial plan. Consciously, such a woman fears being dependent on men, because experience has taught her that rescue is tantamount to control. She believes the last thing in the world she wants is for someone to come along and help beef up her 401(K). But she sabotages herself with the fantasy that "everything will turn out all right." The end result? She neither gets taken care of nor does she take care of herself.

"I honestly don't think that anybody's going to bail me out," says a long-divorced mother of three grown children and self-employed provider of services to writers.

Elena has a master's degree in education and an IQ in the Mensa league. But she's not using her intelligence to create security for herself. Like so many women, her all-out terror about self-sufficiency stymies her.

"I actually believe that when I die, I'm going to be all alone. It's kind of depressing to think that, but I just somehow think that. I'm going to be alone."

Who among us doesn't think that, deep down? "What do you imagine your life will be like?" I ask. "Do you ever look at these old women around Woodstock and think . . ."

"That that could be me?"

"Or, she has to crawl through a blizzard for her bread each morning because she doesn't have a car?"

This image, so appalling to me, apparently isn't so deterring to Elena. "What's going to save me is that I can live very simply and very minimally," she says, enthralled by an almost romantic image of an impoverished old woman trying to tough out her last years in our little mountain town.

"So your fantasy is that you'll just cut back?"

"If I have to. I mean, if I had a lot of money coming in right now, I'd be thinking, 'How much do I need to live in a certain lifestyle?' I'd be putting money away. I would definitely be doing that. But it's a kind of moot point for me right now since I'm not making all that much. . . ."

"But don't you think that if you saw it as truly important, you'd find a way to earn more?"

"Maybe. But I really value my lifestyle now, which is pretty relaxed. I'm not working all that many hours. If I had to stop working, eventually I could collect Social Security, right? And they have housing for the elderly where they only charge you a percentage of your income."

"They have that around here?" I'd never heard of such a place in our neck of the woods.

"Oh, yeah, I'm sure. I think they probably have it all over, housing for people on very limited incomes. And they can only charge this percentage. And then you collect your food stamps, and you have your Medicare, and you have everything you need."

How cozy, I think. Elena continues, with mounting enthusiasm, "And you're not going to be driving, anyway. Hopefully, I'd still be able to do some of the things that I enjoyed. Like read or write or watch movies or see my friends. But I think, yeah, my sphere would probably become very limited."

Elena pops up with a notion that perfectly rationalizes the circumscribed existence she's assigned for her future. "The thing is, you don't want too much room when you're old, anyway. I think old people like smaller spaces."

"Like cats."

"Yeah."

She ponders this. Surely there must be some alternative. "Another idea I've had is that there might be a communal-type arrangement, you know, where I would share with someone and maybe feel less of a need to have a lot of space and a lot of privacy. As a matter of fact, it might even be advantageous to have another person around. Where I could be of help to them and they could be of help to me, that kind of thing. Maybe one person drives and the other one doesn't. Or one person . . ."

"Gardens."

"Or one person sees well and the other one doesn't. So that's a solution that might work for me."

But now we get down to it, the secret ace-in-the-hole of the modern liberated woman who did so damn much to rear those kids, and understand and often support them, and develop her own life to boot: "To tell you the truth, if it came down to it, I wouldn't hesitate to ask my kids to contribute a small amount to me. If I really needed it. And I'm sure they would be willing to do it. So, I don't feel like — I don't worry about being out on the street. Some people worry about being out on the street. I don't worry about being out — I just don't worry about that."

Elena is equivocating, trying to convince herself she's not concerned about her future. She likes her easy, stress-free life and doesn't want to have to do anything differently. But she's in limbo, financial and emotional.

Linda Sapadin, a clinical psychologist in Valley Stream, New York, with a specialty in helping people overcome self-defeating problems, describes women like Elena as "dreamer procrastinators," coasting through day-to-day life in a dreamy state of disengagement. Ironically, it's often stress the woman is trying to avoid, imagining the ideal life to be one that is comfortable and nonthreatening. "She resists accepting the fact that a real, substantial life brings with it a certain number of non-dream-like chores, problems, hardships, and responsibilities that are necessary — and even worthwhile — to address."[1]

But as anyone struggling with procrastination knows, the less we do, the more stress mounts. Procrastinators may *think* they're being active because their minds are so plagued by anxiety, but really they're spinning in the cage of compulsive avoidance.

TERMINAL VAGUENESS

There is a way of functioning that Debtors Anonymous calls "terminal vagueness." Psychologists have another term for it: learned helplessness. Says James W. Gottfurcht, a Los Angeles psychologist who helps people with money problems, "They have this paralysis, this shutdown. They get foggy and bleary-eyed when they look at financial reports. They feel trapped."[2] People who start going to DA meetings because of panic over money soon learn that profligate spending isn't their only problem: a fuzzy, dissociative way of functioning infiltrates every aspect of their lives. More than anything, their vagueness flags: *Help me. I need rescue.*

I had always liked working as a freelance. Over the years I'd dismissed the precariousness of my position — no health insurance, no pension plan, no taxes taken out of the paycheck because there was no paycheck. Freelance writers get paid fees, not salary. We consider the financial trickiness of working as freelancers a trade-off for independence. But in the sleepless nights after I'd begun living alone, I sometimes wished that instead of becoming a writer in my twenties I'd gone to work for some big patriarchal corporation. Yet I realized, watching friends get "downsized," that an actual job guaranteed no safety, either.

Then my father died, and four years later, my mother. I no longer had any illusion of protection, of financial backup should I need it.

Their deaths also brought me up against the extremely discomfiting fact that I wasn't immortal. That wonderful energy I'd always been able to tap into wasn't going to be around forever. Maybe I could keep on pumping out the work for another decade or two, but maybe not. I had to face the fact that I was without a plan. In my forties I'd earned a very good income, but I'd spent it as if there were no tomorrow. I'd never really thought about having to do it myself — forever.

"The biggest barrier to women's financial security lies in our deeply internalized feeling of incompetence," financial counselor Donna Boundy told me. "Many of us have incorporated a stereotype of women as inept with money."

As if to live out this stereotype, a surprising number of bright, competent, and otherwise responsible women glaze over when the subject turns to money. They don't balance their checkbooks, they don't invest, and when it comes to thinking about retirement, they run in the opposite direction as if chased by buckshot. "Women get good-paying jobs but spend everything they earn," says Boundy. "We're competent bookkeepers for others' businesses but 'fog out' whenever we have to deal with our own money. We go into business partnerships the same way many of us went into marriage, feeling grateful someone will have us. Somehow, we never consider our own talents and hard work to be worth much."

Many women describe a debilitating sense of financial impotence. "I feel like I cannot generate wealth on my own," said Dacy. "I feel like it has to come from outside of me — a parent, a husband, the lottery."

In Dacy's house, growing up, she remembers getting the message that only her father had access to the mysterious world of money. "It was a secret. We were not allowed to know how much he made. He was really the king of the house. It was sort of an obscure thing, the knowledge he had. It was not knowledge to be shared, taught, and given to others to empower them. It was his power, to be kept for him. Actually, as it turns out, he was pulling it all off by the skin of his teeth. But what got communicated to us was something entirely different."

Dacy is still paralyzed by the sense that she doesn't have what it takes to deal with money. Her father, after all, kept his power to himself, and her mother insisted she had none. "I grew up thinking that there was some special skill that I just didn't have. It was something I thought was innate, and that it would always elude me. My mother never seemed to have that power either. When I'd ask her for something, she'd always say, 'Maybe your father will give it to you,' or 'When we win the Lotto.' Always, something's going to happen. There was no sense of her own power. Now I do the same thing. Money isn't something I feel I can use my own powers to get. I'm still waiting for it to happen to me."

When I was thirty I went to work part-time for a very successful New York photographer and discovered that I could keep his checkbooks balanced to within a nickel. That's what he required of me, and that's what I did. But I never kept my own checkbooks balanced. It seemed an overwhelming and useless task. To this day, it amazes me that I could do it for *him* — but not for me.

INTERNALIZED INCOMPETENCE

Earning a living is not the same as assuming full responsibility for oneself. Teenagers earn money, sometimes plenty of it. Yet they still need their parents to put on brakes — to provide checks and balances against the unruly impulses they have not yet learned to manage.

Rather than grapple with the demands of protecting their money, some women — especially if they have no husband looking over their shoulders — " 'just piss it away,' " as physical therapist Carol Greenberg put it, in her confession to a Merrill Lynch financial seminar for women. Greenberg said she spends it all because she's afraid of investing. " 'Now, does that make any sense?' "[3]

The women attending the seminar ranged in age from twenty-seven to sixty-seven and included teachers, corporate executives, entrepreneurs, and other professionals. Meeting weekly in the conference room of an elegant New York club, they raised questions about how to get out of debt, how to take responsibility for their financial future, how to make money grow. They learned that they were overly conservative, wanting to keep their money "safe" in savings accounts and money market funds (which these days is almost like throwing it away). They learned they would not have enough to live on, no matter how much they earned, if they didn't become more aggressive as investors. They learned they had to stop leaving things in the hands of their husbands and take control of their own earnings and investments.

Charlotte London, who once wrote and hosted her own network radio finance program, stopped investing when she married, preferring to let her husband do it. When he died, he left "a very uninteresting portfolio. I had to do something if I wanted to live off the income." Luckily for her, there was a stock market surge going on at the time; she plunged in and tripled her holdings in four years. The paradoxes resulting from money phobia rarely make sense. An unmarried thirty-four-year-old executive secretary told the group she was "risk averse." Brought up by Depression-era parents, she was taught to view investing with a skeptical eye. So she keeps her money in a savings account and owes more on credit cards than she's saved. The interest she pays is 19.8 percent. Like many women, her goal is "not to have to worry," but she doesn't see how she can accomplish this. Apprehension clouds her life. (The goal of not having to worry is not necessarily the same as the goal of financial independence.)[4]

The three dozen women attending Merrill's seminar discovered that belief in their incompetence was deep. And it had nothing to do with how brilliantly they might conduct themselves in other areas. "No matter what I do with money, I feel I'm doing something wrong," said Muriel Bernstein. When her husband died, she had two young children, a mortgaged house, five hundred dollars in the bank, no life insurance, and a part-time job with a company that manufactures chemicals used in precast concrete. Today she is a vice president of the company and has been named a Fellow of the American Concrete Institute. "But I haven't learned to manage money."[5]

At one time or another in their lives, 80 percent of American women become wholly responsible for their financial welfare. But the new financial reality notwithstanding, women tend to be more comfortable working their backs off than spending a few months learning how to make their money *work* for them. It's not the time required, but the fear of failure that inhibits them.

Typical is the single mother with fifty thousand dollars in a 401(K) that she's got invested in a money market fund at a paltry 4 percent. "She knows she has to do something," reports Cynthia Kling, "but is afraid brokers will rip her off. So she does nothing."[6]

Says Corinne Smith, a senior vice president at Paine Webber, "The first time, female clients often walk into my office with their shoulders up around their ears. They always say 'I don't know anything.'" But she assures them she'll "take care of them," and they "walk out with tears of relief in their eyes."[7]

For many women, paralysis resulting from pure fear is the culprit. "I add, subtract, and multiply, but I never take any action," said a furtive soul who sat in the back row of the Merrill seminar punching numbers into a calculator. "I know I should do something with my savings, but I seem to be waiting for someone else to do it."

Carmine Dell'Orefice, the model from the forties and fifties who, though white-haired, is still drop-dead beautiful, knows what it's like to beg off entirely, letting "someone else" do it. She was set to marry David Susskind nine years ago when he died of a heart attack. One of his investment pals offered to help her take care of her savings, which amounted to about two hundred thousand dollars. Three years later her account was wiped out — the result of poor management.

"I was asleep at the job of my life," says Dell'Orefice, today. At sixty-five, she has learned the hard way to keep a sharp watch on everything and is a big believer in second opinions. Besides her broker, she has a certified financial planner, Melissa Levine, to double-check her investment decisions.

"Experts think that most women will outlive their retirement money," Levine commented to Dell'Orefice; they were having scones and tea together at the Mayfair Hotel.

"Then there are going to be a lot of old whores running around," Dell'Orefice mused delicately.[8]

WHY WOMEN FEAR THE POWER OF MONEY

Not surprisingly, many women think that if they become competent with money, it will drive men away. Again, as with sex, we believe that men have to feel in control, that if we deprive them of that feeling, we'll emasculate them.

"Because success in the marketplace, particularly in male-dominated professions, is attributed to self-seeking personality traits, such as ruthlessness and competitiveness, women at the top may be perceived as extraordinary, or not typically feminine, and singled out for attention that is not altogether flattering," write Annette Lieberman and Vicki Lindner, the authors of *Unbalanced Accounts*.[9]

Lieberman and Lindner asked scores of women to imagine they'd been invited to a chic dinner and seated next to a woman in their own field who was earning half a million dollars a year. Then they asked the women to describe the conversation they had with this fireball and what she looked like. The women imagined her as cold, hard, forbidding, even "evil." Dava, a video writer, said of her projected dinner-table companion: " 'She's wearing black and pearls. Extremely plain and kind of severe, with a thin, slightly drawn face.

I can't relate to her at all. She feels I'm some underling that might want something from her that she doesn't want to give. I'm very reserved.' "

Some of the participants were envious of the tycoon and tried to bring her down to size by uncovering her " 'human' " side. One very low earner had the plan of drawing her out and getting her to confide " 'her abortions and other tragedies in her life.' "

Even high earners rejected the successful woman. Georgette, who earned over one hundred thousand dollars a year, responded, " 'She'd probably be awful. She'd be very cold, very driven, not very nice, and very snotty. I would be uncomfortable because I would feel that . . . there would be an ax coming my way at some point, and it would be coming from this woman.' "

The authors of the study observe that while Georgette's distrust of successful women may have had some basis in past experience, her quick, reflexive negativity indicated she has trouble internalizing her own success — "integrating her concept of her own femininity with her income-producing powers."

Being truly financially independent feels too risky. The women in the study who were intimidated by an image of a self-sustaining woman had put unconscious boundaries on the amount of success they felt they could achieve. They rejected the self-made woman — not only in fantasy, but in themselves — and instead angrily accused *her* of rejecting *them*.

Encouragingly, Lieberman and Lindner found women with healthy attitudes toward money. These women were happy, in general, and communicated satisfaction with their lives. "Because money in our society spells power — a power women have long been denied — those who had learned to deal with it effectively radiated an aura of confident self-assertiveness."

They had found a way to "feminize" the meaning of money — that is, to integrate wanting money and financial independence with their sense of being acceptable and desirable as women. Nor did they sacrifice their relationships with others to become driven workaholics. "For women, we found there was a definite connection between a healthy financial identity and a healthy sexuality." Contrary to what many women fear — that high earnings and competence with money will make them threatening to men — the women in this study who dealt effectively with money also tended to have good relationships. "In general, it was the seriously moneyphobic who either had no men in their lives or who had troubled marriages and love affairs."

Typically, women are better at managing someone *else's* money — a husband's, a client's — than they are at managing their own. "We're not supposed to look like we can take care of ourselves," says Susannah, a southern belle with a fierce appreciation of the bottom line learned at her daddy's knee.

For years, Susannah did a great job managing her lover's business while she spent all her own income, putting nothing away. And then, with a booming business of his own, he left her. Today, she ruminates, "We can take care of others. We can be prosperous by virtue of a *man's* success, by manipulating him. We can be prosperous by luck, or by accident, or by marrying a rich man. But I don't feel I can be prosperous because of my own competence. I'm supposed to make myself useful, not rich."

At fifty-five, Doris looks back on her success — and how quick she was to give it up. Doris was valedictorian of her college class. She went on to have two marriages and two sons, and to create three successful businesses designing jewelry that she sold in top galleries. But she says, "Each time I'd have my business up and running, I'd meet a guy and become vanilla. Nothing. Nobody. I'd be there in case he wanted a lasagna made, or a shirt ironed. I let my business go in each case. It was like I threw my own talents and money-making abilities out the window. I think I assumed that my success would threaten him, and I'd end up alone."

WATCHING OUR MOTHERS

Women of our mothers' generation often paid the bills and worked out the budgets, but it wasn't *their* money they were taking care of. Nor were even they getting paid to take care of it. For all their hand-wringing and penny-pinching, their self-denial and tendency to spend on anyone but themselves, they often got little appreciation. And we, their daughters, looked at them and found their lives depressing. Not for us, we said. And yet, in strange ways, we end up duplicating their situations.

There is an uncanny connection between the way women view and handle money and their feelings about their mothers. Evelyn, whom we read about in the previous chapter, doles out twenties to her mother in Florida at a time when she herself is in the worst financial situation of her life. "She wanted me to pursue a career of artistic expression, but her view of this was very romanticized," recalls Evelyn. "And it was always in there that I would provide for her, through a man. I would be the one to get the big house and take care of her, in her old age, through the comfortable life I would one day have with my husband."

But if that was mama's plan, it backfired, leaving Evelyn almost as ill-equipped as she to fend for herself.

Phyllis spends lavishly, she says, so that she won't live like her mother, penurious to the end in her desire "not to be dependent" on anyone. (Phyllis doesn't understand this ardent desire older women have "not to be dependent" on anyone. She thinks it must have to do with the Great Depression.)

And Susan. The example set by Susan's mother left her feeling confused and abandoned. After supporting a family with eight children, Susan's physician father left a limited inheritance when he died. Susan, the youngest, was only fourteen. "My mother," she says, "took the money and ran."

Mother left Brooklyn and bought a house in Vermont with the

hundred thousand dollars from her husband's insurance policy. The children, including Susan, scattered hither and yon. Susan got into a special course and skipped the last year of high school. At sixteen she entered college with two plastic garbage bags of clothes and a milk crate of books. "It was sad not to have any-one take me, to get off at a bus station with no one picking me up and no clear idea of where I was going," she says now. "But it was also a great relief after the previous two years of turmoil."

This was a girl who'd been earning her own money since she was a child, and now she continued to do so with a vengeance. This was a survivor. At the point at which I heard her story, she was thirty-nine and feeling financially comfortable for the first time in her life. She'd done her graduate work, getting her Ph.D. in cultural anthropology while supporting herself with grants and part-time jobs. She'd faced the early postdoctoral years of discovering there were few decent jobs available for anthropologists — even those who'd been chosen for grants by the National Science Foundation. And now, finally, she was earning fifty-three thousand a year as a drug abuse researcher.

She was also thinking about why, for the past year, she'd been willing to fully support her boyfriend, a man who didn't seem to be able to get a job and hadn't been able to bring himself to look for part-time work.

A man who was "constitutionally" a good house husband, as Susan put it, though she didn't really need a house husband. What she needed was a man who was paying his own way so that she could afford to have a baby. She had moments of anger, but mostly, she says, she's outgrown these. She feels happy to have enough to share with someone else. It's not unlike how she denies her anger toward her mother for abandoning her when her father died.

She felt that her mother had done what she had to do. Susan's mother had grown up with money, and then met and married a man and had all those children. Dutifully, she fed them, ironed their clothes, and cleaned the house, all three floors of it, in a neighborhood where everyone else had servants. "My father had his medical practice in a poor and working-class neighborhood of Staten Island, where he'd grown up. People couldn't always pay him. Or they'd barter for services. We lived in this great neighborhood, but we couldn't afford to keep the house maintained. So we were like the local haunted house."

Susan says it must have been hard on her mother.

RAGE AND REVENGE: "I'LL MAKE YOU GIVE IT TO ME"

We might wonder what happens to the anger women experience over what happened to them during childhood and adolescence. Many repress their knowledge of being angry. Others vent it in misplaced aggression. Evelyn told me she was so angry over her father's objectifying treatment of her, the loss of the theatrical career that seemed possible when she was seventeen, her abandoning a practice as a massage therapist to become her husband's helper, that her attitude became, "I'll *make* you give it to me."

What follows is a conversation with a self-described feminist who, out of anger at her entire history, has made her husband pay. Rachel is a native New Yorker who in the seventies moved to Washington, D.C., where she married, had children, and worked part-time for a number of years. Today, she is a consultant for the Office of Substance Abuse Prevention for the federal government. But she hastens to tell me, right from the beginning, that her jobs have never interested her much.

"I was trained as a teacher. I did that for about ten years, ran a tennis club for about five years, and for the last twenty-five years have been working. . . . Basically, I was a full-time feminist activist, and none of the jobs was as relevant as my working in the women's movement."

"As a feminist activist, did you work as a volunteer?"

"I don't like the word 'volunteer.' "

"Were you getting paid?"

"No, most of the time not."

"Why don't you like the term 'volunteer'?"

"Because 'volunteer' connotes that people are putting Band-Aids on the sores instead of trying to kill the cancer."

Rachel conducts herself with a certain swagger, so that at first you think, "Here is a woman who knows how to take care of herself."

"In the early seventies I headed the Homemakers' Rights Task Force. It wasn't a salaried job. Mostly, I've been real lucky. We're upper middle class. But I own it."

"You own —"

"Everything! I own all the stock. I have all of the money. He has half of the house. I thought that was only fair."

"Everything's in your name, and not his?"

"Yeah."

"How did you manage that?"

"I said, 'It's mine.' I put it to him exactly the way it was. If I didn't work, I had no income and no pension. And if he wanted to work and I had to take care of the children, then I had to have some guaranteed security. So I own the insurance policies. He pays the premiums. They're on his life, because he's the major breadwinner. But I own them. If he dumped me on the street, as long as I could pay the premiums, I would still own the insurance on his life."

"If he decided to leave you —"

"I own it all."

"No matter what?"

"No matter what. So I've always been — I wouldn't say

financially independent. That's not quite what it is. But financially secure, yes; as secure as one can be."

Rachel says it was a consciousness-raising group in the seventies that convinced her she needed to protect herself.

"I kept listening to what women were getting stuck with. It didn't make any difference what they were promised, they always got stuck. So I changed my name, legally, back to my maiden name, because I found out I had no credit. That's the way it was then, before the laws changed; my whole credit record went under his name. So I changed that. I opened bank accounts in my own name, so I had credit."

She felt that getting a full-time job, however, was more problematic. "I *wanted* to go back to work, but the kids had to come home for lunch. So I organized the community to get a lunch program in the schools."

It seems clear that Rachel was able to work part-time and as a volunteer because she didn't have to rely solely on her own income. She persists in seeing this, however, not as an advantage, but as a liability, one for which she is due just compensation.

"Do you imagine yourself always being married?"

"I don't see any reason to get rid of Ben. He doesn't get in my way. But if he gets sick and old and infirm, I'm going to put him in a home. He knows that. I've already told him that."

Though Rachel likes to present herself as tough and savvy, her facade of invulnerability gives her away.

"At this point in your life, do you have any sense of disappointment, of having missed out on anything?"

"There's been a sense of anger for a long, long time," she says, and now she looks sad. "Probably that's what fuels me, that *who* I could have been, or *what* I could have been *was* never, and would never be."

"And what was that?"

"I don't even know any more. I think back to the things I wanted when I was a little girl. I had a lot of big dreams, but I didn't *do* any of them. And that makes me angry. Because what I've come to realize is, I *could* have. I mean, I have the abilities to do those things, but the opportunities to do those things, I never would have had. And if I *had* gotten anywhere, the price I would have to have paid wouldn't have been worth it."

Why, I wonder, did the picture always look so bleak to her? Had she never seen other women managing families and professions?

"The role models I had were always 'yes, buts.' My mother and everybody else were schoolteachers. They were professionals, but they always had a family that they took care of, too. And the profession was not primary. And the family was always — whatever. So those role models were . . . compromised. I knew a woman doctor when I was growing up; it didn't matter. It was always a 'yes, but.' I don't see that that's terribly much different now. I still think role models that exist today have 'yes, buts' attached to them. Nobody judges a woman by what she does. They always ask who she's married to. Or does she have children. That's a way of detracting from her. I mean all we remember about Geraldine Ferraro was that she cried. Or was it the other one? Pat Schroeder. Pat Schroeder cried. Geraldine Ferraro got blamed for her husband. It wasn't who she was or what she was or what she had accomplished or where she had come from. It had to do with her husband, who was a big-time troublemaker."

"You're saying those were put-downs?"

"Put-downs."

What about the woman she'd mentioned earlier in our conversation, a childhood friend who became a lawyer? She, too, Rachel saw as an exception that proved nothing.

"Marcy Blackstone became a lawyer because she *had* to become a lawyer. Her father died and her mother raised her. She had this single focus, that she never wanted to be in the position her mother'd been in. But Marcy Blackstone is a loophole woman.

She's one of the ones you can point to and say, 'She did it.' There are lots of women like that, but . . ."

Somewhere beneath Rachel's monumental system of defenses lay a kernel of bitterness, and finally it revealed itself.

"I don't know if you ever had anything like this said to you directly. I once complained to a math professor at Queens College about Hyram Milford getting a grade higher than I did, when I did better than he on the exam. The professor told me flat-out that Hyram Milford was going to get into medical school and I wasn't. And that's when my grades at college became a straight C. And I didn't figure out for another ten years that the reason I lost interest in school was because of what that professor had said to me. But instead of being angry and putting it out in the world, the way I learned to do later, I turned it in on myself."

"So you have this anger that you might have become something different if things had been different when you were younger."

"I made a conscious choice in my mid-thirties not to go back to school. What I chose then was to take the anger and become a political activist. That's what I chose to do. Rather than become President of the United States, which is really what I wanted to be."

"Where are you at this point in your life? Do you have any fears about the future?"

"Not about money. My fear is that it's not real."

"What's not real?"

"My approach to life, my attitude."

"Are you afraid that all of a sudden it may turn around and start looking different?"

"Yeah. Am I crazy? The only thing I worry about is getting sick, and that's not something I can control."

It's said that those who fear the future most are those who feel they haven't fully lived. Women who try to gain control in their lives by emulating the power-dominance behavior they've witnessed in men end up not developing their own talents. In the paranoid scramble not to be taken advantage of, they give up on their dreams, becoming hardened and cynical. Inside, there is always that little fear: *Maybe it's not real. Maybe my putative strength is only a facade. Maybe I've gone against myself.*

Chapter 9

BUILDING YOUR OWN CASTLE: GETTING OVER THE FEAR OF FINANCIAL INDEPENDENCE

When I think of beginning to invest, the first thing that comes to mind is that I have to find someone good, someone I can trust, to invest *for* me. But how can I when I believe there is no one who's trustworthy? The whole system is a crapshoot, that is. (If you can't control it, you can't trust it.)

But I know that people make money in the stock market, and not just tycoons, ordinary people. In fact, more and more, ordinary people are convinced that they can make their money grow by investing and that the system works.

This leads me to two conclusions. I have a major issue with trust. If I'm ever going to gather the courage to start with this, I'm going to have to go after more information on the market, learning how it works, why it works. I need to treat it like any other subject I research.

My reticence to do this shows the influence of my father, who thought the market was fraudulent, something like today's pyramid schemes. People who "played" the market were moneygrubbing and foolhardy. My fear of investing has to do with my dependence on my father. His way is the right way. *He* is the one I have to rely on for protection and guidance. I can't rely on myself or anyone else, only him.

Whenever I think of putting aside money and investing it, I feel tremendously inadequate. The prospect is not exciting for the simple reason that I expect failure. There is a great mystery here, which eludes me, the mystery of turning risk into probability. I feel safer, more likely to survive, if I don't invest.

And yet I *know*, because it's talked about everywhere, that if I don't invest, I won't have enough money. If I don't invest, I won't even survive. I'll be out on the streets, penniless, at sixty-five. I'm so convinced I can't succeed at investing I can't bring myself to try. And so, emotionally, I'm trapped. I tell myself I've done all I can. If I don't have enough money for my future, what can I do? I blame the business, the media, the producers (who are too young), the publisher, the publicist, my agent — everyone. To some extent, all of these *are* involved. But above and beyond all of this there had remained a simple truth: I don't fight for myself.

I have finally allowed myself to see that I could end up in dire straits if I don't change, take hold. There *isn't* any more time. Money needs time in order to breed more money. I have just enough time, now, to invest, and thereby protect myself. If I don't, I'm consigning myself to anxiety and fear from here on out. It's *entirely* in my hands.

FEAR OF INVESTING

"I don't like it that I have to take the money I've really worked hard for and put it away instead of spending it, so I'll have money when I'm sixty-five or seventy. But if I don't do it," says Molly, whose day of reckoning came when she turned forty, "there's not going to be anything there."

It was not until she began changing her relationship to money that she started questioning her rescue fantasies. "I've given my-self a budget for the first time in my life. The reason I never had a savings account was partly because I was afraid that if I had one, I would really save. It was that part of me that says, 'Why do I have to do it all? Why doesn't someone come along and take care of me?' There's not much there yet, but I like having the savings."

It often takes a crisis — job loss, illness, divorce, impending retirement — to prompt women to start saving and investing. And rather than make high-return investments in stocks, we tend to keep our nest egg fairly liquid and available.[1] One reason for this may be our ongoing caretaking role. We tend to want to keep our savings available in case it's needed for the household. A Merrill Lynch survey found that women were more likely to save for their children's education, a home, or a car, while men saved for retirement. Only 30 percent of those aged forty-five to sixty-four — compared with 47 percent of the men — were saving for retirement. Of those who were saving, the average portfolio of the women was $25,700, while the men's was double that — $52,500.[2]

At New York dinner parties, lately, people are frantically trying to come up with The Number. "The figure tossed out as the amount of savings necessary for a comfortable retirement: three million dollars. That's the myth currently causing insomnia," writes Leslie Dormen, in *Mirabella*.[3]

" 'You won't need that much,' " she was told by Ginger Apple-garth, personal finance correspondent for CNBC, who hears from a lot of women "suddenly overcome by fear of turning into a bag lady." But the figure Applegarth recommends is still high. Assuming that a woman has no pension plan or other significant assets but can still count on Social Security, how much must she invest annually, beginning at the age of thirty-five or forty-five or fifty-five, in order to retire at sixty-five and have enough to generate a pretax income of $80,000 a year?

According to Applegarth, you'd need at least $800,000. To amass that amount — and then leave it untouched while living on the 10 percent it can earn in interest and dividends — here's what you'd need to invest *annually*: at thirty-five, $4,424; at forty-five, $12,696; at fifty-five, $45,632.

However, how much interest you earn is crucial, and some financial planners advise counting on only 7.5 percent. At that rate, the amount you'd need to have invested at retirement zaps to a little over a million dollars. At 7.5 percent, here's what you'd need to get your $80,000 annually, starting at sixty-five: at thirty-five, $9,596; at forty-five, $22,913; at fifty-five, $70,138.

Needless to say, the longer you wait to get started, the more gargantuan the amount you have to come up with each year.

" 'I'm totally depressed,' " Dormen told Applegarth.

" 'You're not alone,' " said Applegarth.

Almost 60 percent of Americans in their forties, including those with household incomes of over $75,000, think they may out-live their savings. At the same time they feel too discouraged and paralyzed to do much about it.[4]

GETTING STARTED

Historically, women have been taught that "preserving principal" is the best financial strategy they can hope for. *Don't take chances; don't live off your capital* (if, in fact, you were lucky enough to have been left any). In part, the idea was that we couldn't be trusted to do anything creative with our money. This attitude has prevailed until quite recently.

In the early eighties I had an accountant who advised me not to attempt buying a co-op in New York. He said I should keep my money liquid in case my kids needed it. I knew I couldn't afford to buy in Manhattan, but why not go across the bridge, to Brooklyn? There I bought a garden duplex. Twelve months later I sold it, at a profit of $57,000.

To achieve this, I had gone against the advice of the experts by setting an asking price higher than any suggested by three local real estate agencies. It was my conviction that the higher I started, within reason, the higher I'd end up. The outcome vindicated, gloriously, my assessment of the situation. This was my first experience of playing financial hardball and I can tell you the sense of power it gave me was thrilling.

The willingness to take calculated risks has become essential for creating money in the current economy. Anyone staying in CDs and money market funds hoping she'll again hit the 13 to 15 percent levels of the early eighties has a long wait, experts say. At least through the nineties, interest rates aren't expected to rise past 8 percent. "If a woman pays 40 percent of her income in federal, state and local taxes (as is common in New York City) that yield drops to only 4.2 percent — not enough to keep pace with a 6 percent inflation rate, let alone to amass new wealth for an improved standard of living or retirement," says a senior research analyst at Merrill Lynch.[5]

Women have learned to earn, but most haven't learned to manage. Today, being responsible with money requires aggressiveness. As long as interest rates remain low, a fixed-income portfolio isn't going to supply the rate of growth needed to stay ahead of inflation. A percentage of a woman's money has to be in growth investments where there's some risk if she's going to be able to create enough money to protect her future. Psychologically, that means being able to tolerate anxiety — the anxiety involved in giving up the money to the investment *and* the anxiety involved in riding out market volatility.

There's a conundrum here. Today, in order to be financially *conservative* (which is what we used to mean by taking responsibility for oneself), one has to fly. It means leaving the realm of the "feminine," if, by that, we ever meant playing it safe. We can't just be good girls, paying our bills on time, to be counted financially responsible. We have to use our money to create more, and this involves calculated risk taking. It involves learning whatever's necessary in order to be able to make these calculations, at least in a general way.

Nor can we rise to the occasion by dumping everything into the hands of a broker without in the least understanding the fundamentals of investing. It leaves us too vulnerable. " 'I once had a broker who urged me to buy put options just before the market took off,' " recalls the controller of a shipping company. " 'At the time I didn't realize that his recommendation made no sense. The puts expired worthless.' "[6]

" 'No matter what I do with money, I feel I'm doing something wrong,' " the sixty-year-old vice president of a chemical company admitted. At the Merrill Lynch seminars for women discussed in the previous chapter, a woman who kept all her money in a savings account and owed more on her credit cards than she'd saved, confessed that her main goal was " 'not to have to worry' " but she didn't believe she could accomplish this.

As the seminars progressed, it became apparent that the women were paralyzed by their ambivalence. "Asked to explore what money means to them, many women said 'freedom': or 'independence,' with an air of longing," Anne Conover Heller wrote, reporting on the seminars for a women's magazine.[7]

But why were these teachers, corporate executives, entrepreneurs, and other professionals so limited in their ability to act?

Gradually, during the course of their meetings, they began to see that to become free and independent meant they had to be willing to take responsibility — which, as one of them pointed out, meant " 'giving up the fantasy that someone is going to come along and take care of me.' " She added: " 'I'm fifty; I'm in the second half now. It's time.' "

Gay-Darlene Bidart, a widowed painter and writer for whom money had long been " 'a moral puzzle' " — she had never felt she deserved it — learned, at the seminars, to stop feeling guilty about money. " 'Women were invited to come up to the front of the room and claim what was theirs: the right to learn, the right to *have,* empowerment. Don't hold back, we were told.' "

By the end of the four seminars, these women had gotten the message: ambivalence is wasteful. Greater affluence is a perfectly reasonable goal, and a knowledge of sound investing is there for the asking. " 'Learning not to be afraid has changed my life," said Bidart. "For once I feel free to claim what's mine.' "

One of the first rules of investing is to start early. If you've managed to reach midlife without investing, the first rule is to start, period. The vast majority of women I interviewed for my book on women in their fifties, *Red Hot Mamas,* had done no investing at all. Often, they believed, "It's too late." But if you start now, no matter *when* now is, you'll end up with something; if you don't start, you won't. It's that simple.

One thing to get over is the Spilled Milk Syndrome. Occasionally I used to pick up *Money* magazine when there was nothing else to read on an airplane and I would find the story of some chipper young nurse who'd started investing $2.50 a week in a mutual fund when she was twenty years old and now, at the ripe old age of thirty-five, was a millionaire. It made me feel like I'd lost my chance.

But there are more positive ways of assessing such a story. No matter how old she is when she starts, a woman investing $5,000 a year at an average annual yield of 10 percent and paying 35 percent in taxes on the interest (assuming a 5 percent inflation rate), will have, at the end of ten years, $78,057.61. At the end of forty, she'll have $1,015,732.80. I used to read such figures and rue the fact that I hadn't begun forty years earlier instead of acknowledging there was a great deal I could do for myself if I began now.

"You must be willing to put yourself on the line and be wrong," says psychologist Ruth Ross. "We too often decide that the man will risk — what we don't see is that the man then develops the skills, earning power, and confidence that is created in taking the risk. The non-risker just gets older."[8]

INVESTMENT CLUBS: WOMEN TEACHING THEMSELVES

"Women are just as capable as men, the major difference being that if a man doesn't like to manage the family money, it's not socially acceptable for him to say so," observes the noted financial writer Jane Bryant Quinn in an interview in *Hudson Valley* magazine. "Whereas a woman can say, 'Oh, I hate all those investments and stuff, I don't understand it,' and it's considered cute. I think it's very destructive. It takes away from a woman's self-confidence, her self-esteem, and it makes her dependent in a way she shouldn't be."[9]

It wasn't until my second meeting with the Overlook Mountain Money Managers that I saw how influenced I'd been by cultural stereotypes. My bias about women's ability to invest had held even after reading about the success of the Beardstown Ladies. It came bubbling to the surface when some woman with a breathy voice left a hasty message on my answering machine with no return phone number and only the first name of the person at whose office the meetings were held. Typical! I was tempted to forget the whole thing. What could I learn from a group of silly females playing tiddledywinks in the market?

But I made myself go to the meeting and was struck by the intelligence of the women and the orderly way in which they conducted business. That month there was nothing particularly exciting on the agenda, but I learned a lot. The group had been organized for a year and a half and had spent a year studying up before beginning to invest. A rotating stock selection committee researched purchase possibilities and brought the information back to the group to consider. So far, the group had bought three stocks, all of which were making money.

The second meeting had more edge. We were going to discuss whether or not to dump Albertson's, the largest grocery store chain in America. There was a bit of an emergency atmosphere at the meeting, since it had recently come to light that five thousand employees had filed claims that they were forced by Albertson's to work off-the-clock (meaning they got paid only straight time for overtime work). Our group was committed to socially conscious investing. It was also committed to making money.

A call to the union seemed to confirm our fears. "This is the worst case of this sort of thing I've ever seen," the union representative told Maya. Maya, in her late forties, was in the process of adopting her second child, had her own educational video business, a dog, a cat, a live-in lover, a house she'd just purchased, and a bunch of notes she'd taken down from her phone conversation with the union guy. He'd said four class action suits were in the works. And Albertson's prior reputation was not exactly unsullied. A year earlier the company had paid $29 million to settle a race- and sex-discrimination suit in California. *Newsweek* was due to come out with a story on the company in a week, the union man said. A fall in the stock price seemed imminent.

Someone had brought in an issue of *Boise*, an alternative newspaper in Albertson's home town, with a scathing story of the heinous happenings since "old Joe," the company founder, had died. We passed the paper around and thought of old Joe turning over in his grave upon learning how much had gone to the dogs in the mere four years since he'd died. We were unmoved. A call to Albertson's damage control team had not uncovered any hardcore evidence that they were being unjustly accused. The PR man said only that the reports were "grossly exaggerated." He did not say the claims against the company were unfounded. At the moment, our stock was $4 a share higher than when we bought it. The mandate seemed clear: sell now to avoid loss (and be socially conscious in the process).

The problem was, we didn't have a quorum that night. We weren't even sure we could have a meeting, much less vote on something. Only seven women were in attendance, plus me — and

I couldn't vote, since I was still new to the group. What to do? If we waited until next month's meeting, the stock would likely have crashed, and there we'd be with a thousand shares of socially unconscious trash on our hands.

There ensued a scramble to look up the by-laws and amendments. Several women had brought proxy votes with them. Could we use proxies to vote when we didn't have enough people even to have a meeting? Clearly not, if we played it straight. The by-laws said proxy votes could be used for business, but not to make up a quorum. "This is it," I thought. "They'll play by the rules and lose the chance to sell for a profit."

I was wrong.

Several points were brought up. All members of the group had been apprised of the Albertson situation before the meeting. Among the seven who'd attended, the wish to sell was unanimous. If we *didn't* sell, there was a good chance we'd be sorry. We were being handicapped by by-laws that had been written long before we could have contemplated such a dilemma. Discussion of the law on how many needed to be present for a meeting to occur should be on the agenda of the next meeting. In the meantime — in the interests of the group, whose commitment was to educate itself and earn money investing in a socially conscious way — we were selling!

Judy, tall and athletic-looking, wearing a T-shirt, sneakers, and a mop of curly white hair, carefully wrote down, for the minutes, our rationale for going against the by-laws. Someone made a motion to end the meeting. It was seconded. Next day, the deal would be executed by Rita, our broker at Merrill Lynch. With fresh cash in our coffers we'd be ready to start thinking about another stock.

I went out into the early summer evening and got in my car. I rolled back the sunroof to let in the light of a full moon, and drove home with a feeling of exhilaration. It seemed it was actually going to be possible to learn about this stuff. And I would be learning it not from men, but from women!

Compared to New York's 008 Investment Club, which began several years ago, the Overlook Mountain Money Managers looked positively cozy. But like OMMM, the women in the 008 club, with high-profile jobs in fashion and real estate, board positions at Mount Sinai Hospital and the Guggenheim, have followed the lead of the Beardstown Ladies. " 'Whether you come from Beardstown or you come from New York, you're in the same boat,' " Diane Terman Felenstein, the club's founder and president, told the *New York Times.* " 'Women should be caretakers of their own financial future.' "10

It's a concept that at last is catching on. When thinking about one's own financial security, husbands and boyfriends — even rich ones — aren't to be counted on. The 008 group included Carol Safir, a real estate agent whose husband was New York City's fire commissioner, a woman married to a powerful takeover lawyer who asked not to be identified and does not vote on stocks to avoid conflicts with her husband's business, and Marilyn Hope Crockett, a broker at Paine Webber. Crockett offers her story as a prime example of a Cinderella who got radicalized. When she was forty, she broke up with a man she had lived with for nineteen years and realized for the first time that she had little financial security. Her job-related retirement money, at the time, would have amounted to $100 a month. Now she specializes in women's investment decisions and feels she's on a mission to get women to stabilize their own futures.

It's the edge of what could be a revolution: women have started to realize that they haven't been cutting it. Although the group's president, Diane Felenstein, has owned her own public relations firm for two decades, she had only recently come to recognize how little she knew about investing and estate planning. And she was watching other women — those, in particular, who were recently widowed or divorced — struggling with the most fundamental aspects of finance. "I can't believe how deficient we are," she told the *Times* reporter, incredulously.

Investment groups constitute a serious attempt to make up for the deficit. Among the 17,004 investment clubs that belong to the National Association of Investors Corporations, nearly 42 percent are all women, 46 percent are mixed, and just 13 percent are all men. The all-men percentage is half of what it was ten years ago.

A big reason why these clubs have become so popular among women (and why the Beardstown Ladies' guidebook became a best-seller) is fear of the financial difficulty that many women, even some who have been well off, fall into in old age. Thus, learning to invest has become, for women in particular, a mandate.

The 008 Investment Group is one sleek-looking bunch of dames. Short skirts revealing long legs. Do's. Consistently straight white teeth. Women who take care of themselves. Women who, in an earlier time, would have been content merely to be taken care of. Among its founding members, for example, were Carol Levin and Pat Weinbach, whose husbands respectively head Revlon and Arthur Andersen. The minute she suggested forming an investment group, says Felenstein, "the answering machine was full of messages. It didn't matter whether we were single, widowed, married, or divorced. We were all seeking knowledge."

To get it, they were willing to pay annual dues of $1,000 and pay $100 each month. (OMMM requires $25 a month and has no dues.) With an initial investment of about $30,000 in six stocks, they soon were up and running. But they rely on information of specific members more than some groups do. Crockett, for example, is not the group's broker, but she keeps them on their toes with questions. Have the company's earnings increased over the past three quarters? What's the outlook for a company's industry?

She also lines up expert speakers for the group and formed committees to research different industries. The group is lucky to have among its members someone as informed as Crockett, but there's a potential downside. The National Association of Investors Corporation, a nonprofit group that represents the clubs, cautions against using any particular member as a crutch. If there is "a perceived financial expert" in a club, warn the N.A.I.C. guidelines, "in all probability other members will lean on such an individual and know no more after years of membership than they did upon joining!"

Skipping over the hard stuff is another temptation for novices. For example, this particular group got glassy-eyed as a Paine Webber analyst gave a presentation of annual reports and didn't wake up until she began reading names off the firm's "buy" list. There's a tendency to go with what you know — or think you know. At first the women were most enthusiastic about the companies they liked as consumers and businesswomen. Home Depot was an early selection — "an emotional decision," said one member. "All of us understood the company."

But the understanding had a romantic tinge. No one could answer Ms. Crockett's question about why Home Depot's earnings had recently fallen. Eventually the stocks had to be sold at a loss.

Women's close-up observations of how certain manufacturers are doing is often valuable, on the other hand. Carole Black, a fifty-nine-year-old divorced retiree from California noticed several years ago that her grandsons were absolutely fanatical about having Reebok sneakers. Carole, taking this as a clue that Reebok was becoming a major fashion fad, analyzed the company's annual report, read everything she could about the firm, and talked to her broker and even her health-club instructor. Then she bought Reebok at $16 a share. Nine months later she sold it at $27.75.[11]

A broker at Smith Barney told *Money*, " 'Most of the time when a male client has an idea, he's heard it at the office, at the club or from a friend. With my female clients, it's a company or a product they've had some experience with. And generally, that's the smarter way to go.' "12

On a hot morning in August, the 008's sat around a conference table clutching containers of coffee. The issue for discussion was CSX Corporation, a transportation company. The decision of whether or not to buy had been high on the agenda for the July meeting, but all the time had been taken up by the guest speaker — a man who'd droned on so long they didn't have time to make a decision about the stock. " 'We were ready to stab him,' " said Diane Felenstein.13

Ready to stab him mentally, perhaps, but compliant in the here and now. The women hadn't held to their own agenda, so that a month later, at their August meeting, they were scrambling. The stock had risen $7 since early July, to $82 a share. They wanted to buy it anyhow. " 'What's the high and low for the year?' " Marilyn Crocket asked.

" 'Give me a moment,' " said Carol Greenberg, looking it up. Unfortunately, the stock was then trading near its fifty-two-week high — not a great time to buy with a profit in mind. Had they bought in July . . .

" 'I'm getting heartburn,' " said Ms. Felenstein. " 'I'm going to get physically sick.' "

In spite of misgivings, the women voted to buy at $82.

BEYOND THERAPY

Our psyches are affected by the social messages that bombard us, but they are also affected by the hidden conflicts we develop to defend ourselves against what's negative and disturbing. These hidden conflicts, I believe, are as important for women to understand as the social conditions that brought them about in the first place. We *incorporate* social conditioning into our psyches and it becomes invisible. We don't even know that we're reacting to, building our lives around, falsehoods.

Thus, while it's important to address the ways in which women have been hurt by social injustice, we need also to change the ways in which blind conditioning hurts us *psychologically*. We must face our defenses, which may have allowed us to survive emotionally but do not permit us to thrive.

More and more therapists are recognizing that overspending, debting, and even the compulsive fear of investing have much in common with addiction processes. The individual becomes reliant on spending for feelings of well-being. Serious negative consequences ensue, which the person denies. She may not deny that there *are* consequences, but she sees them as anomalous — a function of some circumstance, but nothing, certainly, that has anything to do with *her*.

Like a problem with substance abuse, reliance on debt builds gradually, its damages, for the longest time, invisible. Spending and spending seems normal, necessary. Few of us have "enough." Few save.

If anything, my first analyst was comfortable with this way of thinking. Certainly he didn't *dis*courage it. I think he viewed my spending as a healthy expansion. To spend was tantamount to saying, "There's more where this came from. I believe in myself, my skills, talent, energy — my ability to keep generating income." To hoard would have been like saying, "I don't trust myself. It could all dry up tomorrow."

Meanwhile, the analyst was busy expanding his own horizons. He was buying up properties on the Lower East Side and selling them when the time was right. I sensed that he was losing interest in the more mundane things of life — if not his patients, at least the money he made from them. He had long since stopped billing me. For years he presented me with a bill on the last session of the month. Then one day it stopped. Initially, he said it was because he'd moved his office and was disorganized.

In the beginning I asked him regularly for the bill; he'd apologize and promise to get it together. After a while I stopped asking. His seeming casualness became to me a sign that he knew I was earning enough to come up with the money whenever he asked for it. I was successful, that is, and he trusted me. Eventually he'd say, "Oh, by the way, you owe me fifteen hundred," and I'd write a check on the spot. We were two who didn't have to worry about money. We were hot.

By the end, I was angry about what was happening; very angry. What had changed in our relationship that wasn't being spoken about? Why had he allowed this to go on? I confronted him a number of times. Finally I asked him if he realized what the effect was on *me* of essentially not being charged for my sessions. He said that actually he hadn't thought about the effect on me. It was one of those truths the analyst might better have kept to himself.

Finally, it was the way money was being avoided that made me see there was no point in continuing treatment with this man. By the time I left, he had accorded me thousands of dollars worth of sessions. Briefly, I thought, "Should I try to estimate the amount that's accrued and give it to him?" I decided not. It was his problem, and it had affected our sessions negatively. One of the effects was that I felt more colleague than patient. I began feeling I had to listen to him as much as he listened to me. He started bringing up problems with his children and asking what I thought. I enjoyed that. It supported a defense I'd relied on since childhood, that of feeling "special" as a substitute for not feeling loved.

Later, I discussed what had happened with other therapists. One said that what I'd experienced with the analyst was a form of abuse. (I thought that was a bit extreme.) The other said, "He stopped feeling that what he was giving you in the therapy was worth any money."

That seemed closer to the mark. Something about his own sense of values had shifted or perhaps simply emerged. Although he'd mentioned his real estate projects only obliquely, I still sensed that he'd become a wheeler-dealer in New York real estate. I imagined that fed him in ways that doing therapy with a woman he'd been treating for years didn't — or didn't any longer. I had made my big gains already, after all. Other of his long-term patients had as well, I surmised. He was on to bigger fish.

(Ten years after I left this analyst, my daughter pointed out an article in the *New York Times* describing a real estate development firm belonging to a psychoanalyst that he and a partner had begun in the early eighties. It was my analyst. Since then, they had purchased a total of twenty properties, including nightclubs and restaurants — an average of two buildings a year, I figured. It was like something out of a Woody Allen film!)

Coming to grips with the *me-ness* of a problem with debting is sobering, and it doesn't happen as the result of one swift shaft of insight. The neurotic impulses that have come into play are so myriad, and so intertwined, disentangling them can take months. Only sturdy and regular self-assessment will break through the morass of old habits and entrenched beliefs. Generally, this means tracking — day-to-day, moment-to-moment — our thoughts and feelings and behaviors in relation to spending.

Therapy has not been notoriously helpful with people's money problems. Today, therapists will often tell a patient with a pattern of compulsive behavior to get into a twelve-step program. They know they have a better chance of doing effective therapy if the patient isn't using. "Using" doesn't just refer to substances that alter mood, but behaviors that have the same effect. It has only recently come to light that compulsive debting is a form of *using*.

LOSING EVERYTHING

Profound loss creates profound vulnerability. Out of that, if we can admit the need for help, healing can come.

It was shocking to lose everything it had taken me years to put together: two houses, beautiful land, my studio. The furniture. The retirement fund that was pushing a quarter of a million, now empty. Even my old Saab, which I could drive proudly when I had property and substance, now seemed vulnerable and untrustworthy. If it broke down, I had no money for expensive repairs.

Once the IRS moved in, it all happened quickly. I mounted the energy to sell the houses. The IRS — or at least its agent, Mark Hinds — was pleased. He approved of my effort and focus. He also considered that everything that there was to be gotten had been gotten. But once the closings occurred, I had nothing more to distract me. It was then that I had to begin facing what had happened to me — and what could happen again, I felt quite sure, if I didn't change.

I had been stripped of the accoutrements of success and had returned to the basics. Who was I without the trappings? Could I be happy without them? I had worked so long and hard for a good space in which to write. My beautiful, high-ceilinged studio with its books and tall, custom-built shelves, air-conditioning when I needed it, the sound of the stream when I didn't — everything organized, everything where it belonged. Except that I had not been organized, not in any internal sense.

I had been trying to build my own life, separate from L., separate from my grown children. During the first year, not a day went by that I didn't say to myself, at some point, "I am alone." It was as if I had to keep repeating it to make myself believe it. For the first time in my life empty days rose up before me, demanding that I — and I alone — give them structure and meaning. I would sit at the big kitchen table and watch the birds. I reveled in the silence but also feared it. The small church on the hill, off in the distance, became a steadying sight, its evening chimes a reminder that someone was nearby. Not that there weren't people in the houses up and down the road, but they were locked behind their doors, or at least that's how I thought of them, as I was locked behind mine.

Not that the lock was physical. I had taken trips to Europe without locking my doors. The distancing I experienced was psychological. I imagined units, couples, families, lovers — and myself alone. Time passed. I had built things to remind myself of my place in the world. The day after my last child graduated from college, a team of gardeners had arrived with three dozen peony bushes to plant in my driveway circle. It was a big operation. They came in their pickups and broken-down Chevies and soon were turning up the earth, digging huge holes. I stood with my father, watching them from the upstairs window. "It's something, isn't it?" I said.

He turned and walked away. Earlier that morning, when he'd asked if he could come with me to the store, I'd snapped, "No. I haven't even had my coffee yet." I was stressed, having just returned from a promotion trip in Europe and hosted a graduation party for my daughter, and I was leaving immediately to give a commencement address at my alma mater. The simple request of my father, always needy, felt like the final straw. My parents were in the way. I took no pleasure in having them. I was functioning like an automaton, the beleaguered matriarch who, one way or another, was supporting a lot of people and getting little in return. Doing my duty. Going through the motions.

Loss crashes through all that, strips you of illusion, peels away your defenses. Within six months I had given up my lover, and also my analyst of fifteen years, and was struggling to make it on my own. I tried doing it the way I had done everything else, triumphing over stress through sheer strength of will. But this time, the old strategy wasn't working. My father was not impressed by hordes of landscapers transforming my yard. He was stung by the inhumanness of my response. I had pushed myself to my limits. My brittleness was no longer defensible.

Loss creates vulnerability. When everything went, I had to recognize my vulnerability, my powerlessness, without the help of others, to survive. I had spent my life pretending that it was possible to live otherwise.

SURRENDER

There is this notion of "surrender" that sticks in the craw of the uninitiated. Surrender one's control? Admit powerlessness? Give it up? It sounds weak, New Agey. It sounds victimized. Why should one have to prostrate oneself on the dirt floor of Debtors (or any other) Anonymous just to deal with some problem behavior?

None of this, of course, is actually what is meant by surrender. Surrender, if anything, is the natural condition. We simply lose sight of it as we go through life, growing defenses we think we need in order to get by. We become judgmental, evaluating others according to a hierarchical scheme that puts us on top. We revere control, the idea of being on top of things. And we come to believe that we can not only take actions, we can control the outcome of those actions. We believe that in order to get through the barriers that others — life! — have put before us, we need to barrel full-steam ahead with the sheer power of our will. We become veterans at secretly trying to get our way. We keep our agendas hidden. We manipulate. Distrust of others becomes savvy. We never take anyone at face value but look always for the hidden other, the unspoken motive. As distrust of others builds, so does distrust of ourselves. Life becomes a complex web of suspicions and projections. It gets hard to know where reality ends and our projections of our own values onto others begins.

The odd thing is that throughout this process of moral deterioration we still think we have the values we grew up with. We think we believe in love, goodness, concern for the welfare of others. We don't. We have lost this. We can't have others' welfare at heart because we have given them too much power. We fear them. In a sense, we have created monsters and we spend our lives dodging and bobbing, in the hope of escaping their evil wills. But it is our own will to power that does us in, and we no longer have any way of knowing that.

This will to control is what we are up against when we first begin to take on a destructive pattern of compulsive behavior. Perhaps the most brilliant insight of Bill Wilson, the founder of AA, was recognizing that an addiction doesn't stand alone, to be cleft neatly from one's life like a clean-edged tumor. By the time it has become visibly destructive, addiction has already intertwined itself amongst the other threads of one's personality, and it will not go away until the sham of our self-defensiveness is seen for what it is: a destructive strategy that keeps us isolated and alone.

Unlike therapy, which carefully and over time attempts to unravel the threads of self-delusion, the twelve-step approach urges relinquishing the posture of control the way some people teach swimming: jump into the pool. *Give it up.*

"But my sister needs me. She won't stop drinking without my help," says the "co-dependent" one, who is considered as addicted as the user.

Give it up.

"I can get control of this; I'll just cut back."

Give it up.

"Surely I can keep one credit card, just for emergencies?"

Give it up.

For me, as for others entering a twelve-step group for the first time, the mandate seemed radical, and even dangerous. How can you *stop* advising your sick child? *Stop* paying your drinking spouse's debts? *Stop* making debt payments because you don't have enough money and making the payments will force you into further debt? How, in short, can you get off the merry-go-round?

By getting off the merry-go-round. That is the radical message of AA, and CoDa, and Al Anon, and DA. You stop by stopping. You get off. You say, "I'm outta here."

Recognizing how overwhelming this can seem, groups like Debtors Anonymous advise that change be approached One Day at a Time. It is fine and solacing advice. And it is realistic. To know what you're doing and why, on almost a molecular level — and *that* is the degree of consciousness necessary for this sort of change — you have to manage life meticulously. But a calm, reasonable existence — the oft-prayed-for serenity — isn't something you *will* into being. It comes by means of a process: by admitting to being out of control, by committing yourself to change, by documenting your day-to-day behavior, and by sharing your goals and actions with others and asking for help from those who've been through it before you.

When I sold my house to satisfy the IRS, I wasn't sure where I would live. There are always plenty of overpriced rentals on the market in Woodstock, places that would make you resent shelling out the money. Two women, friends of a friend, had an old house in the village that they weren't using for the winter. They rented it, furnished, for $500 a month. I thought, How wonderful! This will give me a breathing space while I start to get my affairs in order.

I put the furniture I'd managed to salvage in storage, bringing only my desk and computer into the rented house. One of the oldest in the village, it had its charms: small, low-ceilinged rooms, a fireplace, beautiful old floors. But it had been neglected. It took me a week to clean it and rout the rodents.

The house was right on the road, as old homes often are. From seven in the morning until eleven at night, the noise of cars outside the house was constant. I tried to ignore it, to scold myself into submission. For nine years I'd lived with only the sounds of the stream, the snorting of deer, raccoons mating in the spring. My soul resonated to silence, to sun, and to the view of peaceful, open vistas. Clearly, I had been very fortunate. Now there were neighbors close on either side and no views from the windows. Because of the traffic, I couldn't let out my cats, who paced importunately and took to peeing in my workroom to show their displeasure. I rolled up the women's Native American rugs and blankets and tried to concentrate on my work, but I felt confined, hemmed in.

During that long winter I entertained twice, serving coffee and bagels for breakfast in front of the fire. There was no table. I began living in the same old jeans and sweatshirt to cut down on trips to the Laundromat. I didn't miss the dishwasher, the washer-dryer, my big new refrigerator. I missed the silence, and on Christmas Eve morning the bleakness I was feeling was heightened by a whim of Mother Nature's. At eight in the morning a freak storm hit Woodstock. I awoke to loud cracks and the smell of burning electrical wires. "Gaby," I yelled to my daughter, who was visiting. "Get up, get up." We were supposed to drive, that morning, to my son's house, in Massachusetts.

We looked out onto the street from my bedroom window and saw that lines were down, flares of fire sizzling at their ends. Firemen had cordoned off the block and weren't permitting traffic in or out. A huge old tree was lying across the road. People were standing outside in their yards with mugs of coffee watching the firemen work and wondering when we'd be able to get out. It was cloudy and gray but oddly warm. Gaby and I wrapped packages in silence. I had been sick with a bronchial infection and felt depleted. It was almost noon before we were told we could exit the area and be on our way.

That Christmas the kids knew I had little money, and we had agreed to spend no more than thirty dollars per present. It removed a lot of anxiety for all of us. We had a nice time and I was happy just to be with them.

When the holidays are over, the real hard work of winter in

Woodstock begins. Heavy snows and ice. Entertaining comes to a dead halt. Restaurants close. With relatively little to live on — I was paying $760 a month to the IRS, in addition to keeping up with current quarterly payments — I tried to keep my fuel bills low. Plastic got stretched over the large artist's window in my workroom. A heater blasted away under my desk and the rest of the house was kept cool. There was an old woodpile out back and I made fires in the fireplace in the late afternoons to keep my spirits up. Weekends were better because the creditors stopped calling then, but they were also lonely.

I hadn't the least idea how to handle the creditors — Sears, the bank that had lent money for my daughter's college education, the mortgage and management companies for my co-op studio in the city. When they called demanding payment, I at first made promises I couldn't keep. I was afraid *not* to. I owed the electric company a huge bill left from the house I'd sold. I tried to chip away at that bill. I got three months behind on the maintenance payments for the New York co-op (I had a tenant in it but the rent didn't cover expenses) and had an extremely unpleasant conversation with the man who owned the management company. Like Jekyll turning into Hyde, he swung into monster mode as soon as I hit the three-month mark. That, apparently, was the point at which I'd become a "bad" — no longer deserving of civility or even reason. "Forget it, you're out, you've lost the apartment," he snarled, meanly. I knew he was lying but I didn't say that. Instead, I reminded him that he had a duty to remain civil. He screamed that he had no such duty since he wasn't dealing with a civil person. I maintained my dignity throughout, but when the conversation ended I was deeply shaken. What had happened here? I was trying to make good on my debts. I was doing the best I knew how.

The traffic, the horns, the cats peeing on the floor, the phone I never answered, and the cold messages being left on the machine were pushing me to the brink. I had to do something. I had to make some change. I needed to create some space between me and It.

LEARNING TO COPE: DEBTORS ANONYMOUS

Someone once described Debtors Anonymous as the graduate school of twelve-step programs. I wouldn't know about that, having only Al Anon to compare it with.

Several years before bottoming out with debting, I had gone to Al Anon for help getting out of an obsessive pattern of worrying about a family member's drinking. It taught me to begin focusing, instead, on my own problems. Having left the Church years earlier, and not even knowing whether I believed in God, I found I had no trouble standing in a circle at the end of meetings, holding the hands of people on either side of me, and saying the serenity prayer: God grant me the serenity to accept the things I cannot change, the courage to change the things I can, and the wisdom to know the difference. I felt both humbled and exalted by my connection with these courageous souls.

I think by the time I broke down and entered a Debtors Anonymous program, I was beyond needing to profess my allegiance to atheism. I felt, when I said the prayer, gratitude to the people in the room who'd come together for an hour and a half to listen quietly to one another's experiences. Each week one person "qualified" — told, from the vantage point of where she or he was in the recovery process, his or her own story of debting and decline. The meetings had no leader, no one lassoing participants into a particular behavioral corral. Yet the honesty and dignity of virtually everyone who spoke, the unwillingness to wander into victimization or blame, was striking.

From the beginning I identified with the people in my group. Some had little money, some had had a lot, some were very young, some were very old, but we were all fighting the same demons. There were strong similarities among the messages about money and control we'd received from the families we grew up in, and the ensuing wish to blame our problems on anything, or anyone, but ourselves.

There was no harshness expressed in these meetings, only gentle respect. People were encouraged to speak up (ours had voted on a three-minute limit per speaker), but you could go weeks without opening your mouth and still be held in gentle regard. In the meantime, you saw that when others told their stories or revealed their latest struggles, they were given minute attention at the same time that they were embraced in a comforting silence. Five people weren't jumping in to interact with you when you finished speaking. The *point* of speaking was not to open up your story to the interpretation of someone else, but simply to *hear* yourself and to be heard. Knowing you wouldn't have to defend yourself against others' ideas about you, you gradually became freer in what you revealed. You learned what you really thought about the situation you'd put yourself in, how you got there and why you were experiencing so much resistance to doing what needed to be done to change it.

Of course you also learned from, and were supported by, how others were coping with their own self-defeating patterns. At the beginning of meetings each person would say what goals he or she had accomplished that week. A goal could be anything from paying off a loan to getting the cat to the vet. It could be simply getting to the meeting.

At the end, each person said what her goals were for the upcoming week. At first I made a mad dash to scribble down some items before it was my turn to announce my intentions. Thinking of a week's activities ahead of time? I wasn't used to this kind of planning. But somehow it was relieving — relieving just to put things down, to begin looking at life day by day, week by week. Eventually a shape began to emerge, one I was actually *making*. Simple though it may seem, it was surprisingly gratifying.

* * *

WORKING THE PROGRAM

A comforting aspect of being in a twelve-step program is its leveling effect. It helps to see that you're not unlike others who've gotten themselves into similar situations, to recognize, lest you'd forgotten, that you, too, are a member of the human race.

It helps, as well, to see that those who've been "working the program" for a while treat themselves with dignity and humor. But what does the most for the shame and guilt associated with debting is *stopping* debting — and *that* you can do from Day One. In that regard, DA is like other twelve-step programs: *Just for today I will not borrow. Not two dollars, or ten, not "a hundred 'til payday."*

For me, the biggest challenge was taking actions so that I could discover how and where I was scattering my money. I began to keep a daily spending record. After six months I organized all my figures and saw how much I'd spent on magazines and newspapers, how much on eating out, how much on clothes. Going through my checkbook, I could see patterns — for example, how frequently, on a whim, I hit up Marshalls, going in and picking up sheets or shoes or cheap sunglasses. The very fact of doing it at Marshalls, where everything is discounted, seemed to validate the purchase of whatever, whenever. I was spending smartly, after all. And how much could you spend at Marshalls at any given time? Not a whole hell of a lot.

In going through my figures, I glimpsed a method in this apparently random shopping. I rarely went out looking for something I needed. I went out hoping to make myself feel better. I reached a point where just going through the door of Marshalls, with its harsh fluorescent lighting, bare white walls, and racks of same-old same-old, felt comforting. I'd take the shopping cart from its harbor and grow calm as I started down the aisles. A package of tube socks. A jar of strawberry jam. (Marshalls is nothing if not eclectic.) I have to say that the shopping carts of other women, once we were lined up at the cashier, looked much the same as

mine: the out-of-season down vest ("Ah, this will be good for John-
nie, come winter"), the Rubik's cube made in Taiwan, the Calvin
Klein sheets (60 percent off but still thirty dollars a sheet). Men's
shopping carts don't look like this. Men come in for a coat or a
couple of packages of boxer shorts and leave. You don't see them
gliding along behind their shopping carts in a kind of blank-faced
trance. (Of course they could shop differently at electronics stores;
I wouldn't know.)

An accurate spending record involves "keeping your numbers" — writing down each cash expenditure as it's made: every
cup of coffee, every newspaper, every seemingly minor or infre-
quent outlay — the $7 rental fee on my P.O. box, the annual
twenty-dollar contribution to the local volunteer firemen, every
bus or subway token. It's a process I hated and probably always
will, but as soon as I began it, I was able to expand my horizons.
Out went the daily cup of lousy coffee I bought each morning
with my newspaper and into my pocket went $30 a month. Thirty
dollars!

I saw what my restaurant expenses were — I eat out almost
every night — and I knew if I wanted any other recreation in life
besides eating, I'd have to cut those expenses radically. Just by
ordering on the right-hand side of the menu, I dropped this expense by half, without having to give up my social life! With the
money saved, I could afford to study Pilates at the movement studio
in Woodstock. The mere *awareness* of what and how you've been
spending (like keeping a record of what you eat), starts the process
of change.

It's interesting how, as you document your spending pattern,
its essential joylessness becomes apparent. Why am I living my
life so compulsively? What gratification would be more meaningful to me than the daily, disappointing coffee in its paper cup?
What, seriously? Stretching my body? Sex? A relationship? And

why have I been willing to make do with such paltry compensations?

I used to have a four-woman cleaning service that whipped through my house like the white tornado. Now I've cut out the cleaning service and bought a vacuum cleaner with fabulous suction. (Vacuuming — I'd forgotten this — can actually be meditative.) I bought a pair of excellent scissors and started cutting my own hair. I became fascinated by the aesthetics of haircutting, how changing the angle alters my profile. I never understood these things before. The salon, the hairdresser, the arcane intricacies of the cut, had always held an intimidating mystique. This was liberating! Before long I was cutting sharp, clean angles into the hair along the sides of my face, making me feel like Matisse doing his paper cutouts. I saw, clearly, what needed to be done to rebalance the profile: *snip*. The ritual of cutting my hair became almost addictive.

Before the crash I'd been going to a Madison Avenue salon and dropping $160 every six weeks for cut and color. Even so, the cut lost its edge between visits. And the salon prices were so high I couldn't afford highlights, so I could never get past the dowager blond effect of every damn hair being the same glintless shade of medium ash. Now I trim my hair almost weekly and touch up the color twice a month. *Plus* I do my own sexy highlights, having had the mysteries of double process divulged to me by my mother's pedicurist.

The exciting part about going through columns of figures, as I compile my spending report, is that it gives me the understanding that there are choices. Also, it's not so much a question of giving things up as of rearranging — and getting more bang for the buck.

Doing my numbers made clear where I was dribbling money away. But how could I learn what might give me real pleasure? The truth was, I knew very little about pleasure unless it came in the form of great sex or a hot fudge sundae.

A major part of my healing, it would turn out, would come from learning to live in an entirely different way.

For a woman who's been taught that pleasing others is the road to survival, the lessons of DA can be especially challenging. We are so used to scurrying to placate. It is our own special method of control. I'll-be-nice-to-you-and-you'll-behave-toward-me-in-a-certain-way. DA says: Surrender your idea that you can control others. Instead, take care of yourself.

When you begin to do that, begin to give up your attempts to control, gratitude and contentment flood in. Life seems simpler. You go to bed without anxiety because you've done it for one day: taken care of yourself; surrendered to a higher power.

The notion of a higher power is the sticking point, for many, on the question of whether to join a twelve-step program. My own way of interpreting the concept is that there's something bigger going on, here, than just me. I don't think of a higher power with capital letters, because to me it's not a deity as we've been taught to think of deity. It's not someone "up there" watching out for me. And whatever it is, it certainly isn't a "he."

I can accept, personally, the notion of a natural order of which I am a very small part. That is my "higher power." My hope, in relating to others within this order, is to be as simple and direct as I can. I accept the other as being as important as I am. I don't expect the other to take on my responsibilities, and I will not take on *her* responsibilities.

One of the great outcomes of working the DA program is that you reconstitute a sense of boundaries that began to blur for you when you were a girl. Those boundaries turn out to be the greatest gift of all, for they allow you, safe within them, to reach out and love. They allow you to stop judging because you don't need the protection of judging. Judging, actually, creates a kind of pseudoboundary that we feel we need when there is no real sense of ourselves as whole and individuated.

With boundaries intact, one can maintain one's sense of self even when the environment becomes toxic. I listen to the co-op managing agent yelling at me that I'm a scurrilous debtor and I retain my dignity. I know I am facing something directly: I have to save enough money to eat, to keep the roof over my head, without borrowing. I *don't* fire off a check to him to get him off my back because the guilt of not doing so is too much to bear. At this point, I feel relatively little guilt. I am facing my problem. I'm taking responsibility. I'm putting myself first.

He's doing what he needs to do, or *thinks* he needs to do. He's yelling at the debtor because someone told him that's what you do to get the money you're owed. He's on the merry-go-round. I'm not, and I don't get back on it with him just because it will appease him if I do.

"Focusing on yourself," says Donna Boundy, "can sound like the self-obsessed 'me first' rhetoric of the 1970s and 1980s, but it isn't. Self-obsession is what you've *been* doing. The ultimate aim of the codependent, after all, is not altruistic, but self-serving. She wants to covertly control the relationship, elicit approval, and hang on to the hostage. *That* is self-centered."[14]

RESISTANCE

I still struggle with all of this — the disinclination to open bills, keep up with the listing of my expenditures, reconcile my bank statements. A lifetime of resistance is powerful. Insight alone isn't enough. It never is.

In the time since I have stopped going to DA meetings, things have slid backward. They haven't slid to where they were before — I'm more conscious of what I'm *not* doing than I used to be — but the backward slide has made me realize that achieving true financial independence may be the major challenge of my life.

"Sometimes denial goes dormant for a while, only to pop up again later," says Jerry Mundis, who has become a kind of Moses of DA. "It often reappears when you've begun to reverse your situation and the stress is easing — or simultaneously with a large influx of money, from whatever source. The old attitudes and behavior patterns don't die easily. They may simply have gone into hiding, marking time, only to break into the open again at the first opportunity."[15]

This past year I did it again. I got myself into *more* debt with the IRS. And I did it in a year when my income improved. I can tell myself — and have been telling myself — that the debt occurred because my income went up and I had been paying quarterly estimates based on the previous year's income without realizing how *much* my current income was going up. But there was something more destructive happening than mere distractedness. *I've actually come to think that I think I don't want to be financially independent.* I brought the house down again, after all. I put myself in a situation where I not only have to come up with thousands in taxes for last year, I have to pay new and higher estimates for the current year, *plus* my monthly installments for paying off 1992–1993. There is no question that I have dug myself back into a hole — not through wild spending, this time, but through a profound disinclination to continue to keep paying the kind of attention that's required.

" 'Goal planning has no respite, no relief,' " says Kit Cole, a financial investment advisor in Kentfield, California. " 'If you want to be financially successful you can't retire from thinking. You must accept that you are accountable for your fate.' "[16]

So how did this happen? Nineteen ninety-five was the first year since my crash in which I made a good income — the first year in which there seemed to be enough money to buy a few clothes, a washer/dryer, a new computer. I paid off quite a bit of debt. I had begun, through dint of hard work and painful care, to rebuild my life. I had been reading up on investing, looking forward to rebuilding my Keogh account, and learning how to invest, or at least finding out enough to be able to supervise someone else doing the investing for me. I had been off on a new track, the track toward independence.

And then, I began "forgetting." No more keeping my numbers. No more spending plan. Terminal vagueness. And then I screwed up again. "This financial fog, this cloud of unknowing, is catastrophic," says Mundis. "It leads almost inevitably to new debt."[17]

After I got the bad news from my accountant, my shoulder seized up. I had to stop exercising. Low-grade chronic pain temporarily distracted me from a more disturbing reality: I had done this to myself. I had actually said, *No, You're not going to stay on the independence track. You're not going to make this happen. Get back down again. Make yourself small. Make yourself insecure. Put yourself where it's comfortable, where it feels familiar, where you know how to function, and where you feel sure what the outcome will be.*

It was amazing. It was like clockwork. Immediately I began staying down in these old ways.

- Though a session with a Rolfer made my injured shoulder feel much better, I was afraid of spending the money to have another session with him. (Better to limp along trying to heal the shoulder on my own than invest precious money in my own health.)
- I spent an afternoon ironing clothes I was handing down to my daughter when I should have been working on a deadline. This simple, heartwarming act — the iron humming smoothly over the linens and silks — allowed me to (1) identify with my daughter, who, at twenty-nine, was having a hard time making ends meet; (2) wallow in the

self-pity of remembering that my mother never helped *me* when *I* was in need of money; (3) pretend to myself that I was doing something active and constructive in the way that women always have — helping others. Essentially, putting myself last.

- I visited a rehearsal of the dance company whose board I'm on and spent two days obsessing about how I could help *them* make money.
- I offered to spend half a day accompanying my daughter to court to fight a landlord. (She said, "Mom, you have enough on your plate already." I stood corrected.)

This is resistance, big time. The feeling is: I want out. I want *anywhere* but being in charge of my own welfare. Let me be a helper, let me be a caretaker *par excellence,* let me work for others, enhance the image of others. Let me do *anything* but look clearly at what I have to do to take care of myself — and do it. Accept it. Accept responsibility for myself for the long haul.

Yet I didn't want to return to the old place. I didn't want to feel stressed out, isolated, grasping at a few meals out a week with friends to compensate for all my hard work and solitude. I didn't want to feel put upon and out of touch. I didn't want to feel *victimized by having money.* I didn't want to feel childish in relation to managing and investing it. I didn't want to feel that *life* was going to begin sometime in the future.

But how could all this change at a time when I was more strung out with anxiety than I'd ever been before? Wouldn't I have to pay back everything and *know,* always, where my next nickel was coming from, before I could relax and begin to enjoy life?

Oddly, the answer was no. It was in extreme adversity that I began to learn things for the first time that no analysis or group therapy or talk with a priest in confession had ever gotten across.

"You must know what you truly want — what your intention is — or you end up setting off kegs of dynamite in all directions as if they were firecrackers on the Fourth of July," writes Ruth Ross, in *Prospering Woman*. "Everybody enjoys firecrackers — but their effect is short-lived. Getting what you want out of life requires aligning thoughts, beliefs, and intentions."[18]

It has a nice, Zen sound, but just how does one do this? Surely wishing for such congruence isn't enough.

The DA "pressure relief group" suggested that I make a wish list. Simply being in debt to credit card companies, banks, and the IRS didn't mean I was to forget about the things I wanted for myself. That would be unhealthy. What was healthy was acknowledging my wants and working toward getting them, making them a part of my plan.

"Wants are thoughts, and thought — as mind energy — is creative power," says Ross. "When we become specific about what we want, we are focusing the power of thought on our desires."

Studies have shown that most of us have not formulated what we want in any precise way. We let our wants remain nebulous. "It seems easier to live with the vague sense that something is missing, and to make do, rather than define what that something is."[19]

Weeks went by before I sat down to write my list. I was offended even by the idea of doing it. It seemed a silly task. I had no extra money and wouldn't, I imagined, for years. What was the point of acknowledging my burning desire for the big overstuffed armchair from the Crate and Barrel catalogue that cost seven hundred dollars? There was no point. It was stupid. Worse than stupid, depressing. If I were to actually look at, *name*, everything I wanted, I would drown in a sea of acknowledged deprivation. Better not to acknowledge. Better to pretend I wanted *nothing*.

The real power of manifestation comes from the state of expectation. What we *wish for*, and what we *expect*, must be consciously combined — made one, advises Ross. "Actually, our whole concept of reality is limited until we experience the fact that *the only reality there is, is what we tell ourselves.* What we believe, we become."[20]

NO MORE DRESSING THE PART

"Whenever I show my husband some wonderful new outfit I salvaged on the markdown table, he asks, 'But do you need it?' He doesn't understand," says the British playwright Tina Howe. "It's not about need, but being prepared. There's a reason the fashion industry spends so much money trying to woo us. It knows women are constantly trying to define themselves. Who am I? Siren? Mystic? Innocent? Warrior?"

Howe, a serious artist, says she enjoys her "fantasy wardrobe" and its potential for what she calls "transformation." "I spend nine-tenths of my waking hours schlepping around in jeans, but like Cinderella, I can turn into a glamour queen with the stroke of a wand. And I don't need any fairy godmother to wield it. I'm the mistress of my fate because I've appropriated the means of my success. My glass slippers and ball gown are in the closet!"[21]

I could only assume, when I read Howe's article in *Allure* magazine, that she had needed a little more money for feathering her nest. Could she possibly be serious when she says the means of her success is the fantasy wardrobe in her closet?

I used to feel, when I had a big party to go to, that I had to buy a special outfit for it. Here was my chance to make a splash, some kind of *statement* about myself. I felt I needed props for this — jewelry, décolleté, attention-grabbing shoes. I was afraid I wouldn't be *seen* without my props. That's what I really wanted, not to make a statement so much as *to be seen, acknowledged, recognized.*

Now I live my life differently because I *feel* differently about myself. I regard myself well. I create calm and peace in my environment because I need it and deserve it. And I recognize that I am the only one who can create that calm and peace. It is not *about* someone doing that for me. If I meet someone now, and come to love that person, it will be to share the inner peace I've created for myself, not expect it to be provided for me.

Which is not to say I don't like getting dressed up and going out. I do. I think it's fun to put on high heels and eyeliner and go out looking good. But I am not self-conscious about creating an effect, because there's more congruence between how I look when I dress to go out and how I feel about myself when I'm at home during the day.

HEALING

"What we're after in this program," writes Jerry Mundis, "is nothing less than a major shift in consciousness — in the attitudes, beliefs, and ideas you have about yourself and your money. This can be the single most important factor in improving the quality of your life and in determining the ease and comfort with which you liberate yourself from debt."[22]

You can succeed without such a shift. If you use nothing but the practical techniques of Debtors Anonymous, you can probably *still* bring your debting to a halt and eventually pay off all your creditors, "but without a shift in consciousness you'll have a harder time of it, you'll deprive yourself of a great deal of emotional and material gain, and you may well get into trouble again later."

I think it was the extraordinary feeling of connectedness I got in the DA meetings that led me to wanting deeper connections in other realms of my life. Within a year I had started a journal-writing group and joined a group of women who analyzed their dreams. I want to tell you in particular about the dream group, because its effects on me have been profound and I think many women would find the experience similarly supportive.

In the dream group, five women meet weekly. Each meeting is devoted to one person's dream and can last from two to three hours. The one who brings a dream to work on reads it from her dream book while the rest of us write it down.

We are given no information on the dream, just the dream itself. Then we take turns making statements of association, always starting the sentence with "I" and in this way revealing what feelings and thoughts the dream brings up in us.

The group association process may go on for twenty or thirty minutes. During it, the dreamer just listens, taking down our statements in her journal. When she is ready to speak herself she does so, "taking back" the dream.

First she responds to any associations of ours that were meaningful to her. Then she tells us her own thoughts about the dream. This, often, is a time when painful feelings come up, or fears and anxieties. The format for our group doesn't allow for interacting until the end, so we are all thrown deep into our own processes. We do not create fancy interpretations, telling the dreamer what we think her dream is "about," recognizing that the dreamer knows best what the meaning of the dream is for her. Our associations might resonate with her own, or tip some of her feelings closer to the surface. Some pattern or story usually emerges from the process of working on the dream. It takes on a dynamic richness, through the group process, allowing the dreamer to take home more than she came with.

In all my years of therapy, I had never worked with dreams in any deep, systematic way. Immediately I found myself remembering more dreams as I began writing them down in the mornings. At first I would take my dream to the group like a child making an offering. I had no idea what the dream meant. I felt I was giving it to them to work on for me. After about a year, during which I had worked maybe ten times in the group, my relationship to my unconscious shifted. The dreams no longer seemed like weird, alien artifacts; they were from me, part of me, an important part I'd

never had access to before. Instead of feeling afraid of my unconscious I began to embrace it as a holder of important information.

How could I have lived so long without knowing how to make
use of this passageway to my inner self? Even the oddest, and most
magical, parts of the dream were *of* me, made by me. Somehow
these dreams, even the worst, most grotesque nightmares, were
giving me a new affection for myself, a feeling of tenderness and
appreciation. I could acknowledge the secret struggle, the dark
shadows, the lascivious id (although we didn't use Freudian terms.)
I saw that I had depths and complexities that I hadn't been aware
of. I grew to like myself more. In the mornings, rather than shove
away some haunting residue of the night before, I would take out
my journal and work the dream.

Squaring myself with a dream, first thing upon arising, set me
up for the day. I *always* felt better for it, clearer, more grounded,
less anxious. I liked starting the day knowing where I was. Tremendous gratitude for the new tool filled me, also gratitude toward the
women in the group, whose integrity and respect for one another
allowed me to trust this opening up to my inner self.

At this point, my relationships with other people became a true
mainstay in my life. I recognized that I needed them. I began
revealing myself. I still had a lot of information to spout off at the
drop of a hat, but I didn't feel buttoned up and in control. I began
appreciating my friends, idiosyncrasies and all. I began seeing how
much *alike* we all were, rather than how different. (I used to use my
perceived *difference* from others to feel superior to them.) I began
understanding that pleasure was there to be had, if only I would
make myself available to it. Through Pilates, I learned new pleasure
in and appreciation of my body. I went on to sports, taking up things
I'd long since thought were in the past: biking, Rollerblading, dancing. I took a trip to Vietnam, going solo, savoring Southeast Asia but
savoring even more learning what it felt like to be alone in a foreign
culture with no one telling me what I should be doing or feeling
or learning about. I found that what I desired, most, was to write

in my journal and think about my childhood! I befriended a young man, Vu, who drove me everywhere on the back of his motorbike and took me to local restaurants and other places I wouldn't have gone to on my own. I learned the currency exchange, something I'd always left to whomever I was traveling with.

I don't believe in simple willpower or tricky techniques. The effects of these never last. It's like dieting. You can lose pounds temporarily, but you'll gain them back, and probably sooner rather than later.

Today, nutrition experts advise against diets in favor of lifestyle changes. Changing the way you think about food. Changing the way you think about your body and yourself. Creating a new value system that will guide you in traveling comfortably and healthily forward, over the long haul of a productive life.

And so it is with money. There are no quick fixes. A whole lifetime of attitudes and habits and techniques of denial are at issue here.

But in looking at them and where they come from and why their appeal is so great, we stand to gain more than just straightening out our finances. We stand to gain feelings of comfort and security and, yes, *gratitude,* that we may never have known before.

One thing I came to understand was true pleasure from spending; it isn't unrelated to the pleasure of paying one's bills. In both instances, one is taking care of oneself.

Pleasure from spending is not the same as buying on impulse in the frantic effort to lift one's spirits. It was when I discovered I had trouble taking pleasure from responsible spending that I learned this.

After much thought and planning, I had taken occupancy of a small apartment in New York, one my daughter had lived in first, and which I later rented out. Now it was my turn. It had long been my dream to have a place in the city as well as a house in the country. To be able to afford it, I had seriously cut back on my overall living expenses. It was the first time in my life I had financially planned for and worked toward something I wanted.

The apartment needed furnishing. I thumbed through catalogues, visited all the low-end furniture stores, and made a budget. "Spare and functional" would be my decorating scheme. It was only a room and a foyer that needed furnishing. I bought a futon couch and made a simple desk. Then, in one fell swoop, I got everything else during an afternoon at . . . Crate and Barrel!

The shopping blitz was distinctly *un*like a spree. First I went around the store checking prices and jotting down in a notebook the things I was interested in. I sat on a display sofa, went over my list, and saw how the money was adding up. To lower the total, I crossed some things off and made some substitutions.

Then, *before buying anything*, I left the store and went across the street to a coffee shop where I sat and rechecked my list. Too much money. I crossed off the sisal rug and rug pad. The wood floor was good enough. Five hundred dollars saved. Finally I went back to Crate and Barrel, paid cash for my purchases, and arranged for everything to be sent the following day. I was thrilled with what I'd gotten, but the thrill didn't last long. I went home that night and began to worry. *Was I fooling myself? Could I afford to do what I was doing? Was this my old predisaster grandiosity returning?*

I kept waking up at night, turning it over in my mind. Did I really need two lamps for the console in the foyer? Did I really need the console? Et cetera, et cetera. I was in a quandary. It was as if I didn't *know* what I could afford.

And then, finally, at about four o'clock in the morning, a new train of thought trickled into my mind. This act of moving into a new apartment was causing me to regress to an earlier time in life, a time when I felt I didn't deserve nice things. A time when

I didn't have the power to go out and furnish an apartment. Guilt was ruining my pleasure in being able to provide for myself. My mother would have *sewn* the duvet and the shams. She would have discussed each furniture purchase with my father. And of course *he* would have had veto power. My mother never knew the joy — or the terror — of going out and furnishing a place on her own, without someone else to mediate her decisions.

Thus, my afternoon at Crate and Barrel had tremendous symbolic meaning. I was a woman alone, a woman with hard-earned cash in her bank account that she was about to spend on herself.

A woman who didn't have to ask anyone's permission.

A woman who had only to answer to herself.

But what a frightening thing that can be, to have only to answer to oneself. In making my purchases carefully, in extending the process to give due weight to my decisions, I had put myself in touch with that fear. Grandiose fantasies no longer buoyed me up, diluting my anxiety. I didn't imagine dinner parties with the literati or huge Christmas festivities with the family. This apartment was only for me. Anything I did to make it attractive was purely for myself.

Was it possible that I was afraid of all that implied?

These were the thoughts and fears of a woman with no rescue in sight. And it was this — the clear recognition that the buck stopped with me — that had me tossing and turning. Spending thirteen hundred dollars to furnish a studio caused me more anxiety, in my new, conscious state, than spending a hundred thousand dollars to renovate a house had caused me back in the days when I was blindsided by illusion.

Getting it together financially doesn't have to mean becoming a workaholic who sacrifices relationships for more and more money, like the male role models we've observed. By taking care of ourselves we are "feminizing" the meaning of money. We are seeing to it that we have all the resources we need to take care of ourselves, our families, our causes — whatever it is that's important to us as women. Ross differentiates between the aggressive power that money has been used for and the inner power that managing our money supports. "Personal power is not aggressive, muscular, manipulative or authoritative power, but an inner power that comes from knowing we have all the resources we need to handle whatever happens in life. When we have personal power we shift from the pseudo-strength of appearing strong to the real strength of feeling strong."[23]

Judy Collins, speaking to three thousand women at a conference held by American Women's Economic Development Corporation, gave testimony to her former financial dependency. For over twenty years she'd left her finances in the hands of her business manager. One day he came and told her she had no money to pay her taxes. The end of innocence!

Today she is her own manager. But getting there took effort. "I broke personal barriers to learn how to do it," she told the audience. "As women we are raised to have rescue fantasies, but I'm here to tell you" — she paused and waited, while laughter erupted in the hotel ballroom — "no one is coming."

Having learned, now, to manage her affairs responsibly, Collins is exhilarated by the experience of being in charge of her life. "Nothing thrills me more than to pay my quarterly taxes. I sing with joy."

It is the embracing of personal responsibility, not performance for approval, that makes us want to dance and sing.

Today, women are at a new stage. We have the ability not only to earn our money but to manage it.

To have an overview of our financial situation.

To see the larger picture.

To include the final years in our plans.

To be able to say no to the impulse to have, to buy, to spend, recognizing that "No" does not deprive us; it serves, instead, a larger interest — our sense of being balanced, someone who is making real choices, someone who feels she can control the situation so that it works on her behalf. It is self-management and self-regulation that is required if we are to emerge free from patriarchy. But before that is possible, a sense of self must be regained. This, no less, is what is required for independence and autonomy. Otherwise, we are still subservient, enslaved by our fears, if not by our fathers and husbands.

NOTES

CHAPTER I

1. Margaret Randall, *The Price You Pay* (New York: Routledge, 1996), p. 9.

CHAPTER 2

1. Saul Hansell, "A Shaky House of Plastic with No Quick Fix in Sight," *New York Times*, Dec. 28, 1995, section D1, p. 1.

2. Donna Boundy, *When Money Is the Drug: The Compulsion for Credit, Cash, and Chronic Debt* (San Francisco: HarperSanFrancisco, 1993), p. 78. Boundy based her picture of American capitalism in the '70s and '80s on Adam Smith's *The Roaring Eighties* (New York: Penguin, 1988).

3. Robert D. Hershey, Jr., "At College, Many Learn How to Plunge into Debt," *New York Times*, Nov. 10, 1996, section D, p. 1.

4. Jerrold Mundis, *How to Get Out of Debt, Stay Out of Debt, and Live Prosperously* (New York: Bantam, 1990).

5. Sana Siwolop, "Genius Grant Patches Up Family's Frayed Finances," *New York Times*, August 4, 1996, section F., p. 3.

6. Sana Siwolop, "For a Choreographer, a Chance to Leap Out of Debt," *New York Times*, July 20, 1997, section F, p. 4.

7. Mundis, *How to Get Out of Debt* . . .

CHAPTER 3

1. Donna Boundy, *When Money Is the Drug: The Compulsion for Credit, Cash, and Chronic Debt* (San Francisco: HarperSanFrancisco, 1993), p. 117.

2. Annette Lieberman and Vicki Lindner, *Unbalanced Accounts* (New York: Viking Penguin, 1988), p. 151.

3. Cynthia Kling, "Why Are Women Still Afraid of Money?" *Harper's Bazaar*, January 1997, p. 24.

4. Sarah Lyall, "A Duchess: Her Life in Debt," *New York Times*, February 4, 1996, section 4, p. 4.

5. Geraldine Fabrikant, "New Chapter for a Serial Spender," *New York Times*, March 23, 1997, section D, p. 6.

6. Martha McPhee, "My Favorite Store: Agnes B," *New York Times Magazine*, April 6, 1997, p. 74.

7. Meghan Daum, "Losing My Shirt," *Self*, April 1996, p. 157.

8. Walter Kirn, "Going Postal," *Vogue*, March 1996, p. 204.

9. David J. Morrow, "To Shop, Perchance Nonstop," *New York Times*, Dec. 29, 1996, section 3, p. 1.

10. Susan McElroy, M.D., et al. "Pharmacological Treatment of Kleptomania and Bulimia Nervosa," *Journal of Clinical Psychopharmacology* 9, no. 5 (October 1989).

11. Susan McElroy, M.D., James I. Hudson, M.D., Harrison G. Pope, Jr., M.D., and Paul E. Keck, Jr., M.D., "Kleptomania: Clinical Characteristics and Associated Psychopathology," *Psychological Medicine* 21 (1991), pp. 93–108.

12. I had a number of discussions with Hudson and Pope in their office at McLean Hospital, outside Boston, while researching my book *You Mean I Don't Have to Feel This Way?: New Help for Depression, Anxiety and Addiction* (New York: Bantam, 1993).

13. McElroy et al., "Pharmacological Treatment of Kleptomania and Bulimia Nervosa."

CHAPTER 4

1. Jennifer Dunning, "Dance Notes," *New York Times*, June 18, 1996, section C, p. 18.

2. Barbara Kerbel, "Ill Suited for This," *Newsday*, January 18, 1997, section B, p. 5.

3. Rosalind C. Barnett, "Women in Management Today," Center for Research on Women, No. 249 (Wellesley, Mass.: Wellesley College, 1992), p. 2.

4. Maggie Mahar, "The Truth About Women's Pay," *Working Woman*, April 1993, pp. 52–55.

5. Tamar Lewin, "Equal Pay for Equal Work Is No. 1 Goal of Women," *New York Times*, September 5, 1997, section A., p. 20.

6. Charlotte Kinstlinger-Bruhn, "Singled Out," *Woodstock Times*, July 25, 1996, p. 12.

7. Namkee G. Choi, "Correlates of the Economic Status of Widowed and Divorced Elderly Women," *Journal of Family Issues* 13, no. 1, (March 1992), p. 48.

8. Sharon Hicks and Carol M. Anderson, "Women on Their Own," in Monica McGoldrick, Carol M. Anderson, and Froma Walsh, eds., *Women in Families* (New York: W. W. Norton, 1991), p. 318.

9. Dirk Johnson, "No Fault Divorce Is Under Attack, *New York Times*, February 2, 1996, section A, p. 10.

10. Barbara Ehrenreich, "Whose Gap Is It, Anyway?" *Time*, May 6, 1996, p. 36.

11. Diane P. Holder and Carol M. Anderson, "Women, Work and the Family," *Women in Families*, p. 376.

12. Charlotte Kinstlinger-Bruhn, "Singled Out," p. 12.

13. A. O'Rand and J. Henretta, "Women at Middle Age: Developmental Transitions," *Annals of the American Academy of Political and Social Science* 404 (1982), quoted in *Women on Their Own*, p. 310.

14. Barnett, "Women in Management Today," p. 21.

15. Sharon Hicks and Carol M. Anderson, "Women on Their Own," p. 330.

16. Choi, p. 38.

17. Anita Jones-Lee, *Women and Money* (Happauge, N.Y.: Barron, 1991), p. 4.

18. Figures from NOW, reported by Annette Lieberman and Vicki Lindner in *Unbalanced Accounts* (New York: Viking Penguin, 1998), p. 179.

19. "Equity Eludes Women," *AARP Bulletin*, November 1991, p. 1.

20. Jones-Lee, *Women and Money*, p. 6.

21. Ibid.

22. Seventeen percent of American women over sixty-five have incomes below the poverty line, as opposed to 10 percent of men. This and other statistics on income of older women: McGoldrick, Anderson, and Walsh, *Women in Families*.

23. "Equity Eludes Women."

24. Gary Belsky, "The Five Ways Women Are Often Smarter Than Men About Money," *Money*, June 1992, p. 82.

25. Beth B. Hess, "Aging Policies and Old Women: The Hidden Agenda," in Alice Rossi, ed., *Gender and the Life Course* (New York: Aldine, 1985), p. 323.

26. Carol M. Anderson and Susan Stewart, with Sonja Dimidjian, *Flying Solo* (New York: W. W. Norton, 1995), p. 104.

27. Ibid., p. 265.

28. Ibid.

29. Hicks and Anderson, "Women on Their Own," p. 318.

30. Ibid., p. 317.

31. Ibid., p. 309.

32. "An Income of Her Own: Summary Update, January 1994," p. 1, An Income of Her Own, P.O. Box 987, Santa Barbara, CA 93102.

33. Belsky, p. 82.

34. Leslie Brenner, "When Smart Women Aren't Smart About Money," *New Woman*, August 1996, p. 102.

35. Ibid.

36. Ibid.

37. Hicks and Anderson, "Women on Their Own," p. 331.

CHAPTER 5

1. Carol Gilligan, "Prologue," in Carol Gilligan, Nona P. Lyons, and Trudy J. Hanmer, eds., *Making Connections: Notes from the Underground of Female Adolescence* (Cambridge: Harvard University Press, 1990), p. 1.

2. Carol Gilligan, *In A Different Voice* (Cambridge: Harvard University Press, 1993), p. xx.

3. Carol Gilligan, "Teaching Shakespeare's Sister," in *Making Connections*, p. 14.

4. American Association of University Women, *Shortchanging Girls, Shortchanging America: Executive Summary* (Washington, D.C.: American Association of University Women), p. 4.

5. Jane Brody, "Girls and Puberty: The Crisis Years," *New York Times*, November 4, 1997, section F, p. 9.

6. Lyn Mikel Brown, "Telling a Girl's Life: Self-Authorization as a Form of Resistance," in *Women, Girls and Psychotherapy* (New York: Haworth Press, 1991), p. 73.

7. Lyn Mikel Brown and Carol Gilligan, *Meeting at the Crossroads* (New York: Ballantine Books, 1992), p. 55.

8. Gilligan, "Teaching Shakespeare's Sister," p. 9.

9. Unpublished paper, "The Life and Death of Prunella: A Psychological Study of My Imaginary Twin," by Elizabeth McLeod.

10. *Shortchanging Girls, Shortchanging America: Executive Summary*, p. 10.

11. Brown and Gilligan, p. 58.

12. Teresa Bernardez, "Adolescent Resistance and the Maladies of Women: Notes from the Underground," Carol Gilligan, Annie G. Rogers, Deborah L. Tolman, eds., *Women, Girls and Psychotherapy: Reframing Resistance* (Binghamton, N.Y.: Haworth Press, 1991).

CHAPTER 6

1. Valerie Saiving, "The Human Situation: A Feminine View" in *Womanspirit Rising: A Feminist Reader in Religion,* Carol P. Christ and Judith Plaskow, eds., (San Francisco: Harper, 1989), p. 26.

2. Elizabeth Debold, Marie Wilson, Idelisse Malavé, *Mother Daughter Revolution* (New York: Bantam Books, 1994), p. 212.

Wilson and Malavé were president and vice president of the Ms. Foundation for Women; Elizabeth Debold was a member of the Harvard Project. Debold expanded on Carol Gilligan's working theory of women's development, explaining the psychological dynamics of power, knowledge, and desire that come into play as girls begin to understand that they are becoming women in this culture. She integrated the work of other researchers in the new feminist psychology — Annie Rogers, Dana Jack Crowley, and Deborah Tolman among them — as well as research on trauma and cognitive development.

Debold, Wilson, and Malavé incorporated into the study the latest Harvard Project research with an inner-city population of adolescent girls "at risk" and with preadolescent girls at both a public and a private school. These studies, and the American Association of University Women's nationwide survey on girls' self-esteem, begin to confirm what has long been suspected but until recently was not studied — that "adolescence is also a time of crisis and concern for girls of color."

3. Debold, Wilson, and Malavé, p. 202.

4. Annette Lieberman and Vicki Lindner, *Unbalanced Accounts* (New York: Viking Penguin, 1988.)

5. Greenberg-Lake Analysis Group, *Shortchanging Girls, Shortchanging America: A Nationwide Poll to Assess Self-Esteem, Educational Experiences, Interest in Math and Science, and Career Aspirations of Girls and Boys Ages 9–15* (Washington, D.C.: American Association of University Women, 1991), p. 6.

6. Debold, Wilson, and Malavé, p. 11.

7. The American Association of University Women, Educational Foundation, *The AAUW Report: How Schools Shortchange Girls* (Washington, D.C.: The AAUW Educational Foundation and National Educational Association, 1992), p. 79.

8. Peggy Orenstein, *SchoolGirls: Young Women, Self-Esteem, and the Confidence Gap* (New York: Anchor Doubleday, 1995), p. xxvii.

9. Clifford Adelman, "Women at Thirtysomething: Paradoxes of Attainment" (Washington, D.C.: Office of Educational Research and Improvement, 1991).

10. Linda Matthews, "Making Math Add Up for Girls," *New York Times*, March 31, 1996, section 4 A, p. 10.

11. Debold, Wilson, and Malavé, p. 59.

12. One out of three girls has an unwanted sexual encounter with an adult male before the age of eighteen, and roughly a quarter of the abuse occurs before puberty, according to Judith Herman, *Father-Daughter Incest* (Cambridge: Harvard University Press, 1981), p. 12.

13. Orenstein, p. 61.

14. Daniel P. Orr, Mary L. Wilbrandt, Catherine J. Brack, Steven P. Rauch,

and Gary M. Ingersoll, "Reported Sexual Behaviors and Self-Esteem among Young Adolescents," *American Journal of Diseases of Children* 143 (1989), p. 86.

15. Orenstein, p. 55.

16. Nan Stein, Nancy L. Marshall, and Linda R. Tropp, *Secrets in Public: Sexual Harassment in Our Schools — A Report on the Results of a "Seventeen" Magazine Survey* (joint project of NOW Legal Defense and Education Fund and Wellesley College Center for Research on Women, March 1993.)

17. Debold, Wilson, and Malavé, p. 63.

18. Mindy Bingham and Sandy Stryker, *Women Helping Girls with Choices: A Handbook for Community Service Organizations* (Santa Barbara, Calif.: Advocacy Press/Girls Club of Santa Barbara, 1989).

19. Girls Count, *In America's Future, in Tomorrow's Workforce, in Colorado's Classrooms* (Denver, Colo., 1992).

20. Linda K. Christian-Smith, *Becoming a Woman Through Romance* (New York: Routledge, 1990), p. 108.

21. Debold, Wilson, and Malavé, p. 86.

22. Sharon Thompson, "Search for Tomorrow: On Feminism and the Reconstruction of Teen Romance," in Carol S. Vance, ed., *Pleasure and Danger: Exploring Female Sexuality* (Boston: Routledge & Kegan Paul, 1984), p. 351.

23. Christian-Smith, p. 108.

24. Debold, Wilson, and Malavé, p. 85.

25. Rebecca Johnson, "For Love or Money," *Vogue*, August 1997, p. 78.

26. Debold, Wilson, and Malavé, p. xxi.

27. Erik Erikson, "Identity and the Lifecycle," *Psychological Issues* 1, 1959, pp. 18–164.

28. Debold, Wilson, and Malavé, p. 211.

29. Louise Kaplan, *Female Perversions* (New York: Doubleday, 1991), p. 232.

CHAPTER 7

1. Robert Lypsyte, "Married to the Game," *New York Times*, June 1, 1997, section 8, p. 1.

2. Ibid, p. 2.

3. Martha Kirkpatrick, M.D., "Some Clinical Perceptions of Middle-Aged Divorced Women," in Judith Gold, M.D., ed., *Divorce as a Developmental Process* (Washington, D.C.: American Psychiatric Press, 1988).

4. Jean Baker Miller, M.D., *Toward a New Psychology of Women* (Boston: Beacon Press, 1977), p. 84.

5. Karen Horney, *Self-Analysis* (New York: W. W. Norton, 1942).

A biography of Horney appearing after her death revealed "Clare" to be none other than Karen Horney herself as a young woman. Horney must have felt she would undermine the value of her insights were she to have presented them as having been gleaned from her own analysis. She made up a "patient" and devoted much of a book to her "case."

6. Miller, p. 32.

7. Horney, p. 199.

8. June Singer, *Boundaries of the Soul: The Practice of Jung's Psychology* (New York: Doubleday Anchor, 1994), p. 185.

9. Miller, p. 50.

10. Miller, p. ibid.

11. Singer, p. 194.

12. Ibid.

13. Miller, p. 34.

CHAPTER 8

1. Dr. Linda Sapadin and Jack Maguire, *It's About Time: The Six Styles of Procrastination and How to Overcome Them* (New York: Viking Penguin, 1996), p. 74.

2. Kirk Johnson, "Sit Down. Breathe Deeply. This Is Really Scary Stuff," *New York Times,* April 16, 1995, section F, p. 5.

3. Merrill Lynch seminar reported by Anne Conover Heller, in "How to Make Money by Risking It," *Lear's,* September 1991, p. 73.

4. Ibid.

5. Ibid.

6. Cynthia Kling, "Why Are Women Still Afraid of Money?" *Harper's Bazaar,* January 1997, p. 26.

7. Ibid.

8. Ibid.

9. Annette Lieberman and Vicki Lindner, *Unbalanced Accounts* (San Francisco: Viking Penguin, 1988), p. 127.

CHAPTER 9

1. Allen R. Myerson, "Wall Street Addresses Women's Needs," *New York Times,* July 31, 1993, section C, p. 1.

2. Ibid.

3. Leslie Dormen, "Will Your Money Last As Long As You Do?," *Mirabella,* May/June 1996, p. 80.

4. Ibid.

5. Anne Conover Heller, "How to Make Money by Risking It," *Lear's,* September 1991, p. 74.

6. Ibid.

7. Ibid.

8. Ruth Ross, *Prospering Woman* (San Rafael, Calif.: New World Library, 1982), p. 151.

9. Kate Stone Lombardi, "Not an Advice Column," *Hudson Valley Magazine,* March 1993, p. 29.

10. Reed Abelson, "Our Portfolios Ourselves," *New York Times,* October 15, 1995, section 3, p. 1.

11. Gary Belsky, "The Five Ways Women Are Often Smarter Than Men About Money," *Money,* June 1992, p. 81.

12. Ibid.

13. Abelson, "Our Portfolios Ourselves."

14. Donna Boundy, *When Money Is the Drug: The Compulsion for Credit, Cash, and Chronic Debt* (San Francisco: HarperSan Francisco, 1993), p. 202.

15. Jerrold Mundis, *How to Get Out of Debt, Stay Out of Debt, and Live Prosperously* (New York: Bantam, 1990), p. 74.

16. Ross, p. 92.

17. Mundis, p. 143.

18. Ross, p. 92.

19. Ibid., p. 132.

20. Ibid., p. 141.

21. Tina Howe, "Hangers-On," *Allure,* May 1997.

22. Mundis, p. 143.

23. Ross, p. 105.

BIBLIOGRAPHY

BOOKS

Anderson, Carol M., and Stewart, Susan, with Dimidjian, Sonja. *Flying Solo*. New York: W. W. Norton, 1995.

Boundy, Donna. *When Money Is the Drug* (San Francisco: HarperCollins, 1993).

Brown, Lyn Mikel, and Gilligan, Carol. *Meeting at the Crossroads: Women's Psychology and Girls' Development*. New York: Ballantine Books, 1992.

Bingham, Mindy, and Stryker, Sandy. *Women Helping Girls with Choices: A Handbook for Community Service Organizations*. Santa Barbara, Calif.: Advocacy Press/Girls Club of Santa Barbara, 1989.

Christian-Smith, Linda K. *Becoming a Woman Through Romance*. New York: Routledge, 1990.

Dowling, Colette. *You Mean I Don't Have to Feel This Way?: New Help for Depression, Anxiety and Addiction*. New York: Bantam, 1993.

Debold, Elizabeth, Wilson, Marie, and Malavé, Idelisse. *Mother Daughter Revolution: From Betrayal to Power*. New York: Bantam Books, 1994.

Gilligan, Carol, Lyons, Nona P., and Hammer, Trudy J., eds. *Making Connections: Notes from the Underground of Female Adolescence*. Cambridge: Harvard University Press, 1990.

Gilligan, Carol. *In a Different Voice*. Cambridge: Harvard University Press, 1993.

Gilligan, Carol, Rogers, Annie G., and Tolman, Deborah L., eds. *Women, Girls and Psychotherapy: Reframing Resistance.* Binghamton, N.Y.: Haworth Press, 1991.

Gold, Judith, M.D., ed. *Divorce as a Developmental Process.* Washington, D.C.: American Psychiatric Press, 1988.

Herman, Judith. *Father-Daughter Incest.* Cambridge: Harvard University Press, 1981.

Horney, Karen. *Self-Analysis.* New York: Norton, 1942.

Jones-Lee, Anita. *Women and Money.* Happauge, N.Y.: Barron, 1991.

Kaplan, Louise. *Female Perversions.* New York: Doubleday, 1991.

Lieberman, Annette, and Lindner, Vicki. *Unbalanced Accounts.* New York: Viking Penguin, 1988.

McGoldrick, Monica, Anderson, Carol M., and Walsh, Froma, eds. *Women in Families.* New York: W. W. Norton, 1991.

Miller, Jean Baker, M. D. *Toward a New Psychology of Women.* Boston: Beacon Press, 1977.

Orenstein, Peggy. *SchoolGirls: Young Women, Self-Esteem, and the Confidence Gap.* New York: Anchor Doubleday, 1995.

Ross, Ruth, Ph.D. *Prospering Woman.* San Rafael, Calif.: New World Library, 1982.

Rossi, Alice, ed. *Gender and the Life Course.* New York: Aldine, 1985.

Sapadin, Linda, Ph.D., and Maguire, Jack. *It's About Time: The Six Styles of Procrastination and How to Overcome Them.* New York: Viking Penguin, 1996.

Vance, Carol S., ed. *Pleasure and Danger: Exploring Female Sexuality.* Boston: Routledge & Kegan Paul, 1984.

Walters, Marianne, Carter, Betty, Papp, Peggy, and Silverstein, Olga. *The Invisible Well.* New York: Guilford Press, 1988.

Randall, Margaret. *The Price You Pay.* New York: Routledge, 1996.

PERIODICALS

Abelson, Reed. "Our Portfolios Ourselves." *New York Times* (October 15, 1995): section 3, p. 1.

Adelman, Clifford. "Women at Thirtysomething: Paradoxes of Attainment." Washington, D.C.: Office of Educational Research and Improvement (1991).

Barnett, Rosalind C. "Women in Management Today." Center for Research on Women, No. 249, Wellesley College, Wellesley, Mass. (1992).

Belsky, Gary. "The Five Ways Women Are Often Smarter Than Men About Money." *Money* (June 1992): p. 82.

Brenner, Leslie. "When Smart Women Aren't Smart About Money." *New Woman* (August 1996): p. 102.

Brody, Jane. "Girls and Puberty: The Crisis Years." *New York Times* (November 4, 1997): section F, p. 9.

Choi, Namkee G. "Correlates of the Economic Status of Widowed and Divorced Elderly Women," *Journal of Family Issues* 13, no. 1 (March 1992): p. 48.

Daum, Meghan. "Losing My Shirt." *Self* (April 1996): p. 157.

Dormen, Leslie. "Will Your Money Last As Long As You Do?" *Mirabella* (May/June 1996): p. 80.

Dunning, Jennifer. "Dance Notes." *New York Times* (June 18, 1996): section C, p. 18.

Erikson, Erik. "Identity and the Lifecycle." *Psychological Issues* 1 (1959): pp. 18–164.

"Equity Eludes Women." *AARP Bulletin* (November 1991): p. 1.

Fabrikant, Geraldine. "New Chapter for a Serial Spender." *New York Times* (March 23, 1997): section D, p. 6.

Greenberg-Lake Analysis Group. "Shortchanging Girls, Shortchanging America: A Nationwide Poll to Assess Self-Esteem, Educational Experiences, Interest in Math and Science, and Career Aspirations of Girls and Boys Ages 9–15." Washington, D.C.: American Association of University Women (1991): p. 6.

Hansell, Saul. "A Shaky House of Plastic with No Quick Fix in Sight." *New York Times*, Dec. 28, section D 1, p. 1.

Heller, Anne Conover. "How to Make Money by Risking It." *Lear's* (September 1991): p. 73.

Hershey, Robert D., Jr. "At College, Many Learn How to Plunge into Debt." *New York Times* (Nov. 10, 1996): section D, p. 1.

Howe, Tina. "Hangers-On." *Allure* (May 1997).

Johnson, Dirk. "Sit Down. Breathe Deeply. This Is Really Scary Stuff." *New York Times* (April 16, 1995): section F, p. 5.

Johnson, Dirk. "No Fault Divorce Is Under Attack." *New York Times* (February 2, 1996): section A, p. 10.

Johnson, Rebecca. "For Love or Money." *Vogue* (August 1997): p. 78.

Kerbel, Barbara. "Ill Suited for This." *Newsday* (January 18, 1997): section B, p. 5.

Kinstlinger-Bruhn, Charlotte. "Singled Out." *Woodstock Times* (July 25, 1996): p. 12.

Kirn, Walter. "Going Postal." *Vogue* (March 1996): p. 204.

Kling, Cynthia. "Why Are Women Still Afraid of Money?" *Harper's Bazaar* (January 1997): p. 26.

Lewin, Tamar. "Equal Pay for Equal Work Is No. 1 Goal of Women." *New York Times* (September 5, 1997): section A, p. 20.

Lombardi, Kate Stone. "Not an Advice Column." *Hudson Valley Magazine* (March 1993): p. 29.

Lyall, Sarah, "A Duchess: Her Life in Debt." *New York Times* (February 4, 1996): section 4, p. 4.

Lypsyte, Robert. "Married to the Game." *New York Times* (June 1, 1997): section 8, p. 1.

Mahar, Maggie. "The Truth About Women's Pay." *Working Woman* (April 1993): pp. 52–55.

Matthews, Linda. "Making Math Add Up for Girls." *Education Life. New York Times* (March 31, 1996): section 4A, p. 10.

McElroy, Susan, M.D., et al. "Pharmacological Treatment of Kleptomania and Bulimia Nervosa." *Journal of Clinical Psychopharmacology* 9, no. 5 (October 1989).

McElroy, Susan, M.D., et al. "Kleptomania: Clinical Characteristics and Associated Psychopathology." *Psychological Medicine* 21 (1991): pp. 93–108.

McPhee, Martha. "My Favorite Store: Agnes B." *New York Times Magazine* (April 6, 1997): p. 74.

Morrow, David J. "To Shop, Perchance Nonstop." *New York Times* (Dec. 29, 1996): section 3, p. 1.

Myerson, Allen R. "Wall Street Addresses Women's Needs." *New York Times* (July 31, 1993): section C, p. 1.

O'Rand, A., and Henretta, J. "Women at Middle Age: Developmental Transitions." *Annals of the American Academy of Political and Social Science* 404 (1982).

Orr, Daniel P., et al. "Reported Sexual Behaviors and Self-Esteem among Young Adolescents." *American Journal of Diseases of Children* 143 (1989): p. 86.

Stein, Nan, et al. "Secrets in Public: Sexual Harassment in Our Schools — A Report on the Results of a *Seventeen* Magazine Survey." Joint project of NOW Legal Defense and Education Fund and Wellesley College Center for Research on Women (March 1993).

Siwolop, Sana. "Genius Grant Patches Up Family's Frayed Finances." *New York Times* (August 4, 1996): section F, p. 3.

Siwolop, Sana. "For a Choreographer, a Chance to Leap Out of Debt." *New York Times* (July 20, 1997): section F, p. 4.